PATHWAYS

Reading, Writing, and Critical Thinking

2

Laurie Blass   Mari Vargo
Keith S. Folse
Series Consultant

NATIONAL GEOGRAPHIC LEARNING | HEINLE CENGAGE Learning

Australia • Brazil • Japan • Korea • Mexico • Singapore • Spain • United Kingdom • United States

NATIONAL GEOGRAPHIC LEARNING | **HEINLE** CENGAGE Learning

Pathways 2: Reading, Writing, and Critical Thinking
Laurie Blass, Mari Vargo, and
Keith S. Folse / Series Consultant

Publisher: Andrew Robinson

Executive Editor: Sean Bermingham

Associate Development Editor: Sarah Tan

Contributing Editors: Bernard Seal, Sylvia Bloch

Director of Global Marketing: Ian Martin

Marketing Manager: Caitlin Thomas

Marketing Manager: Emily Stewart

Director of Content and Media Production:
  Michael Burggren

Senior Content Project Manager: Daisy Sosa

Manufacturing Manager: Marcia Locke

Manufacturing Buyer: Marybeth Hennebury

Associate Manager, Operations: Leila Hishmeh

Cover Design: Page 2 LLC

Cover Image: Patrick McFeeley/
  National Geographic Image Collection

Interior Design: Page 2, LLC

Composition: Page 2, LLC

Library of Congress Control Number: 2012932717

International Student Edition:

ISBN-13: 978-1-133-31287-1

ISBN-10: 1-133-31287-X

U.S. Edition:

ISBN-13: 978-1-133-31708-1

ISBN-10: 1-133-31708-1

National Geographic Learning
20 Channel Center Street
Boston, MA 02210
USA

Cengage Learning is a leading provider of customized learning solutions with office locations around the globe, including Singapore, the United Kingdom, Australia, Mexico, Brazil, and Japan. Locate your local office at **ngl.cengage.com**

Cengage Learning products are represented in Canada by Nelson Education, Ltd.

Visit National Geographic Learning online at **elt.heinle.com**

Visit our corporate website at **www.cengage.com**

Printed in the United States of America
6 7 18 17 16 15

▲ Tornado Alley in the U.S. has the world's most extreme weather. **page 125**

▲ Chichén Itzá in Mexico has been called one of the Seven Wonders of the World. **page 155**

▲ Barcelona's La Sagrada Família will finally be complete in 2026—more than 100 years after it began. **page 145**

Gold miners in Choco are using old mining methods with new innovations. **page 195**

PATHWAYS

▲ 13,500-year-old Göbekli Tepe in Turkey may be the oldest religious building in the world. **page 154**

▲ In Singapore, laws are strict and working hours are long. So why are Singaporeans so happy? **page 5**

What is the secret to long ▲ life? Ask the people of Japan's Okinawan islands. **page 9**

On the island of ▲ Vorovoro, Fiji, an online community has created its own tribe. **page 52**

A remarkable world exists beneath the waves of Australia's Coral Sea. **page 63**

Madagascar is home to some of the world's most poisonous species. **page 109**

Scope and Sequence

Unit	Academic Pathways	Vocabulary
1 **Happiness** *Page 1* **Academic Track:** Health Science 	**Lesson A:** Identifying an author's main ideas Guessing meaning from context **Lesson B:** Understanding a classification text **Lesson C:** Introduction to the paragraph Writing a topic sentence	Understanding meaning from context Using new vocabulary in an everyday context **Word Partners:** *factor*
2 **Big Ideas** *Page 21* **Academic Track:** Interdisciplinary 	**Lesson A:** Understanding a biographical text Identifying supporting ideas **Lesson B:** Ranking ideas in order of priority **Lesson C:** Supporting the main idea and giving details Writing a descriptive paragraph	Understanding meaning from context Identifying part of speech from context Using new vocabulary in an everyday context **Word Link:** *-tion, -able*
3 **Connected Lives** *Page 41* **Academic Track:** Anthropology/ Sociology 	**Lesson A:** Skimming for gist Making inferences **Lesson B:** Reading a magazine article **Lesson C:** Writing a concluding sentence Writing an opinion paragraph	Understanding meaning from context Using new vocabulary in an everyday context **Word Link:** *-inter, -al* **Word Partners:** *environmentally*
4 **Deep Trouble** *Page 61* **Academic Track:** Interdisciplinary 	**Lesson A:** Interpreting visual information Examining problems and solutions **Lesson B:** Understanding graphic information Reading an interview **Lesson C:** Explaining a chart or graph	Understanding meaning from context Using new vocabulary in an everyday context **Word Partners:** *reduce, informed* **Word Link:** *mini-*
5 **Memory and Learning** *Page 81* **Academic Track:** Health Science/ Psychology 	**Lesson A:** Identifying cause and effect in an expository text **Lesson B:** Synthesizing information from multiple texts **Lesson C:** Using an outline to plan a paragraph Writing a paragraph with supporting information	Understanding meaning from context Using new vocabulary in an everyday context **Word Link:** *-ize, trans-* **Word Partners:** *stress*

Reading	Writing	Viewing	Critical Thinking
Interpreting infographics Predicting for main idea Understanding the gist Identifying key details Using clues in opening sentences **Skill Focus:** Identifying main ideas	**Goal:** Writing a paragraph **Grammar:** Using simple present tense **Skill:** Writing a topic sentence	**Video:** *Longevity Leaders* Guessing meaning from context Viewing for general understanding Viewing for specific information	Inferring word meaning from context Analyzing and discussing information Synthesizing information to identify similarities **CT Focus:** Inferring meaning from context
Interpreting survey information Predicting for main idea Understanding the gist Identifying key details **Skill Focus:** Identifying supporting ideas	**Goal:** Writing a descriptive paragraph **Grammar:** Using simple past tense **Skill:** Supporting the main idea and giving details	**Video:** *Solar Cooking* Viewing for general understanding Viewing for specific information	Identifying problems and solutions Synthesizing information to identify similarities Analyzing and ranking ideas and providing reasons **CT Focus:** Deciding on criteria for ranking
Interpreting maps and charts Predicting for main idea Understanding the gist Identifying key details Scanning for key details **Skill Focus:** Skimming for gist	**Goal:** Writing an opinion paragraph **Grammar:** Using present perfect tense **Skill:** Writing a concluding sentence	**Video:** *Lamu: Tradition and Modernity* Guessing meaning from context Viewing for general understanding Viewing for specific information	Synthesizing information to identify similarities Synthesizing information for group discussion Analyzing text for function and purpose **CT Focus:** Making inferences from a text
Interpreting maps Understanding the gist Identifying main ideas Identifying purpose Identifying key details **Skill Focus:** Interpreting visual information (graph/map)	**Goal:** Writing a paragraph that explains a chart or graph **Grammar:** Describing charts and graphs **Skill:** Explaining a chart or graph	**Video:** *Saving Bluefin Tuna* Viewing to confirm predictions Viewing for general understanding Viewing for specific information	Inferring word meaning from context Evaluating author arguments Synthesizing textual and visual information for discussion Analyzing text for key information **CT Focus:** Analyzing and evaluating problems and solutions presented in a text
Interpreting infographics Understanding the gist Identifying key details Classifying information using a T-chart Identifying main ideas **Skill Focus:** Identifying cause and effect	**Goal:** Writing a paragraph with supporting information **Grammar:** Using *by* + gerund **Skill:** Using an outline	**Video:** *Memory School* Viewing to confirm predictions Viewing for general understanding Viewing for specific information	Inferring author opinion from the text Synthesizing information for group discussion Analyzing text for function and purpose **CT Focus:** Applying a new method for internalization

Reading	Writing	Viewing	Critical Thinking
Comparing text and images Understanding the gist Identifying key details Understanding references in the text **Skill Focus:** Identifying pros and cons	**Goal:** Writing a persuasive paragraph **Grammar:** Making concessions **Skill:** Convincing a reader that something is true	**Video:** *The Frog Licker* Viewing to confirm predictions Viewing for general understanding Viewing for specific information	Synthesizing information to identify similarities Synthesizing information for group discussion Analyzing and organizing information into an outline Analyzing text for function and purpose **CT Focus:** Identifying figurative language
Interpreting maps and captions Understanding the gist Identifying main ideas Identifying key details Identifying supporting examples **Skill Focus:** Identifying sequence	**Goal:** Writing a process paragraph **Grammar:** Verb forms for describing a process **Skill:** Organizing a process paragraph	**Video:** *Lightning* Viewing to confirm predictions Viewing for general understanding Viewing for specific information	Synthesizing information to identify similarities Analyzing and discussing content Inferring and identifying reasons **CT Focus:** Evaluating sources for reliability and purpose
Analyzing and relating textual information Understanding the gist Identifying main ideas Identifying supporting details **Skill Focus:** Scanning for specific information	**Goal:** Writing a comparison paragraph **Grammar:** Using comparative adjectives **Skill:** Identifying and writing about things you wish to compare	**Video:** *The Pyramids of Giza* Viewing to confirm predictions Viewing for general understanding Viewing for specific information	Using prior knowledge to reflect on content Evaluating arguments Analyzing information to complete a Venn diagram **CT Focus:** Identifying and analyzing similarities and differences (e.g., using graphic organizers)
Interpreting text and images Understanding the gist Identifying main ideas Identifying supporting details **Skill Focus:** Identifying and differentiating theories from facts	**Goal:** Writing a summary **Grammar:** Using synonyms **Skill:** Explaining key ideas of a passage in your own words	**Video:** *Flying Reptiles* Using prior knowledge Viewing for general understanding Viewing for specific information	Applying theories to different scenarios Synthesizing information to identify similarities Analyzing and discussing content Analyzing text for function and purpose **CT Focus:** Evaluating evidence
Interpreting maps, charts, and captions Understanding the gist Identifying main ideas Identifying sequence **Skill Focus:** Taking notes and using graphic organizers	**Goal:** Writing a problem-solution paragraph **Grammar:** Using modals to discuss abilities and possibilities **Skill:** Describing a problem and suggesting a solution	**Video:** *Cell Phone Trackers* Viewing to confirm predictions Viewing for general understanding Viewing for specific information	Synthesizing information to identify similarities Analyzing and discussing information Identifying problems and solutions **CT Focus:** Relating information to personal experience

EXPLORE A UNIT

Each unit has three lessons.
Lessons A and B develop academic reading skills and vocabulary by focusing on two aspects of the unit theme. A video section acts as a content bridge between Lessons A and B. The language and content in these sections provide the stimulus for a final writing task (Lesson C).

The **unit theme** focuses on an academic content area relevant to students' lives, such as Health Science, Business and Technology, and Environmental Science.

Academic Pathways highlight the main academic skills of each lesson.

Deep Trouble

UNIT 4

Think and Discuss

1. What ocean or sea is nearest your home? When was the last time you saw it?
2. Do you eat seafood? If yes, what types do you eat? If no, why not?

▲ A school of barracuda surrounds a diver off New Hanover Island, Papua New Guinea.

61

Exploring the Theme
provides a visual introduction to the unit. Learners are encouraged to think critically and share ideas about the unit topic.

Exploring the Theme

Look at the map and read the information. Then discuss the questions.

1. What do the colors of the map show? What kinds of "activity" does this refer to?
2. Which areas have the highest impact, or effect, of human activities?
3. How is human activity affecting, or changing, the four places described? How are the effects similar and different?

Ocean Impact

Human activities are affecting, in some way, all of the world's oceans. These activities include fishing, farming, manufacturing, and offshore gas and oil drilling.

Impact of human activity

- Very high
- High
- Medium high
- Medium
- Low
- Very low

North Sea

Pollution from shipping, farming, and offshore drilling is causing "dead zones"—places without enough oxygen for plants and fish to live. Overfishing adds to the problem.

◄ Pollution from offshore oil and gas drilling is one cause of the North Sea's dead zones.

East China Sea

Several large rivers bring pollution into the sea. It is also a major fishing area and shipping route. Together, these factors cause serious problems for the ocean environment.

◄ Concave ships are a common sight on the rivers that flow from several countries into the East China Sea.

Coral Sea

The Coral Sea has less impact from human activity than other oceans. However, the water is warming and becoming acidic. Plants and fish cannot live in acidic water.

◄ The increased interest is among thousands of fish species living in the Great Barrier Reef in Australia's Coral Sea.

Caribbean Sea

Pollution and overfishing are causing some fish species to disappear. The temperature of the water is increasing, too. The rising water temperature makes it more difficult for species to survive.

◄ Garbage washes ashore on the southern edge of Aruba in the Caribbean.

62 | UNIT 4

DEEP TROUBLE | 63

In **Preparing to Read**, learners are introduced to key vocabulary items from the reading passage. Lessons A and B each present and practice 10 target vocabulary items.

Reading A is a single, linear text related to the unit theme. Each reading passage is recorded on the audio program.

Maps and other graphic formats help to develop learners' visual literacy.

Guided comprehension tasks and reading strategy instruction enable learners to improve their academic literacy and critical thinking skills.

Viewing tasks related to an authentic National Geographic video serve as a content-bridge between Lessons A and B. (Video scripts are on pages 203–208.)

Learners need to use their **critical thinking skills** to relate video content to information in the previous reading.

Word Link and **Word Partners** boxes develop learners' awareness of word structure, collocations, and usage.

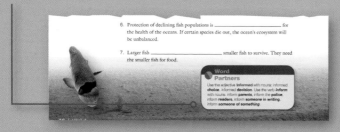

Guided pre-reading tasks and strategy tips encourage learners to think critically about what they are going to read.

LESSON B — READING

An Interview with Barton Seaver

Barton Seaver is a chef and conservationist[1] who wants our help to save the oceans. He believes that the choices we make for dinner have a direct impact on the ocean's health. According to Seaver, individuals can make a big difference by making informed choices.

Q. Should people stop eating seafood?

People should definitely not stop eating seafood altogether. There are certain species that have been severely overfished and that people should avoid for environmental reasons. But I believe that we can save the oceans while continuing to enjoy seafood. For example, some types of seafood, such as Alaskan salmon, come from well-managed fisheries. And others, such as farmed mussels and oysters, actually help to restore declining wild populations and clean up polluted waters.

Q. What kind of seafood should people eat? What should they not eat?

My general advice is to eat fish and shellfish that are low on the food chain and that can be harvested[2] with minimal impact on the environment. Some examples include farmed mussels, clams and oysters, anchovies, sardines, and herring. People should not eat the bigger fish of the sea, like tuna, orange roughy, shark, sturgeon, and swordfish.

Q. Why did you choose to dedicate[3] your life to the ocean?

I believe that the next great advance in human knowledge will come not from new discoveries, but rather from learning how we relate to our natural world. Humans are an essential part of nature, yet humans do not have a very strong relationship with the world around them. I have dedicated myself to helping people to understand our place on this planet through the foods that we eat.

Q. Why do you believe people should care about the health of the oceans?

The health of the oceans is directly linked to the health of people. The ocean provides most of the air we breathe. It has a big effect on the weather that we rely on for crops and food production. It also provides a necessary and vital[4] diet for billions of people on the planet. So I don't usually say that I am trying to save the oceans. I prefer to say that I am trying to save the vital things that we rely on the ocean for.

[1] A **conservationist** is someone who works to protect the environment.
[2] When you **harvest** something, such as a crop or other type of food, you gather it in.
[3] When you **dedicate** yourself to something, you give it a lot of time and effort because you think it is important.
[4] Something that is **vital** is very important.

72 | UNIT 4

Lesson B's reading passage

presents a further aspect of the unit theme, using a variety of text types and graphic formats.

Critical thinking tasks require learners to analyze, synthesize, and critically evaluate ideas and information in each reading.

3. Eating a pound of orange roughy is like eating _____ of shrimp.

4. Barton Seaver says he works to protect the oceans because _____

CT Focus

Examine the problems and solutions in exercise D. Do you think each suggestion is an effective solution to each problem? Are the suggestions realistic?

D | Critical Thinking: Analyzing Problems and Solutions. For each problem below, write one or two of Barton Seaver's suggestions that might help solve it.

Problems	Suggestions
Some wild fish populations are declining.	
People don't have a strong relationship with the world around them.	

E | Critical Thinking: Synthesizing. Discuss the questions in small groups.

1. Barton Seaver recommends that people eat smaller fish. How can this help the ocean's ecosystem?

2. Do you agree with Seaver that "humans do not have a very strong relationship with the world around them"? What are some examples in this unit for or against this idea?

LEVEL 4	TOP PREDATORS	When you eat **1 pound** of a level 4 fish, it's like eating …
LEVEL 3	CARNIVORES	**10 pounds** of level 3 fish
LEVEL 2	HERBIVORES	or **100 pounds** of level 2 fish
LEVEL 1	PLANTS	or **1,000 pounds** of level 1 organisms

But if you consume **1 pound** of level 3 fish, it's like eating … **10 pounds** of level 2 fish or **100 pounds** of level 1 organisms

A top predator needs much more food to survive than fish at lower levels of the food chain do. When we catch or eat top predators, we increase our impact on the ocean.

...hat We ...t Makes a ...fference

Authentic charts and graphics

from National Geographic support the main text, helping learners comprehend key ideas.

LEVEL 4 TOP PREDATORS

LEVEL 3 CARNIVORES

LEVEL 2 HERBIVORES

LEVEL 1 PLANTS

ALASKA POLLOCK

ZOOPLANKTON

PHYTOPLANKTON

PERUVIAN ANCHOVETA

...ean's top predators are the ...t, fastest animals. Some ...les are sharks, tuna, orange ..., and seals. They mostly eat ...r carnivores.

These fish eat smaller carnivores and herbivores such as zooplankton. Examples of carnivores include squid and sardines. They are eaten by top predators.

These are animals that eat plants. They include tiny animals, known as zooplankton, and small fish such as shrimp and clams. They are eaten by carnivores.

Plants, such as seaweed, sea grasses, and phytoplankton, are eaten by herbivores. They produce all the oxygen in the ocean, just as plants on land do.

JAPANESE FLYING SQUID

ORANGE ROUGHY

ATLANTIC SALMON

AMERICAN LOBSTER

ALGAE

DEEP TROUBLE | 73

The **Goal of Lesson C** is for learners to relate their own views and experience to the theme of the unit by completing a guided writing assignment.

Integrated **grammar practice and writing skill development** provides scaffolding for the writing assignment.

The ***Independent Student Handbook*** provides further language support and self-study strategies for independent learning.
► see pages 209–217.

Resources for *Pathways* Level 2

Video DVD with authentic National Geographic clips relating to each of the 10 units.

Teacher's Guide including teacher's notes, expansion activities, rubrics for evaluating written assignments, and answer keys for activities in the Student Book.

Audio CDs with audio recordings of the Student Book reading passages.

A **guided process approach** develops learners' confidence in planning, drafting, revising, and editing their written work.

Unit Quiz provides an opportunity for learners to review some of the key ideas and language from the unit.

Assessment CD-ROM with Exam*View*®

containing a bank of ready-made questions for quick and effective assessment.

Classroom Presentation Tool CD-ROM

featuring audio and video clips, and interactive activities from the Student Book. These can be used with an interactive whiteboard or computer projector.

Online Workbook,

powered by MyELT, with both teacher-led and self-study options. This contains the 10 National Geographic video clips, supported by interactive, automatically graded activities that practice the skills learned in the Student Books.

Text

4-5, 12-13: Adapted from "Thrive: Finding Happiness the Blue Zones Way," by Dan Buettner: National Geographic Books, 2011, **25-26:** Adapted from "Windmills of His Mind," by Karen Lange: http://blogs.ngm.com/blog_central/2009/10/the-windmills-of-his-mind.html, October 2009, **32-33:** Adapted from "Big Ideas, Little Packages": NGM November 2010, and "Hayat Sindi": http://www.nationalgeographic.com/explorers/bios/hayat-sindi/, **45-46:** Adapted from "Michael Wesch": http://www.nationalgeographic.com/explorers/bios/michael-wesch/, **52-53:** Adapted from "Welcome to Internet Island," by James Vlahos: National Geographic Adventure, February 2007, **65-66:** Adapted from "Overfishing": http://ocean.nationalgeographic.com/ocean/critical-issues-overfishing/, **72-73:** Adapted from "Seafood Crisis," by Paul Greenberg: NGM October 2010, **85-86:** Adapted from "Remember This," by Joshua Foer: NGM November 2007, **92:** Adapted from "Memory Boosters: How to Help": NGM November 2007, **93:** Adapted from "Direct Evidence of the Role of Sleep in Memory Formation Uncovered," by David Braun: http://blogs.nationalgeographic.com/blogs/news/chiefeditor/2009/09/sleep-and-memory.html, **105-106:** Adapted from "Zoltan Takacs": http://www.nationalgeographic.com/explorers/bios/zoltan-takacs/, **112-113:** Adapted from "Pick Your Poison," by Cathy Newman: NGM May 2005, **125-126:** Adapted from "Joplin, Missouri, Tornado Strong, But Not Surprising?" and "Monster Alabama Tornado Spawned by Rare "Perfect Storm","" by Willie Drye: http://news.nationalgeographic.com/news/2011/05/110523-joplin-missouri-tornado-science-nation-weather/ and http://news.nationalgeographic.com/news/2011/04/110428-tuscaloosa-birmingham-alabama-news-tornadoes-science-nation/, **132-133:** Adapted from "Fire Season," by Neil Shea: NGM July 2008, **145-148:** Adapted from "Gaudi's Masterpiece," by Jeremy Berlin: NGM December 2010, **154:** Adapted from "The Birth of Religion," by Charles C. Mann: NGM June 2011, **155:** Adapted from "Chichén Itzá": http://travel.nationalgeographic.com/travel/world-heritage/chichen-itza, **167-168:** Adapted from "Evolution of Feathers," by Carl Zimmer: NGM February 2011, **174:** Adapted from "Power Beak," by John Eliot: NGM June 2006, **175:** Adapted from "Beetles Shell Offers Clues to Harvesting Water," by Bijal P. Trivedi: http://news.nationalgeographic.com/news/2001/11/1101_TVdesertbeetle.html, and "How Shark Scales Give the Predators Deadly Speed," by Christine Dell'Amore: http://news.nationalgeographic.com/news/2010/11/101123-shark-scales-speed-animals-environment/, **187-188:** Adapted from "Ken Banks": http://www.nationalgeographic.com/explorers/bios/ken-banks/, and "How To Change the World": http://newswatch.nationalgeographic.com/2010/10/22/how_to_change_the_world_poptec/ **194-195:** Adapted from "Newswatch: Mobile Message": http://newswatch.nationalgeographic.com/tag/mobile-message/, and "Aydogan Ozcan": http://www.nationalgeographic.com/explorers/bios/aydogan-ozcan/

NGM = National Geographic Magazine

Photo Images

Cover: Patrick McFeeley/National Geographic, **IFC:** Katie Stoops, **IFC:** Michael Wesch, **IFC:** Courtesy of Dan Buettner, **IFC:** Tyrone Turner/National Geographic, **IFC:** Kris Krug, **IFC:** Jim Webb, **IFC:** Embrace Global, **IFC:** Rebecca Hale/National Geographic, **IFC:** Bedford, James/National Geographic Stock, **IFC:** Moving Windmills Project, Inc., **i:** Wes. C. Skiles/National Geographic, **iii:** Steve Raymer/National Geographic, **iii:** Ken Eward/National Geographic Stock, **iii:** Lynsey Addario/National Geographic, **iii:** David Doubilet/National Geographic, **iii:** Gerd Ludwig/National Geographic Stock, **iii:** Bruce Dale/National Geographic Image Collection, **iii:** Mark Thiessen/National Geographic, **iii:** Simon Norfolk/National Geographic, **iii:** Joe Petersburger/National Geographic, **iii:** Ken Banks, kiwanja.net, **iv:** Campo, Colorado/National Geographic, **iv:** Simon Norfolk/National Geographic, **iv:** Stephen Chao/National Geographic, **iv:** Frans Lanting/National Geographic, **iv-v:** NASA Goddard Space Flight Center Image by Reto Stöckli (land surface, shallow water, clouds), **v:** ©2011/Vincent J. Musi/National Geographic Image Collection, **v:** Steve Raymer/National Geographic, **v:** David McLain/National Geographic, **v:** Ben Keene, **v:** David Doubilet/National Geographic, **v:** Joel Sartore/National Geographic, **vi:** Michael S. Lewis/National Geographic, **vi:** Moving Windmills Project, Inc., **vi:** Bobby Haas/National Geographic, **vi:** Brian J. Skerry/National Geographic, **vi:** Anne Keiser/National Geographic, **viii:** Bruce Dale/National Geographic Image Collection, **viii:** Mike Theiss / National Geographic, **viii:** National Geographic, **viii:** Robert Clark/National Geographic, **viii:** Guillaume Collanges, **1:** Joel Sartore/National Geographic, **2-3:** Steve Raymer/National Geographic, **5:** Steve Raymer/National Geographic, **6:** Michael S. Lewis/National Geographic, **8:** Stephen St. John/National Geographic, **9:** David McLain/National Geographic Stock, **12:** Sisse Brimberg/National Geographic, **12:** David McLain/National Geographic, **12:** Lynsey Addario/National Geographic, **13:** Image courtesy of Dan Buettner, **21:** Ken Eward/National Geographic Stock, **22:** Ira Block/National Geographic, **23:** Wright, Orville/National Geographic, **23:** Paul Sutherland/National Geographic, **25:** Workshop Loves You, **26:** Moving Windmills Project, Inc., **26:** The Toronto Star/ZUMApress.com, **27:** Workshop Loves You, **28:** SuperStock/Corbis, **29:** Rebecca Hale/National Geographic, **29:** Jodi Cobb/National Geographic, **30:** Michael Melford/National Geographic Image Collection, **32:** Embrace Global, **32:** Rebecca Hale/National Geographic, **32:** Renee Comet/National Geographic, **33:** Renee Comet/National Geographic, **33:** Kris Krug, **33:** Renee Comet/National Geographic, **41:** Susan Seubert/National Geographic, **43:** Lynsey Addario/National Geographic, **45:** Gerd Ludwig/National Geographic, **46:** Peter Essick/National Geographic, **46:** Michael Wesch, **49:** Bobby Haas/National Geographic, **50:** Ben Keene, **52:** James Vlahos, **52:** Ben Keene, **53:** James Vlahos, **53:** James Vlahos,

continued on p. 224

Happiness

Think and Discuss

1. What does it mean to be happy?

2. Think of someone you know who seems happy.
   How do you know he or she is happy?
   Describe the person.

▲ A zebra butterfly brings joy to a young girl in Lincoln, Nebraska.

Exploring the Theme

Look at the information about two surveys and discuss the questions.

1. Where are the happiest places on Earth, according to the two surveys? How do the results compare?

2. Why do you think people from these countries are happy?

3. Imagine you want to find the happiest place in your country. What information would you look at? What questions would you ask?

World Happiness Survey ①
Happy Hot Spots

The **World Database of Happiness** brings together scientific reports on happiness from 149 countries around the world. The researchers ask people to rate their enjoyment of life on a scale from 0 to 10. The top six happiest nations according to the survey (2000–2009) are listed below. The happiest Asian country, Singapore, is 37th in the list; Malawi (62nd) is Africa's happiest nation. The world's richest nation, the United States, placed 21st.

③ Iceland
Rating **8.2**
Pop.: 311,000
GDP pc: $38,300
Avg. Life: 80.9 years

⑤ Finland
Rating **7.9**
Pop.: 5.3 million
GDP pc: $35,400
Avg. Life: 79.27 years

② Denmark
Rating **8.3**
Pop.: 5.5 million
GDP pc: $36,600
Avg. Life: 78.63 years

⑥ Mexico
Rating **7.9**
Pop.: 113.7 million
GDP pc: $13,900
Avg. Life: 76.47 years

① Costa Rica
Rating **8.5**
Pop.: 4.6 million
GDP pc: $11,300
Avg. Life: 77.72 years

④ Switzerland
Rating **8.0**
Pop.: 7.6 million
GDP pc: $42,600
Avg. Life: 81.07 years

Pop.: Population; **GDP pc:** Gross Domestic Product per capita (the value of goods and services produced by a country, divided by the number of people); **Avg. Life:** Average life expectancy.

Source: http://worlddatabaseofhappiness.eur.nl/

World Happiness Survey ②
Happy Planet

The **Happy Planet Index** was started in 2006 by the New Economics Foundation (NEF). It measures average personal happiness together with a country's average life expectancy and environmental impact. The highest-rated countries have happy, long-living people without harming the environment.

The top six countries in the 2009 Index are listed below. Other countries in the top 20 include Brazil (9th), Egypt (12th), Saudi Arabia (13th), the Philippines (14th), Argentina (15th), and China (20th).

1 Costa Rica

2 Dominican Republic

3 Jamaica

4 Guatemala

5 Vietnam

6 Colombia

Source: http://www.happyplanetindex.org/

▲ An elderly Vietnamese woman smiles for a photo. Vietnam was rated #5 in the 2009 **Happy Planet Index**, the highest-placed Asian nation in that survey.

A | Building Vocabulary. Find the words in **blue** in the reading passage on pages 5–6. Read the words around them and try to guess their meanings. Then write the correct word or phrase from the box to complete each sentence (1–10).

access	basic necessities	confident	financial	freedom
poverty	provides	secure	socialize	standard of living

1. When you _____ *socialize* _____, you spend time with other people for fun.

2. A country with a lot of _____ *poverty* _____ has a lot of people who don't have money.

3. If you have _____ *access* _____ to something, you can use it.

4. If you have complete _____ *freedom* _____, you can do anything you want to do.

5. If a government _____ *provides* _____ jobs to people, it gives jobs to people.

6. If you have a high _____ *standard of living* _____, you are very comfortable and wealthy.

7. If you discuss your _____ *financial* _____ situation, you are talking about money.

8. If you are _____ *secure* _____, you feel safe and are not worried about anything.

9. If you have the _____ *basic* *necessities* _____, you have a home and enough food to eat.

10. If you are _____ *confident* _____ about something, you are sure about it.

B | Using Vocabulary. Answer the questions. Share your ideas with a partner.

1. What do you think are the **basic necessities** in life, besides food and a home?
   security – good government – free education – basic health neccesery
2. Do you feel **confident** about your future? Why, or why not?
   Yes, I have Plan A–B and I think I am on the Right way.
3. Who do you **socialize** with?
   my family — my internet friends

All life is not depend on me but

C | Brainstorming. List six things you think a person needs in order to be happy. Share your ideas with a partner.

1. *internet-Hs*
2. *enough money*
3. *happy wife*
4. *eat burger at Resturant*
5. *healthly*
6. *drink beer*

D | Predicting. Read the title and the subheads of the reading passage on pages 5–6. What do you think the reading passage is about?

a. Different things make different people happy.

b. Security is the most important thing for happiness.

c. Everyone needs the same basic things to be happy.

Is there a Recipe for Happiness?

▲ A happy street seller shows off his fruit selection at an open-air market in Singapore.

track 1-01

A
WHAT MAKES US HAPPY? Money? Friends? A good job? Are the answers the same for everyone? According to world surveys, Mexico and Singapore are two happy countries—but their people may be happy for different reasons.

Safety and Security

B
There are more than 19,000 people per square mile[1] in the small nation of Singapore. People on the island work an average of 70 hours per week. The country has strict laws, for example, against littering,[2] graffiti,[3] and even for not flushing a toilet. But according to the World Database of Happiness, Singapore is the happiest country in Asia. Why?

C
One reason for Singapore's happiness is that the government provides the basic necessities, such as jobs and housing. There is almost no poverty, and Singapore has one of the lowest levels of unemployment in the world. The government creates jobs for people who are unemployed. It "tops up"[4] poorer people's income so everyone can have a minimum standard of living. The government also offers tax breaks[5] to people who look after their aging parents. This may be why 84 percent of older people live with their children. The result is a lot of closely connected families with roughly equal standards of living.

D
People may not all be happy about the laws, but they are generally happy with the results—they don't step in litter, the public toilets work, and the streets are safe and clean. So for Singaporeans, it seems that living in a secure, clean, and safe place may be more important than having a lot of personal freedom. As Dr. Tan Ern Ser of Singapore's Institute of Policy Studies explains, "If you are hopeful and confident of getting what you want in life, then you are happy."

---

[1] A **square mile** = 2.59 square kilometers
[2] **Littering** is leaving garbage or trash lying around outside.
[3] **Graffiti** is words or pictures that are written or drawn on walls or other public places.

[4] If you **top** something **up**, you add to it to make it full.
[5] If the government gives someone a **tax break**, it lowers the amount of tax they have to pay.

Friends and Neighbors

In many ways, Mexico is the opposite of Singapore. There are some parts of Mexico where people do not have a safe or secure life. Many people do not have jobs, enough food, or access to education. But, as in Singapore, most people in Mexico feel that they are happy. Why?

One reason is the importance of socializing. According to psychologists, much of our happiness comes from remembering the small joys that happen throughout the day. Simple acts of socializing, such as talking with a neighbor or having dinner with friends, can greatly increase our overall happiness. People in Mexico socialize with family and friends a lot, and this adds to their happiness.

But what about poverty? In Mexico, about half of the population is poor. However, most people in Mexico live near people in a similar financial

▲ About 60 percent of Mexico's population rates itself as "very happy"—about 24 percent more than Mexico's richer neighbor, the United States.

situation. If your neighbor doesn't have expensive items, such as a big house or an expensive car, you don't feel the need to have those things. So money, by itself, may not be so important for happiness. What matters more is how much money you have compared to the people around you.

A Mixed Recipe?

So the question "What makes people happy?" does not seem to have a simple answer. Work, security, safety, freedom, and socializing with friends and family can all play important roles. As the examples of Singapore and Mexico suggest, there may be no single recipe for happiness. The good news is that we can each find our own.

Adapted from *Thrive: Finding Happiness the Blue Zones Way* by Dan Buettner, 2010

A | **Understanding the Gist.** Look back at your answer for exercise **D** on p. 4. Was your prediction correct? *Yes*

B | **Identifying Key Details.** Match each statement (1–7) to the place it describes, according to the reading.

1. Most people here feel that they are happy.
2. Most people have equal standards of living.
3. The government provides the basic necessities.
4. Family is important to people.
5. People spend a lot of time with family.
6. People feel safe and secure.
7. Although many people are poor, most of them are happy.

Mexico · Both · Singapore

C | **Critical Thinking: Guessing Meaning from Context.** Find and underline these **bold** words in the reading on page 5. Use context to identify their meaning. Then match the sentence halves to make definitions.

1. _c_ If you are **strict**,
2. _e_ If you are **flushing** something,
3. _d_ If you are **unemployed**,
4. _b_ If you **look after** people,
5. _a_ If you make something **public**,

   a. you provide it to everyone.
   b. you take care of them and make sure they are well.
   c. you don't allow people to behave badly.
   d. you do not have a job.
   e. you are cleaning or emptying it with a fast flow of water.

> **CT Focus**
>
> **Use the context**—the words around a word—to guess the meaning of a word you don't know. The context can also help you decide the word's part of speech, e.g., noun, verb, adjective, etc.

D | **Critical Thinking: Analyzing.** Discuss your answers to these questions with a partner.

1. Most people in Singapore have financial security and many people in Mexico do not. In what way is their financial situation similar?
2. According to the author, socializing can make people happy. What examples does he give? Do you agree with his view? *Yes*

E | **Personalizing.** Complete the sentences with your own ideas.

1. I think (*safety and security / personal freedom / socializing*) is most important for happiness.
2. I usually socialize about _____ hours a week, and I (*work / study*) about _____ hours a week.
3. I think I would prefer to live in (*Singapore / Mexico*) because _____ _____.

Reading Skill: *Identifying the Main Idea*

The main idea of a paragraph is the most important idea, or the idea that the paragraph is about. A good paragraph has one main idea and one or more supporting ideas. Read the paragraph below and think about the main idea.

> *Researchers have found that the sunny weather in Mexico is one of the reasons that people there are happy. Mexico has many hours of sunlight, so people in Mexico get a lot of vitamin D. Vitamin D is important for overall health and well-being. Also, studies show that when people tan, they make more endorphins—chemicals in our bodies that make us feel happy.*

Which of these statements is the main idea of the paragraph?

> *a. People in Mexico are happy because they get a lot of vitamin D.*
>
> *b. Tanning makes us create more endorphins, which make us feel happy.*
>
> *c. Mexico gets a lot of sun, which may make people there happier.*

The last sentence is the main idea. The other two sentences are supporting ideas that explain the main idea.

A | **Matching.** Look back at the reading on pages 5–6. Match each main idea below to a paragraph from the reading (**A–H**).

_____ 1. One reason that people are happy is the government takes care of them financially.

_____ 2. Socializing is important because it can contribute a lot to happiness.

_____ 3. You do not need to have a lot of money to be happy.

_____ 4. There are different answers to the question "What makes people happy?"

🎧 track **1-02**

B | **Identifying the Main Idea.** Read the information about Denmark. Then write the main idea of the paragraph.

CT Focus

Use context to guess the meaning of new words. What do *fit*, *obesity*, and *recreation* mean?

It's hard to be happy when you're unhealthy. According to the World Database of Happiness, Denmark is the second happiest country in the world, and most Danes are fit. They have a lower rate of obesity than many of their European neighbors. Danish cities are designed so it's easy to walk or bike from one place to another. With a 30-minute walk, you can go from the city of Copenhagen to the ocean, where you can sail or swim, or to the woods, where you can hike. Everyone has easy access to recreation.

Main Idea: _____

_____

Roads in Copenhagen have a special lane just for cyclists. ▲

Longevity Leaders

▲ Not many people live to be 100 years old or older. But there are some places in the world where people—such as this Sardinian farmer—live very long, healthy lives.

Before Viewing

A | Guessing Meaning from Context. You will hear the words and phrases in **bold** in the video. Discuss the meaning of each one with a partner. Write definitions for the words and phrases.

1. Some countries have a lot of **centenarians**. These people live to be 100 years old or older.
2. Dan Buettner wanted to learn the secret of **longevity**. He wanted to know why people in some countries live a very long time.
3. Some young people eat a lot of **processed foods**, such as frozen pizza and soft drinks. These kinds of food often aren't good for you. Natural foods are usually healthier.
4. Many older people have a **traditional lifestyle**. They do things the same way that people have done for a long time.
5. Some older people spend time with friends, exercise, and play games. They like to stay **active**.

B | Brainstorming. What kinds of things do you think centenarians do to stay healthy?

_____eat well_____ _____ _____ _____

While Viewing

A | Watch the video about places where people live a long time. Does it mention any of the things that you listed in exercise **B** above? Circle any items that are mentioned.

B | As you view the video, think about the answers to these questions.

1. How many people are alive in the world now? How many will there be by the middle of the century?
2. Why are there more elderly people now than there were before?
3. What kinds of traditional lifestyles are disappearing? Why? What will happen if they continue to disappear?

After Viewing

A | Discuss answers to the questions 1–3 above with a partner.

B | Critical Thinking: Synthesizing. What do the centenarians in the video and the people in Singapore and Mexico have in common?

A | **Building Vocabulary.** Find the words or forms of the words in **bold** in the reading passage on pages 12–13. Look at the words around the bold words to guess their meanings. Then circle the best definition (**a** or **b**) of each word.

1. A **researcher** who studies happiness might ask people what kinds of things make them happy.

   a. someone who studies something and tries to discover facts about it
   b. someone who teaches subjects such as science and math in school

2. A person's **long-term** goals can include going to college and then medical school.

   a. happening over a long time
   b. traveling for a long distance

3. It's important to live in a **community** that you like. Do you like the people who live near you? Does the area have good places to shop, eat, and socialize?

   a. the place where you live
   b. a place where people meet

4. Most happy people have a **hobby**, such as writing, surfing, or painting.

   a. something that you do for money, such as a job
   b. an activity that you enjoy doing in your free time

CT Focus

Look for key words to help you guess meaning from context, e.g., *help others, no money, work.*

5. Some people **volunteer** to help others who are in need. Although you may get no money for volunteering, the work can make you feel good about yourself.

   a. do something without being paid
   b. go to school with a group of people

6. People feel happier when they are **grateful** for the things that they have. They spend less time wanting things that they don't have.

   a. thankful   b. excited

7. A person's **mood** can depend on many things. For example, if someone says something nice about you, it can make you feel good.

   a. the place where you spend most of your time
   b. the way you feel at a particular time

8. Healthy food, exercise, and friends are important for a person's **well-being**.

   a. health and happiness
   b. the way you spend your time

Word Partners

Use **factor** with:
(*adj.*) **contributing** factor, **deciding** factor, **important** factor, **key** factor;
(*n.*) **risk** factor.

9. In many countries, adult children **support** their elderly parents. The children pay their parents' bills and provide them with food and a place to live.

   a. help   b. teach

10. Good health is one **factor** that can make you a happy person. A close group of friends is another factor.

   a. one of the things that causes a situation
   b. something that is difficult or causes problems

B | **Using Vocabulary.** Answer the questions in complete sentences. Then share your sentences with a partner.

1. What are some of your **long-term** goals?

_____

2. What kinds of opportunities do you have to socialize in your **community**?

_____

3. What is your favorite **hobby**?

_____

4. What are you **grateful** for in your life?

_____

C | **Predicting.** Look at the title, subheads, and opening paragraph on pages 12–13. What do you think is the gist of the reading?

a. Your community is the most important factor for your happiness.

b. Self, home, and financial life are more important for happiness than social life, workplace, or community.

c. There are some small changes you can make in your life to increase your happiness.

D | **Brainstorming.** The reading looks at six factors related to happiness. Write the factors in the word web below. Then, with a partner, brainstorm some words that you think might relate to each one.

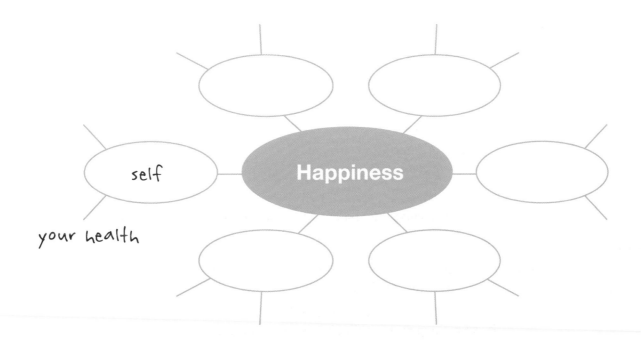

self

your health

Happiness

🎧 Six Keys to Happiness

A RESEARCHERS **HAVE FOUND** that different people need different things to be happy. But there are some basic things that you can do to become happier. According to researcher Dan Buettner, the way to have long-term happiness is to make changes in six areas of our lives: Self, Home, Financial Life, Social Life, Workplace, and Community.

Self

B Your self includes your education, your health, and your sense of purpose—the feeling that you are doing something important. It's important to take care of yourself and to connect with the people around you. First, find a hobby. This gives you a chance to spend time focusing on your interests and talents and to meet people with similar interests. Denmark is one of the happiest countries on Earth, and 95 percent of Danes belong to clubs. You can also volunteer. Volunteering takes the focus off your own problems and makes you feel grateful for what you have.

Home

C How you arrange your home can make you happier. Create a quiet, dark area where you can sit and relax. Paint your living room yellow—it can increase energy and improve mood. It also helps to own a pet. Pets can increase their owners' self-esteem,[1] make them feel calm, and provide love and friendship.

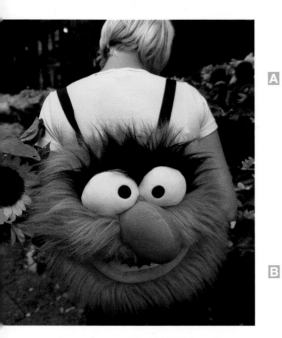

▲ **Copenhagen, Denmark**. According to a global survey, Danish people are among the world's happiest people, second to Costa Ricans.

◀ **Okinawa, Japan.** Close families and friendships help make Okinawa one of the longest-living and happiest places on the planet.

▼ **Paro, Bhutan.** Four rice farmers take a lunch break in Bhutan, a country famous for its GNH, or "Gross National Happiness."

COMMUNITY

SELF

Financial Life

This is the way you think about and spend money. According to Ed Diener, author of *Happiness: Unlocking the Mysteries of Psychological Wealth*, the key to greater **well-being** is to have money, but not to want it too much. Try to spend money on things that give you long-lasting pleasure. Try not to waste money. Buy things that will really enrich your life, such as music lessons and dinners with friends and family.

Social Life

It's important to have a good group of friends and people you see or communicate with regularly. Have friends that encourage you to eat right, to be active, to laugh, and to do your best. Researchers have found that having a close, happy friend can raise a person's mood by nine percent, while each unhappy friend lowers it by seven percent. Create a special group of friends—what Okinawans call a *moai*. Meet with them regularly and share with them when you have more of something than you need. **Support** each other in difficult times.

Workplace

Your office, or wherever you spend your working hours, is a big part of your life. So it should be a place that you like. Find a job with people that you enjoy being around. That includes your boss. You don't want to spend 40 hours a week with people that you dislike. And do something that you feel strongly about. That's more important than a big salary.[2]

▲ Nicoya, Costa Rica. Costa Ricans, such as centenarian Francesca Castillo (pictured with author Dan Buettner), may be the world's happiest people.

Community

The place where you live is probably more important than any other **factor**, including income, education, and religion. If possible, live near people who have about the same amount of money as you. Financial equality with your neighbors makes you less aware of what you don't have. Live in a neighborhood where you feel safe and where you can walk a lot. Walking makes you healthier, and healthier people are happier people.

[1] Your **self-esteem** is how you feel about yourself.
[2] A **salary** is the money that someone receives each month or year from their employer.

Adapted from *Thrive: Finding Happiness the Blue Zones Way* by Dan Buettner, 2010

A | Understanding the Gist. Look back at your answer for exercise **C** on page 11. Was your prediction correct?

B | Identifying Main Ideas. Read the statements below. Circle the main idea in each pair of statements (**a** or **b**).

Self	a. You need to take care of yourself and connect with the people around you. (b.) Focus on your interests and talents and meet people who are like you.
Home	(a.) It's a good idea to paint your living room yellow. b. You should arrange your home so that it makes you feel happy.
Financial Life	(a.) You can be happy if you have enough money, but don't want money too much. b. If you waste money on things you don't need, you won't have enough money for things that you do need.
Social Life	(a.) A good group of friends can increase your happiness. b. Researchers say that a happy friend can increase our mood by nine percent.
Workplace	(a.) You spend a lot of time at work, so you should like your workplace. b. Your boss needs to be someone you enjoy working for.
Community	(a.) The place where you live is more important for happiness than anything else. b. Live around people who have the same amount of money as you do.

Strategy

Look for **clues to the main idea** in the first (and sometimes second) sentence of a paragraph.

C | Identifying Key Details. Complete the following sentences about *"Six Keys to Happiness"*.

1. Volunteering can increase your happiness because _you will focus off_ _your own problems and make you feel grateful for what you have_

2. You should have friends who help you _to eat right to be active_ _to laugh, and to do your best._

3. People are less aware of what they don't have if they have _same financial_ _quality with neighbors._

D | Personalizing. How can you improve each area of your life to become happier? Complete the notes using information from the reading or your own ideas. Write a sentence for each one.

Example: I can take a painting class.

Self _____

Home _I do cleaning of home that make me happy._

Financial Life _when I have enough money._

Social Life _Chat with friends._

Workplace _chose jobs that I like._

Community _I chose place with peaceful neibors_

E | Critical Thinking: Synthesizing. Discuss the questions in small groups.

1. Which of the tips on pages 12–13 do you think the people in Mexico, Singapore, Sardinia, and Okinawa follow?
2. Can you think of other factors affecting happiness that are not mentioned in the reading passages and video?

GOAL: In this lesson, you are going to plan, write, revise, and edit a paragraph. Your topic is:

Do you think people in your community are generally happy or unhappy?

A | **Brainstorming.** Brainstorm a list of things that make people in your community happy and a list of things that people in your community may be unhappy about.

_____   _____

_____   _____

_____   _____

_____   _____

Strategy

When you **brainstorm**, think of as many ideas as possible related to your topic. Don't worry about whether the ideas are good or bad—write down all the ideas you can think of.

B | **Journal Writing.** Use your ideas from exercise **A** to write a response in your journal to the following question. Write for three minutes.

Are the people in your community generally happy or unhappy?

C | Read the information in the box. Use the present tense of the verbs in parentheses to complete the sentences (1–5).

Language for Writing: _Review of the Simple Present_

We use the simple present to talk about facts or things that are generally true.

> _About 5.1 million people_ **live** _in Singapore._
> _Singapore_ **doesn't have** _a high unemployment rate._

We also use the simple present to talk about habits and routines.

> _I_ **spend** _two hours with my friends on most days._
> _I_ **don't see** _my friends on Sundays._

For more explanation and examples, see page 214.

Example: Mike ____loves____ (_love_) his job.

1. Kim ____has____ (_have_) a great job.

2. We _____ (_see_) our friends three or four times a week.

3. My boss and my coworkers _____ (_be_) really friendly.

4. My family and I _____ (_not / feel_) safe in our neighborhood.

5. We ____do not like____ (_not / like_) the city that we live in.

D | **Applying.** Write five sentences using the simple present tense. Write about things you do every day that make you feel happy.

Writing Skill: *Writing a Topic Sentence*

A paragraph is a group of sentences about one topic. Most paragraphs include a sentence that states the main idea of the paragraph. This sentence is called the topic sentence. Paragraphs often begin with topic sentences, but topic sentences can occur anywhere in a paragraph.

A topic sentence should introduce the main idea that the paragraph will discuss or examine.

Below are some examples of strong and weak topic sentences.

Strong Topic Sentences

> *One reason that Singaporeans are happy is that the government provides the basic necessities, such as jobs and housing.*
>
> *People in Mexico socialize a lot, and this may contribute to their happiness.*

Weak Topic Sentences

> *Singaporeans are happy.*

(If the paragraph is about the ways that the government improves people's happiness, this idea should be included in the topic sentence.)

> *People in Mexico socialize a lot.*

(If the paragraph is about how socializing contributes to people's happiness in Mexico, this idea should be included in the topic sentence.)

E | **Identifying Topic Sentences.** Underline the topic sentence in each paragraph. One of the topic sentences is stronger than the others.

1. In Mexico, family is important. Family members provide support to each other during difficult times. Grandmothers take care of grandchildren so the children's mothers can go to work and earn money. When they grow up, children take care of their parents. People in Mexico are generally happy as long as family members are close.

2. Studies have shown that laughter may be an important factor for our happiness, and people who laugh a lot are happier. People who laugh more tend to have higher levels of self-esteem. They also tend to be healthier. Laughter is so important for our general well-being that some people go to "laugh therapy" where they laugh with groups of people.

3. We spend most of our daily lives at work. Our work can increase our happiness. In many countries, a lot of people choose their job based on how much it pays, or on what other people think about that job. But in Denmark, one of the world's happiest countries, most people take jobs that interest them. That gives them a better chance to feel good about the work that they do.

F | Rewrite the two topic sentences that are weak.

1. _In mexico family is important._

2. _we should work can increase our happiness_

A | Planning. Follow the steps to make notes for your paragraph. Don't write complete sentences. Pay attention to the content more than the grammar or spelling.

Step 1 Look at your brainstorming notes on page 15. Do you think people in your community are generally happy or unhappy? Write a topic sentence for your paragraph in the chart below.

Step 2 Choose the best two or three ideas from your notes and write them in the chart.

Step 3 For each idea, write one or two reasons why it makes people in your community happy or unhappy.

Outline

Topic: Are people in your community generally happy or unhappy?

Topic Sentence _Iranian peoples are most socialize and its main reason of their happiness_

Brainstorming Idea 1 _same Financial level_

Reason(s) this makes you happy / unhappy _____

Brainstorming Idea 2 _____

Reason(s) this makes you happy / unhappy _____

Brainstorming Idea 3 _____

Reason(s) this makes you happy / unhappy _____

B | Draft 1. Use your notes to write a first draft of your paragraph.

C | Analyzing. The paragraphs below are on the topic of a happy life.

Which is the first draft? _b_   Which is the revision? _a_

a I think I'm generally happy because I like most things about my life. I have a great job. I do work that I feel passionate about, and I like my coworkers. My family and friends are very supportive. Whenever I have problems, I know that my family and friends will help me. Also, my friends make me laugh a lot. In addition, I'm healthy. I don't have any illnesses, and I play fun sports such as soccer and basketball.

b I think I'm generally happy. I have a great job. I do work that I feel passionate about, and I like my coworkers. I don't make a lot of money, so sometimes I have to do extra work on the weekends. I want to ask for a raise at work. My family and friends are very supportive. Whenever I have problems, I know that my family and friends will help me. Also, my friends make me laugh a lot. In addition, I'm healthy.

D | Analyzing. Work with a partner. Compare the paragraphs above by answering the following questions about each one.

	a		b	
1. Does the paragraph have one main idea?	Y	N	Y	N
2. Does a strong topic sentence introduce the main idea?	Y	N	Y	N
3. Does the paragraph include 2–3 different ideas that relate to the main idea?	Y	N	Y	N
4. Does the paragraph include 1–2 reasons for each one?	Y	N	Y	N
5. Is there any information that doesn't belong?	Y	N	Y	N
6. Is the present tense used correctly?	Y	N	Y	N

Now discuss your answer to this question: Which paragraph is better? Why?

E | Revising. Answer the questions in exercise **D** about your own paragraph.

F | Peer Evaluation. Exchange your draft with a partner and follow these steps:

Step 1 Read your partner's paragraph and tell him or her one thing that you liked about it.

Step 2 Complete the chart with information from your partner's paragraph.

Topic Sentence _____

Idea 1 _____

Reason(s) this makes
people happy / unhappy _____

_____

Idea 2 _____

Reason(s) this makes
people happy / unhappy _____

_____

Idea 3 _____

Reason(s) this makes
people happy / unhappy _____

_____

Step 3 Compare your chart with the chart your partner completed on page 17.

Step 4 The two charts should be similar. If they aren't, discuss how they differ.

G | Draft 2. Write a second draft of your paragraph. Use what you learned from the peer evaluation activity, and your answers to exercise **E**. Make any other necessary changes.

H | Editing Practice. Read the information in the box. Then find and correct one simple present tense mistake in each of the sentences (1–5).

In sentences using the simple present, remember to:

- use the correct verb endings with third person singular subjects (*he likes, she takes*).
- watch out for verbs that have irregular forms in the simple present: *be, have,* and *do.*

---

1. I enjoy the work that I do because it's very challenging, but I doesn't like my boss or my coworkers.

2. My coworkers are supportive, friendly, and fun, and I enjoying spending time with them after work.

3. It's important to me to spend time with my family members when I can, but it's difficult because they don't lives close to me.

4. Although my house is not big and fancy, my neighborhood are safe and beautiful.

5. My friends and I exercises together every day to stay healthy, and that contributes to our happiness.

WRITING TASK: Editing

I | **Editing Checklist.** Use the checklist to find errors in your second draft.

Editing Checklist	Yes	No
1. Are all the words spelled correctly?		
2. Is the first word of every sentence capitalized?		
3. Does every sentence end with the correct punctuation?		
4. Do your subjects and verbs agree?		
5. Did you use the simple present tense correctly?		

J | **Final Draft.** Now use your Editing CheckList to write a third draft of your paragraph. Make any other necessary changes.

UNIT QUIZ

p.2
1. According to the World Database of Happiness, the happiest country in the world is _____.

p.4
2. The level of a person's comfort and wealth is called their _____ of living.

p.5
3. In _____, the government creates jobs and tops up minimum-wage salaries.

p.6
4. In _____, people spend a lot of time socializing, which may contribute to their happiness.

p.8
5. The most important idea of a paragraph is called the _____.

p.12
6. Volunteering can help you forget about your own problems and make you feel _____ for the things you have.

p.13
7. According to researchers, each _____ that we have improves our mood by nine percent.

p.13
8. According to Dan Buettner, your _____ is the most important factor that determines your level of happiness.

Big Ideas

Think and Discuss

1. Do you know any famous inventors?
   What did they invent?

2. What inventions are you using right now?

▲ Tiny silica balls, each one 120 nanometers (0.000000012 m) wide, kill cancer cells in a person's body. Nanotechnology was invented in the late twentieth century and is used in many modern inventions.

Read the information on these pages and discuss the questions.

1. Do you agree with the list of the most important inventions? Can you think of other inventions to add?

2. In your opinion, which inventions made the biggest changes to our daily lives? How?

3. Which inventions saved the most lives? How?

What's the World's Greatest Invention?

A U.K. company, Tesco Mobile, asked 4,000 people to name the world's most important invention. Some inventions—like the washing machine and wheel—make everyday life easier. Some, like the medicine penicillin, save lives. Others—like wireless technology and the Internet—changed the way we communicate. As Lance Batchelor, CEO of Tesco Mobile, says, "All of the inventions in this list have changed the world forever."

1 **wheel**

2 **airplane**

3 **lightbulb**

4 **Internet**

5 **personal computer**

6 **telephone**

7 **penicillin**

8 **iPhone**

9 **flushing toilet**

10 **combustion engine**

Alexander Graham Bell invented the first **telephone** in 1876. His early interest in speech, sound, and music helped him understand how sound might travel along a wire. Later he created the Bell Telephone Company, which became AT&T, the largest phone company in the U.S.

Orville Wright made the first powered **airplane** flight (right) on December 17, 1903, on a windy hillside in North Carolina, USA. The flight lasted 12 seconds for a distance of 120 feet (36.5 meters)—shorter than a Boeing 707's wingspan. To build the *Flyer*, Orville and his brother Wilbur used bicycle technology, parts made from wood, a homemade engine—and no wheels.

The internal **combustion engine** is the main source of power for most cars, planes, and boats. A car's movement comes from burning fuel in the engine, which produces high-pressure gas. Other types of vehicles use electricity stored in batteries, like this solar-powered car.

A | Building Vocabulary. Find the words in **blue** in the reading passage on pages 25–26. Read the words around them and try to guess their meanings. Then write each word next to its definition.

1. _____ (*verb*) have enough money to pay for something

2. _____ (*verb*) gave the energy that something needed in order to work

3. _____ (*adjective*) able to do tasks well without wasting time or energy

4. _____ (*noun*) a form of energy that can be used for heating and lighting and to provide energy for machines

5. _____ (*noun*) energy from the sun's light and heat

6. _____ (*adjective*) having the ability to invent and develop new and original ideas

7. _____ (*adverb*) in the end, especially after a lot of problems

8. _____ (*noun*) the act of making sure that something does not happen

9. _____ (*noun*) the things people need for a job, hobby, or sport

10. _____ (*noun*) a drawing that shows how to make something

B | Using Vocabulary. Answer the questions. Share your ideas with a partner.

1. Describe one way in which you are **creative**.

2. What **equipment** do you use for your job or for your hobby?

3. **Solar power** is one source of energy. What are some other ways to produce **electricity**?

C | Brainstorming. Make a list of things you use every day that require electricity.

1. _____   5. _____

2. _____   6. _____

3. _____   7. _____

4. _____   8. _____

D | Predicting. Read the title and look at the photos on pages 25–26. What do you think the reading is about? Write one sentence.

_____

Word Link

The suffix **-tion** can turn some verbs into nouns, e.g., prevent / preven**tion**, define / defini**tion**, act / ac**tion**, create / crea**tion**, contribute / contribu**tion**.

Malawi

The Power of Creativity

track 1-04

WILLIAM KAMKWAMBA lives in Malawi, Africa, where most people have to grow their own food and have no electricity or running water.[1] Only two percent of Malawians can afford electricity. With no electricity or running water, life is difficult. In 2001, when William was 14 years old, life in Malawi became even more difficult. There was a severe drought[2] and most families, including William's, couldn't grow enough food. He explains, "Within five months all Malawians began to starve to death. My family ate one meal per day, at night."

A

Because of the drought, William's family couldn't afford to send him to school anymore. So one day William went to the library near his home. He wanted to continue his education. William found a science book called *Using Energy*. It included instructions for building a windmill. Windmills can be very efficient sources of electricity, and they can bring water up from underground. William didn't know much English, and he wasn't able to understand most of the book, but it was full of pictures and diagrams.[3] Looking at the pictures, William thought he could build a windmill for his family.

B

William used old bicycle parts and other thrown-away items to build his windmill. The final windmill was 16 feet (5 meters) tall.

[1] **Running water** is water that is brought into a building through pipes.
[2] A **drought** is a long period of time with no rain.
[3] **Diagrams** are drawings that show how something, e.g., a machine, works.

When William went home and started building his windmill, a lot of people laughed at him, including his mother. They didn't think he could do it, but William was confident. He saw the photo of the windmill in the book. That meant someone else was able to build it, so he knew he could build it, too. William was also creative. He didn't have the parts and equipment that he saw in the book's illustrations, and he couldn't buy them. So he looked for parts in junkyards.[4] He explains, "I found a tractor fan,[5] [a] shock absorber,[6] [and] PVC pipes.[7] Using a bicycle frame . . . , I built my machine."

William changed and improved his design little by little. First, the windmill powered only one lightbulb. Eventually, it powered four lights. Then there was enough electricity for four lights and a radio. No one laughed at William after that, and people in his town started to come to his house to get power for their cell phones. Later, William built a second windmill. This one brought water up from underground. After that, William began to teach other people how to build windmills. He also continued to build more of them himself, including one at a primary school in Malawi.

Because of his success with the windmills, William was able to go back to school. He also helped with other projects, including solar power, clean water, and malaria[8] prevention. He wrote a book about his life, *The Boy Who Harnessed the Wind: Creating Currents of Electricity and Hope.* In addition, he uses his website, movingwindmills. org, to educate and give hope to people. His main message is this: "To the Africans, and the poor who are struggling[9] with your dreams . . . trust yourself and believe. Whatever happens, don't give up."[10]

[4] A **junkyard** is a place where old machines are thrown away.
[5] A **tractor fan** is a machine part that helps cool the engine in a tractor (a vehicle used on farms).
[6] A **shock absorber** is a machine part that helps make a car run smoothly over uneven roads.
[7] **PVC pipes** are tubes made from a plastic material (polyvinyl chloride).
[8] **Malaria** is a disease spread by mosquitoes.
[9] If someone is **struggling**, they are trying hard to do something because it is difficult.
[10] If you **don't give up**, you don't stop trying to do something, especially something that is difficult.

A | Understanding the Gist. What is the main idea of the reading? Circle the best answer. Then compare with your prediction on page 24.

1. Windmills can create electricity and bring up water from under the ground.

2. In most parts of Malawi, there is no electricity or running water.

3. A young boy used his creativity to bring electricity to his village.

B | Identifying Key Details. Complete the sentences below with information from the reading.

1. In 2001, life became very challenging for William's family because _____.

2. William found instructions for a windmill in a book called _____.

3. When he started to build his windmill, many people in his village _____.

4. He knew that he could build the windmill because _____.

5. After William built his first windmill, people came to his house to _____.

6. William's second windmill was able to _____.

C | Critical Thinking: Making Connections. Complete the chart below. Fill in the missing problems and solutions.

Problems				
William couldn't afford to go to school.	William couldn't read the book about windmills because he didn't know much English.		The village needed more water.	Other people wanted to build windmills but didn't know how.

Solutions				
		William went to a junkyard.		

D | Personalizing. Write answers to the questions.

1. Name a problem that you solved in your own life. How did you solve the problem? _____

_____

2. Choose one of the inventions from page 22 or use your own idea. Describe the problem(s) that it solved.

Invention: _____

Problem(s) it solved: _____

Reading Skill: *Identifying Supporting Ideas*

Supporting ideas tell more about the main idea. They can do the following:

describe   give reasons   give examples

Look at the paragraph from the reading. What does each colored sentence do?

> *When William went home and started building his windmill, a lot of people laughed at him, including his mother. They didn't think he could do it, but William was confident. He saw the photo of the windmill in the book. That meant someone else was able to build it, so he knew he could build it, too. William was also creative. He didn't have the parts and equipment that he saw in the book's illustrations, and he couldn't buy them. So he looked for parts in junkyards. He explains, "I found a tractor fan, shock absorber, [and] PVC pipes. Using a bicycle frame … , I built my machine."*

The main idea of the paragraph is that William was confident and creative in building his windmill. The green sentences **give reasons** why William was confident. The blue sentences **give examples** of how William was creative. And the purple sentences **describe** how he did it.

A | **Analyzing.** Read the information about seat belts below. Write the main idea of the paragraph and the three supporting details

Main idea: _____

Supporting detail 1: _____

Supporting detail 2: _____

Supporting detail 3: _____

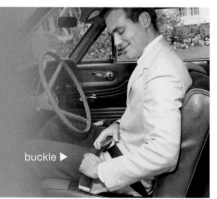

track 1-05

Many inventions change lives, but Nils Bohlin's invention has probably helped to save more than a million lives so far. Bohlin invented a new type of seat belt that is in all cars made today. Before Bohlin's invention, seat belts were buckled across the stomach (see picture). The buckles often caused injuries during high-speed accidents. Bohlin's seat belt holds the upper and lower body safely in place, with a buckle at the side.

buckle ▶

B | **Identifying Supporting Details.** Look back at the reading passage on pages 25–26. Find and underline one supporting detail that gives a reason, one that gives an example, and one that describes.

Solar Cooking

Before Viewing

absorb	alternative
developing world	fuel
pollution	purify

A | Matching. Here are some words you will hear in the video. Write each word or phrase next to the correct definition. Use your dictionary to help you.

1. _____ the process of making things such as air and water dirty

2. _____ to take in something, such as gas, liquid, or heat

3. _____ countries or parts of the world that generally have low standards of living

4. _____ to make something clean by removing harmful or dangerous things from it

5. _____ a different choice

6. _____ things that provide heat or energy, such as oil, wood, or gasoline

B | Brainstorming. Many people in developing countries have to burn wood to cook their food. Why do you think this might be a problem?

can cause air pollution _____ _____

While Viewing

A | Watch the video about solar cooking. Does it mention any of the things that you listed in exercise **B** above? Circle any items that are mentioned.

B | As you view the video, think about the answers to these questions.

1. How do solar stoves work?

2. What can a person do with a solar stove? Who can benefit from them?

3. How much does a solar stove cost and how long can it last?

▲ Cooking in many African countries is done the traditional way, over a wood fire.

After Viewing

A | Discuss answers to questions 1–3 above with a partner.

B | Critical Thinking: Synthesizing. In what ways are William Kamkwamba's windmills and the solar cooker in the video similar?

_____

_____

A | **Building Vocabulary.** Read the sentences below. Use the context to help you identify the part of speech (adjective, noun, verb) and meaning of each **bold** word. Write your answers. Check your answers in a dictionary.

1. Bottles are useful **containers** for water and other liquids. They make liquids easy to carry.

   Part of speech: _____

   Meaning: _____

2. Doctors have many different ways to **detect** diseases. For example, they can do blood tests or listen to your lungs to learn if you are sick.

   Part of speech: _____

   Meaning: _____

3. Solar power can **benefit** people in the developing world by providing them with free electricity.

   Part of speech: _____

   Meaning: _____

4. Cell phones can make a noise to **indicate** that you are receiving a text message.

   Part of speech: _____

   Meaning: _____

5. There have already been several **innovations** in this century. Text messaging and the tablet computer are just two examples.

   Part of speech: _____

   Meaning: _____

6. The cell phone is a popular **device** for things such as communication and Internet browsing. For things such as document creation and movie watching, a computer is a better choice.

   Part of speech: _____

   Meaning: _____

7. The sun is a great source of **renewable** energy because we can't use up all the sun's heat and light.

   Part of speech: _____

   Meaning: _____

Word Link

The suffix **-able** can turn some verbs into adjectives, e.g., renew / renew**able**, detect / detect**able**, afford / afford**able**, prevent / prevent**able**.

8. Before refrigerators were invented, people could not **store** fresh meat. Instead, they had to store salted or dried meat.

Part of speech: _____

Meaning: _____

9. Morse code was invented in the 1930s. It is a **system** of communication that uses long and short sounds.

Part of speech: _____

Meaning: _____

10. The wheel is one of the most **valuable** inventions of all time. Without it, we would probably have to walk or ride on the backs of animals to travel long distances.

Part of speech: _____

Meaning: _____

B | Using Vocabulary. Answer the questions in complete sentences. Then share your sentences with a partner.

1. What do you think is the most **valuable innovation** of the last 10 years? Why?

_____

2. What are some examples of **renewable** energy?

_____

3. What **devices** do you use every day?

_____

4. What kinds of things **indicate** a person's mood?

_____

5. What **system** do you use for remembering your schedule?

_____

C | Predicting. Look at the photos, and read the title, subheads, and opening paragraph of the reading passage on pages 32–33. What do you think is the purpose of each of the items described? Discuss your ideas with a partner.

Infant Warmer _____

Water Container _____

Portable Clay Cooler _____

Health Detector _____

Solar Wi-Fi Light _____

Big Ideas: Little Packages

track 1-06

A

CAN SIMPLE IDEAS change the world? They just might, one new idea at a time. Creative designers and scientists are working to invent products for communities in developing countries. Some of their innovations might solve even the biggest problems—from health care to clean water.

Infant Warmer

B Around 19 million low-birthweight babies are born every year in developing countries. These babies weigh less than 5.5 pounds (2.5 kilograms) when they're born. Low-birthweight babies are often unable to keep their body temperatures[1] warm enough. Many get too cold and die. The Embrace Infant Warmer helps keep these babies warm. Developer Jane Chen says, "Over the next five years, we hope to save the lives of almost a million babies."

◄ "We hope that the Embrace Infant Warmer represents a new trend for the future of technology," says developer Jane Chen. "Simple, localized, affordable solutions that have the potential to make a huge social impact."

▲ Developers of the Embrace Infant Warmer (left to right): Naganand Murty, Linus Liang, Rahul Panicker, Jane Chen.

Water Container

C In poor areas, people often have to walk several miles to get clean water. Usually, women and children have to carry heavy containers of water home every day, and it is difficult work. The Q Drum holds 13 gallons (about 50 liters) in a rolling container. With this innovation, people can easily roll the water on the ground.

[1] Your **body temperature** is how hot or how cold your body is.

Portable Clay Cooler

D The pot-in-pot system is a good way to store food without using electricity. The user puts wet sand between two pots, one fitting inside the other. The water evaporates[2] and keeps food cool. That helps food stay fresh longer. For example, tomatoes can last weeks instead of just days. That way, people can buy more fresh fruits and vegetables at the market, and farmers can make more money.

Health Detector

E Scientist Hayat Sindi's device is the size of a postage stamp, and it costs just a penny. But it could save millions of lives. In many parts of the world, doctors and nurses work with no electricity or clean water. They have to send health tests to labs[3] and wait weeks for results. But this little piece of paper could change that. It contains tiny holes that are filled with chemicals. These chemicals can detect health problems. A person places a single drop of blood on the paper. The chemicals in the paper change because of the blood and indicate whether or not the person has an illness.

▲ Saudi-born inventor, Hayat Sindi, presenting her invention at the 2009 Pop!Tech conference.

Solar Wi-Fi Light

F The StarSight system is an innovation that can benefit millions of people around the world. It absorbs solar energy during the day to power streetlamps at night. The solar panels also power wireless Internet access. The result: renewable electricity for better street lighting and faster communication. This can be extremely valuable in places where it is difficult to get electricity.

[2] When a liquid **evaporates**, it changes to a gas as its temperature increases.
[3] **Labs** are laboratories, places where scientific research is done.

A | **Understanding the Gist.** Look back at your answers for exercise **C** on page 31. Were your predictions correct?

B | **Identifying Key Details.** Read the following sentences about the reading on pages 32–33. For each sentence, circle **T** (true), **F** (false), or **NG** (the information is not given in the passage).

1. The infant warmer was invented to help low-birthweight babies.   **T**   **F**   **NG**

2. In poor areas, men and teenage boys usually carry water home.   **T**   **F**   **NG**

3. The portable clay cooler will cause farmers to make less money because people won't have to buy vegetables every day.   **T**   **F**   **NG**

4. Hayat Sindi's low-tech diagnostic device is made of paper.   **T**   **F**   **NG**

5. Each solar Wi-Fi light can provide electricity for 10 to 20 homes at a time.   **T**   **F**   **NG**

C | **Identifying Supporting Ideas.** Find supporting details in the reading to answer each question below.

1. What is the reason that low-birthweight babies need infant warmers?

   _____

2. What can the Q Drum hold?

   _____

3. How does the portable clay cooler work?

   _____

4. What is one reason that people need Hayat Sindi's diagnostic tool?

   _____

5. What is an example of how the solar Wi-Fi light can benefit people?

   _____

CT Focus

To rank items in order, first decide on your *criteria* for ranking, e.g., how many people you think will be able to afford the item, or how many lives might be saved or improved.

D | **Critical Thinking: Ranking and Justifying.** Which of the innovations from pages 32–33 do you think is the most important? Which is the least important? Rank them 1–5, with 1 as the most important. Then talk with a partner and explain your choices.

_____ Infant Warmer   _____ Portable Clay Cooler   _____ Solar Wi-Fi Light

_____ Water Container   _____ Health Detector

E | **Critical Thinking: Synthesizing.** Discuss this question in small groups: How is the clay cooler described in the reading similar to, and different from, the solar cooker shown in the video?

GOAL: In this lesson, you are going to plan, write, revise, and edit a paragraph. Your topic is:
Choose an innovation—one from this unit or one you have used yourself.
Describe the need it filled and how it changed people's lives.

A | Read the information in the box. Then use the simple past tense of the verbs in parentheses to complete the sentences (1–7).

Language for Writing: Review of the Simple Past

We use the simple past tense to talk about events that began and ended in the past.

> *According to historians, a man named Ts'ai Lun* **invented** *paper in China around AD 105.*
>
> *Before that time, people* **didn't have** *inexpensive material to write on.*
>
> *People* **wrote** *on things such as silk and clay, which* **were** *expensive and inconvenient.*

To form the simple past tense of *be*:
• use *was* or *were* to form affirmative statements.
• use *was not / wasn't* or *were not / weren't* to form negative statements.

To form the simple past tense with other verbs:
• add *-ed* to the end of most verbs to form affirmative statements.
• use *did not / didn't* with the base form of a main verb to form negative statements.

Some verbs have irregular past tense forms in affirmative statements:
go—went   have—had   make—made   take—took   do—did   build—built

For more explanation and examples, see page 215.

Example: In 2001, there ____was____ (*be*) a drought in Malawi and most people
__didn't have__ (*not / have*) enough food.

1. Most people in William Kamkwamba's village _____ (*not / have*) electricity.

2. William _____ (*go*) to the library.

3. He _____ (*find*) a book there called *Using Energy.*

4. William _____ (*use*) the information in the book and he _____ (*build*) a windmill.

5. When he _____ (*start*), people _____ (*not / believe*) that he could do it.

6. William _____ (*not / be*) worried. He _____ (*be*) confident.

7. After a while, he _____ (*be*) successful. His windmill _____ (*make*) electricity.

B | **Applying.** Write five sentences using the simple past tense. Describe things that people did not do 50 years ago, but that you do today.

C | Brainstorming. Brainstorm a list of innovations that you think are important. Use ideas from this unit or your own ideas.

_____

_____

D | Journal Writing. Use your ideas from exercise **C** to write a response in your journal to the following question. Write for three minutes.

Which innovations caused the biggest changes in people's lives?

Writing Skill: *Supporting the Main Idea and Giving Details*

Good paragraphs include supporting ideas that give information and details about the main idea. These sentences can give descriptions, reasons, or examples to help the reader clearly understand the main idea.

E | Identifying Supporting Ideas. Match each topic sentence with three supporting sentences. Write **A** or **B** for each one. Two sentences are extra.

Topic Sentence A: About 900 million people need access to safe drinking water, and a simple invention may be the answer to this problem.

Topic Sentence B: The solar-powered MightyLight is a safe and clean source of lighting that can provide light to millions of people around the world.

_____ a.   The LifeStraw provides instant clean water, saving lives during disasters.

_____ b.   You should drink about eight glasses of water a day.

_____ c.   The MightyLight is safer and cleaner than traditional kerosene lamps.

_____ d.   Each straw purifies about 160 gallons of water.

_____ e.   It's easy to carry, and you can hang it on a wall or place it on a tabletop.

_____ f.   Candles don't provide much light.

_____ g.   It also lasts longer—its LED technology is good for up to 30 years.

_____ h.   Thousands of LifeStraws were donated to Haiti after the 2010 earthquake.

F | Now use the sentences in exercise **E** to write two paragraphs.

A | **Planning.** Follow the steps to make notes for your paragraph. Don't write complete sentences. Pay attention to the content more than the grammar or spelling.

Step 1: From your brainstorming notes on page 36, choose an innovation to write about.

Step 2: Write a topic sentence that will introduce your paragraph.

Step 3: Look at your brainstorming notes again. Complete the chart.

Outline

Topic: Choose an invention. What need did it fill, and how did it change people's lives?

Topic Sentence _____

Supporting Idea
What is one
way that the
innovation changed
people's lives? _____

_____

_____

_____

Detail(s)
(one or two points) _____

_____

_____

_____

Supporting Idea
What is another
way that the
innovation changed
people's lives? _____

_____

_____

_____

Detail(s)
(one or two points) _____

_____

_____

_____

B | **Draft 1.** Use your notes to write a first draft of your paragraph.

C | **Analyzing.** The paragraphs below are on the topic of an innovation.

Which is the first draft? _____   Which is the revision? _____

(a)   The car is one of the most important inventions in history. Before the car was invented, most people used horses to travel long distances, and they didn't travel very quickly. For example, a person on a horse could travel an average of 50–60 miles in a day. People traveling by horse and carriage could go 20–30 miles in a day. Because it was difficult to travel far, most people stayed in their own towns and villages their whole lives. Families stayed in the same place for generations. Now that we have cars, it only takes an hour to go 60 miles. Because it's so easy to travel long distances, people can work 60 miles away from home if they want to. And they can live almost anywhere they want. Because of the car, people have many more opportunities to shape their lives than they used to.

(b)   The car is one of the most important inventions in history. The first real car factory opened in 1902. Before the car was invented, most people used horses to travel long distances, and they didn't travel very quickly. For example, a person on a horse could travel an average of 50–60 miles in a day. People traveling by horse and carriage could go 20–30 miles in a day. A horse can go up to 40 miles per hour, but it gets tired after just a few miles. If the horse goes more slowly, it can travel for a longer period of time without getting tired. Now that we have cars, it only takes an hour to go 60 miles. Because it's so easy to travel long distances, people can work 60 miles away from home if they want to. And they can live almost anywhere they want. Because of the car, people have many more opportunities to shape their lives than they used to.

D | **Analyzing.** Work with a partner. Compare the paragraphs above by answering the following questions about each one.

		a		b	
1.	Does the paragraph have one main idea?	Y	N	Y	N
2.	Does the topic sentence introduce the main idea?	Y	N	Y	N
3.	Does the paragraph include 2–3 supporting ideas?	Y	N	Y	N
4.	Does the paragraph include 1–2 details for each supporting idea?	Y	N	Y	N
5.	Is there any information that doesn't belong?	Y	N	Y	N
6.	Does the paragraph use the past tense correctly?	Y	N	Y	N

E | **Revising.** Answer the questions in exercise **D** about your own paragraph.

F | **Peer Evaluation.** Exchange your draft with a partner and follow these steps:

Step 1   Read your partner's paragraph and tell him or her one thing that you liked about it.

Step 2   Complete the chart below with information from your partner's paragraph.

Topic Sentence   _____

Supporting Idea
What is one way that
the innovation changed
people's lives?   _____

_____

Detail(s)
(*one or two points*)   _____

_____

Supporting Idea
What is another
way that the
innovation changed
people's lives?   _____

_____

Detail(s)
(*one or two points*)   _____

_____

Step 3   Compare your chart with the chart your partner completed on page 37.

Step 4   The two charts should be similar. If they aren't, discuss how they differ.

G | **Draft 2.** Write a second draft of your paragraph. Use what you learned from the peer evaluation activity, and your answers to exercise **E**. Make any other necessary changes.

H | **Editing Practice.** Read the information in the box. Then find and correct one simple past tense mistake in each of the sentences (1–5).

In sentences using the **simple past tense**, remember to:

- use the correct past tense forms of *be*: *was*, *wasn't*, *were*, and *weren't*.
- use the correct verb endings; for most verbs, you add *-ed* to form the simple past tense, but some verbs have irregular past tense forms.
- use the base form of the verb with *did not / didn't* in negative statements.

---

1. The people in William Kamkwamba's village wasn't confident about William's plan.

2. When they were young, the Wright brothers had a flying toy.

3. Alexander Graham Bell make the first telephone.

4. The first car didn't went very fast.

5. Ts'ai Lun invented paper in the first century AD, but paper didn't be widely available until many years later.

I | Editing Checklist. Use the checklist to find errors in your second draft.

Editing Checklist	Yes	No
1. Are all the words spelled correctly?		
2. Is the first word of every sentence capitalized?		
3. Does every sentence end with the correct punctuation?		
4. Do your subjects and verbs agree?		
5. Did you use the simple present and simple past correctly?		

J | Final Draft. Now use your Editing Checklist to write a third draft of your paragraph. Make any other necessary changes.

UNIT QUIZ

p.22
1. According to a U.K. survey, the wheel is the world's most _____.

p.24
2. Energy from the sun is called _____ power.

p.25
3. Windmills can create _____ and bring up _____ from under the ground.

p.28
4. Supporting sentences can _____, _____, and _____.

p.29
5. A(n) _____ uses power from the sun to heat food for eating. It is also called a(n) _____.

p.30
6. A new thing or method of doing something is called a(n) _____.

p.33
7. Hayat Sindi's health detector is as small as a(n) _____.

p.39
8. We use the _____ of a verb with *did not / didn't* to make a past tense negative statement.

Connected Lives

Think and Discuss

1. How do you use the Internet to keep in touch with other people?

2. In what ways is the Internet useful for teaching and learning?

Internet users gather at a Wi-Fi cafe on 42nd Street, New York.

Exploring the Theme

A. Look at the information below and answer the questions.

    1. What do the colors on the map show?

    2. Which places are most connected? Which regions had the biggest rise in Internet use?

B. Look at the information on page 43 and answer the questions.

    1. What information does the graphic show? Do you think the connections are different today?

    2. Which social networks are popular in your country today? Why are they popular?

Worldwide Connections

The map shows the density of IP addresses around the world. IP addresses identify personal computers and devices that connect to the Internet. Areas with many large cities are densely populated with addresses. Remote or undeveloped areas are mostly empty. In Canada and the United States, for example, about 75 percent of people are connected to the Internet. In Sub-Saharan Africa, less than 5 percent of people had Internet access in 2007. Some areas, such as South and East Asia, Latin America, and the Middle East, have seen very fast growth in recent years. Internet usage in East Asia rose from less than 2 percent of the population in 2000, to 15 percent by 2007.

NORTH AMERICA

EUROPE

AFRICA

SOUTH AMERICA

ANTARCTICA

IP addresses per populated place, 2009

- More than 10,000
- 300–10,000
- 45–299
- 15–44
- 1–14

Unique visitors age 15 and over, October 2009 (in millions)

0   10   20   30

MYSPACE 110

WER-KENNT-WEN 7

STUDIVZ SITES 17

United States

LINKEDIN 35

HATENA BOOKMARK 4

MIXI 13

Japan

BAIDU SPACE 63

China

Canada

Germany

BHARATSTUDENT 4

DEVIANTART 34

India

FACEBOOK 430

QQ ALUMNI 43

KAIXIN001 24

ORKUT 54

TWITTER 58

HI5 47

VKONTAKTE 17

Russia

Brazil

BEBO 8

United Kingdom

France

VK 14

WINDOWS LIVE PROFILE 164

SKYROCK 16

ODNOKLASSNIKI 10

Worldwide Friends

In October 2009, more than 830 million users visited social networks on their home and office computers. Ten sites (shown in dark blue) had the most visitors. Green lines connect countries to their three favorite sites. The number of social network users continues to grow: By 2012, Facebook alone had more than 800 million active users.

The remote kingdom of Bhutan ▶ introduced its first Internet service in 1999. The country's first Internet café opened a year later. Today, the Internet helps young Bhutanese, such as these college students, stay connected with the rest of the world.

A | **Building Vocabulary.** Find the words in **blue** in the reading passage on pages 45–46. Read the words around them and try to guess their meanings. Then match the sentence parts below to make definitions.

1. _____ When you **edit** something,
2. _____ A **culture** is a society with
3. _____ **Communication** means
4. _____ When you **interact** with someone,
5. _____ The **relationship** between two people is
6. _____ The term **media** includes
7. _____ **Participation** means
8. _____ Something with **potential** has
9. _____ **Technology** is
10. _____ If something is **traditional**,

a. its own beliefs or way of life.
b. you talk, spend time, or work together.
c. the possibility for success in the future.
d. you correct and make changes to it in order to improve it.
e. sharing information with people, for example, by talking or writing.
f. joining in to be a part of something.
g. the way they feel and act toward each other, or the way they are connected.
h. it is connected with customs, methods, or beliefs that have existed for a long time.
i. television, radio, magazines, and other things that provide information.
j. methods, systems, and devices that are the result of scientific knowledge.

B | **Using Vocabulary.** Answer the questions. Share your ideas with a partner.

1. Why do you think classroom **participation** is important for students?
2. What are some of the latest developments in **technology**?
3. What forms of **media** do you use regularly? What do you use them for?

C | **Brainstorming.** Think about how we get and share information by TV and the Internet. How are TV and the Internet similar? How are they different? Write your ideas in the chart.

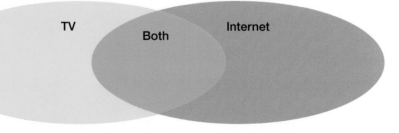

TV   Both   Internet

D | **Predicting.** Scan the reading passage on pages 45–46 quickly. List two other nouns or verbs that appear two or more times.

relationships   _____   _____

Now look at the words you wrote. What do you think the passage is about?

a. how the Internet is changing society
b. how to use the Internet in the classroom
c. why websites are the most important form of media

track **1-07**

The Changing Face of Communication

▲ Students explore the online world at an Internet café in Novosibirsk, Russia.

A Michael Wesch is a cultural anthropology[1] professor who explores the effects of new media on society and culture. He believes that all human relationships depend on communication. Change the type of communication, and you change the relationships. Change the relationships, and you change the structure[2] of society.

B One example of this, he says, is television. When television became the dominant medium[3] in the 1950s, it changed the way families interacted. Family members began to sit in front of the TV to watch rather than face each other to talk. The people on the television spoke, and the TV viewers listened. In this one-way type of communication, only the people on TV had power. Only they had a voice.[4]

Communication Today: The Internet

C Today, the Internet is changing our relationships again. The newest media of communication are on the Internet, and these media change and grow every day. Wesch and his students study social networks and other interactive Internet sites. For example, they studied YouTube, the popular online video sharing site. As Wesch explains, "Instead of simply watching TV, we can create and edit our own videos." Viewers all over the world can watch and write comments. This kind of sharing changes the way we communicate. With the Internet, everyone can have a voice.

---

[1] **Anthropology** is the study of people, society, and culture.
[2] The **structure** of something is the way it is put together or organized.
[3] A **dominant medium** is the most powerful, successful, or noticeable medium (*medium* is the singular form of *media*).
[4] A person's **voice** can refer to his or her opinion about something and the ability to share that opinion.

Wesch created and posted his own short video on YouTube. It has had more than 11 million views. The video asks us to think about how we use and interact with the Internet. The Internet is no longer just connecting people with information. It's connecting people with people. It's a way for us to share our thoughts and ideas with the world. It wouldn't exist without us. In fact, Wesch says, "the Web is us."

▲ A computer brings information and entertainment to a class of young Nigerian students.

Education and the New Media

Wesch wants to make changes in education to fit this new style of communication. He has made some changes in his own classes. For example, in his Introduction to Cultural Anthropology class, he didn't simply teach his students about different cultures. Instead, he asked each student to become an expert in one culture. Then the class used their knowledge to create an online role-playing game. As they learned about the different cultures, they increased their knowledge about global problems.

According to Wesch, activities such as the role-play exercise help prepare students to be active and responsible members of society. "I ask [students] to think not about what new media was designed for," he says, "but how they can [use] it for something else." A great example, he believes, is social media. It was created to help friends connect, but now it also allows people to share and collaborate[5] on projects.

Wesch understands that the new media can provide opportunities for sharing and participation. However, he warns that online content can also be misleading. He believes it is important for everyone, especially students, to understand the dangers of digital media and learn how to use it wisely. In a traditional classroom, for example, the teacher is the main provider of information. Now, information is available to anyone with an Internet connection—and anyone can provide new information at any time. So one of the goals of education should be to prepare students to find, analyze, and think critically about online information, as well as create their own.

Wesch says, "I want to believe that technology can help us see relationships and global connections in positive new ways. It's pretty amazing that I have this little box sitting on my desk through which I can talk to any one of a billion people. And yet do any of us really use it for all the potential that's there?"

"One of the most important skills we must now learn is collaboration. We can learn to listen to one another, use each other's strengths, and practice working together in any environment."

*- Michael Wesch,
U.S. Professor of the
Year, 2008*

[5] If you **collaborate**, you work with other people to achieve a goal or complete a project.

A | **Understanding the Gist.** Look back at your answer for exercise **D** on page 44. Was your prediction correct?

B | **Identifying Key Details.** Complete each statement with information from the reading passage.

1. Some examples of new media are _____.

2. In the 1950s, TV changed _____.

3. The main way that TV is different from the Internet is _____.

4. One way the Internet can benefit us is _____.

5. One way that the Internet can be harmful is _____.

6. Wesch's students shared cultural information by playing _____.

7. Wesch thinks students need to learn how to _____.

C | **Critical Thinking: Making Inferences.** Work with a partner. What can you infer from each statement from the reading passage? Circle the best inference.

1. "When television became the dominant medium in the 1950s, it changed the way families interacted."

   a. Before the 1950s, a different medium was probably dominant.

   b. There were a lot of good television programs in the 1950s.

2. "This kind of sharing changes the way we communicate. With the Internet, everyone can have a voice."

   a. People probably should not share certain things on the Internet.

   b. The Internet is a better medium of communication than TV.

3. "It's pretty amazing that I have this little box sitting on my desk through which I can talk to any one of a billion people. And yet do any of us really use it for all the potential that's there?"

   a. There are a lot of possible uses of the Internet that most people don't really think about.

   b. The Internet is an amazing tool, but most people in the world don't use it very much.

> **CT Focus**
>
> You **make inferences** when you make logical guesses about things a writer does not say directly. This is also called "reading between the lines."

D | **Personalizing.** Write answers to the questions.

1. Do you ever create Web content, write comments on websites, or post things on social networking sites? Why, or why not?

   _____

2. Do you agree with Wesch's views on how we use the Internet? Why, or why not?

   _____

   _____

Reading Skill: *Skimming for Gist*

Skimming is quickly looking over a passage to get the general idea of what it is about. When we skim, we don't read every word. Instead, we look for important words or chunks (pieces) of information. For example, we look for things such as names, dates, and repeated words.

We often skim online news sites to find out the most important news of the day, blogs to choose which posts we want to read, and magazines to decide what we want to read about. But skimming can also help with academic reading. If you skim a passage before you read it carefully, you can get an idea of what the passage is about and how it is organized. This can help you understand the passage more easily when you do read it carefully, because you know what to expect.

A | Skimming. Skim the paragraph below. Read only the darker words. What do you think is the main idea of the paragraph?

For many of us, visiting Facebook, Twitter, or other online social networks has become a regular part of our daily activities. However, we may not have noticed the significant ways that social networks have changed our lives. First of all, they have changed the way we get our news. These days, we often only read the news stories that our friends post online. Second, our relationships have changed. Now, it's easier to keep in touch with new friends and find old friends that we haven't seen for a long time. Third, many of us share thoughts with our online friends that we used to keep private. For example, in an instant, we can tell all our online friends that we think we just failed an exam. Are these changes good or bad? That's for each person to decide. But one thing is certain—as more people join social networks and as new networks continue to appear, we can expect more changes in the future.

B | Skimming. Now read the whole paragraph carefully. Were you correct about the main idea?

track **1-08**

For many of us, visiting Facebook, Twitter, or other online social networks has become a regular part of our daily activities. However, we may not have noticed the significant ways that social networks have changed our lives. First of all, they have changed the way we get our news. These days, we often only read the news stories that our friends post online. Second, our relationships have changed. Now, it's easier to keep in touch with new friends and find old friends that we haven't seen for a long time. Third, many of us share thoughts with our online friends that we used to keep private. For example, in an instant, we can tell all our online friends that we think we just failed an exam. Are these changes good or bad? That's for each person to decide. But one thing is certain—as more people join social networks and as new networks continue to appear, we can expect more changes in the future.

CT Focus

Make inferences as you read. For example, what can you infer from this sentence about how the writer got news in the past?

Lamu: Tradition and Modernity

▲ Traditional houses are tightly packed on the island town of Lamu, Kenya.

Before Viewing

A | **Guessing Meaning from Context.** You will hear these **bold** words in the video. Discuss the meaning of each one with a partner. Write definitions for the words and phrases.

1. When you visit a different culture, it can have an **influence** on the way you think and the things you do.
2. Lamu is having **economic** problems. There are not a lot of jobs, so people can't earn much money.
3. Culture is **dynamic**. It doesn't stay the same forever.
4. Cultures are always changing, but they usually **retain** their most important **features**. For example, language and religion usually stay the same.

B | **Brainstorming.** Why might a traditional culture want to connect to the Internet and become more modern? Why might they *not* want to? List reasons with a partner.

Reasons for: They can learn about other countries.

Reasons against: _____

While Viewing

A | Watch the video about Lamu. Does it mention any of the things that you listed in exercise **B** above? Circle any items that are mentioned.

B | Read questions 1–3. Think about the answers as you view the video.

1. Why do some people want to make Lamu more modern?
2. What are some people doing to help make Lamu more modern?
3. How does Sheik Ahmad Badawy feel about changes to the culture of Lamu?

After Viewing

A | Discuss answers to questions 1–3 above with a partner.

B | **Critical Thinking: Synthesizing.** Nowadays, we think of social networking as something we do on the Internet. What kind of social networking did people in Lamu do in the past? How did it affect their culture?

_____

A | **Building Vocabulary.** Read the sentences below. Look at the words around the **bold** words to guess their meanings. Then circle the best definition.

1. A lot of companies **advertise** their products on TV and online. They have commercials on TV and small ads on websites.

   a. provide a way for people to buy products online or on television

   b. tell people about something so that they might buy it or use it

2. Often, old friends **contact** each other online, for example, by using social networks.

   a. communicate or meet with someone

   b. ask someone to do something for money

3. Companies these days are trying to be more **environmentally** responsible. For example, some use only electric cars and others use solar power.

   a. relating to a company and the employees of the company

   b. relating to the natural world of land, sea, air, plants, and animals

4. You can do a lot of different things on social networks. You can write a **message** to a friend, you can find old friends, and you can make new friends.

   a. a piece of information or a request that you send to someone

   b. a homework assignment for a class

5. One **positive** effect of social networking is that people can easily find other people with the same interests.

   a. good or helpful

   b. bad or unhelpful

6. A lot of people like **posting** articles and videos on social networks. They want to share them with their friends.

   a. sending information by email to share with other people

   b. making something available to other people on the Internet

7. Texting is a good **tool** for communicating with many friends at the same time.

   a. a website that is used by a lot of people for a particular purpose

   b. something that you use to do a particular thing

Word Link

The suffix **-al** often indicates that a word is an adjective, e.g., virtu**al**, trib**al**, environment**al**, cultur**al**, structur**al**, tradition**al**, influenti**al**, economic**al**.

Word Partners

Use **environmentally** with adjectives, for example, environmentally **responsible**, environmentally **sound**, environmentally **friendly**, environmentally **aware**, and environmentally **sensitive**.

8. Tui Mali is the leader of a **tribe** near Fiji. They live on an island called Vorovoro, and they speak Fijian.

    a. a group of people who do the same type of job and who work together

    b. a group of people who usually live in the same place and share customs, beliefs, language, etc.

9. With some online games, you can have **virtual** cities. The places aren't real; they only exist online.

    a. used to describe an activity or a game that you can either play on a computer or in reality

    b. used to describe an activity or a game that you can only do on the computer

10. In most communities, important decisions are made by **voting**. In many countries, this is how people choose leaders or make laws.

    a. giving your opinion about a decision, usually by marking a paper or raising your hand

    b. finding out information about laws in your community or about people who want to lead the community

B | **Using Vocabulary.** Answer the questions in complete sentences. Then share your sentences with a partner.

1. What is something that you do that is **environmentally** responsible?

    _____

    _____

2. What might be one **positive** effect of social networking on people's lives?

    _____

    _____

3. What kinds of things do you usually **post** on social networks? If you don't post things, why not?

    _____

    _____

4. How can you use the Internet as a research **tool**?

    _____

    _____

C | **Predicting.** Skim the reading on pages 52–53. Why do you think the title is "Internet Island"?

    _____

    _____

Internet Island

track 1-09

▲ Ben Keene, co-creator of tribewanted.com, with members of his tribe.

The Idea

ON JANUARY 14, 2006,
Ben Keene received an
email that changed his life.
The message was from
his friend Mark James.
The subject line read: "A
TRIBE IS WANTED."
Keene and James, both
26, wanted to create
A an Internet start-up.[1]
Here was James's new
idea: We will create an
online community and
call it a tribe. We will make decisions about
rules with discussions and online voting. Then
we will do something that no one has ever
done—our virtual tribe will become a real one.
We will travel to a remote island and form a
partnership with a local tribe. We will build an
environmentally friendly community and share it
with the world.

B James's idea came from social-
networking websites, which got hundreds
of millions of visitors a year. People spent
a lot of time online, but they spent most
of that time posting messages and sharing
music. In James's opinion, these sites could
be used for so much more.

The Island

C Keene liked the idea, and he and James
named their website tribewanted.com.
Then they began looking for an island for
their tribe. Around the same time, Tui
Mali, the chief of a tribe in Fiji, wanted
jobs and money for his people. He owned
a small island called Vorovoro. The main
islands of Fiji were becoming very modern,
but Vorovoro was not.

---

[1] An **Internet start-up** is a newly created online business.
[2] If you **lease** a building or a piece of land, you allow
someone to use it in return for regular payments.
[3] **Donations** are money or items that someone gives to an
organization to help it.

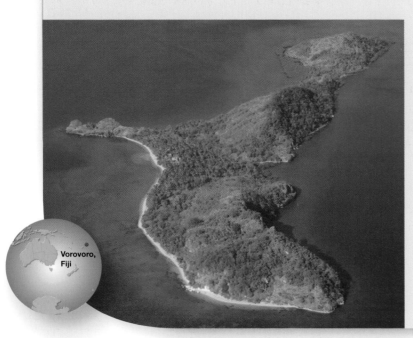

Vorovoro,
Fiji

D On Vorovoro, a few people had cell phones or worked on one of the main islands, but most lived in very small, simple homes with no electricity or running water.

Tui Mali wanted to find someone to develop his island. So he decided to advertise his island on the Internet. A few weeks later, Keene and James contacted him. They agreed to pay $53,000 for a three-year lease[2] of the island and $26,500 in donations[3] to the community. They also promised jobs for the local tribe members. "We are all excited E about Tribewanted," Tui Mali told a local newspaper reporter. "It will provide us with work for the next three years." Tui Mali was happy to have the money, but he also trusted that Keene and James would respect his culture.

▲ Tribal chief Tui Mali hopes the Tribewanted project will provide jobs and income without destroying his people's land or culture.

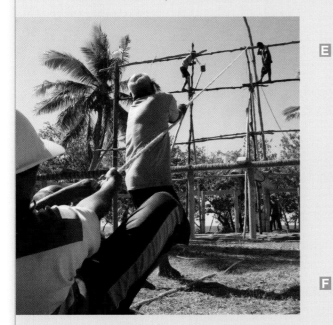
▲ The Vorovoro islanders helped the new arrivals to build a structure for their central meeting place.

The New Tribe

The Internet tribe quickly attracted people. In a few months, it had 920 members from 25 countries. In September of 2006, Keene and 13 of his tribe members, F aged 17 to 59, traveled to the island for the first time. (James stayed at home to manage the website.) When they arrived, the local tribe, along with their chief Tui Mali, were there to greet them.

For several weeks after the newcomers arrived, they G worked with the local tribe members. They built buildings, planted crops behind the village, set up non-polluting sources of energy, such as solar power, and ate fresh fish from the ocean. As they worked together, they became friends. Eventually they became one tribe.

H Through the Internet, the tribe connected with almost a thousand people from all over the world. On the island, it brought together groups of people from very different cultures. Keene and Tui believe the new tribal connections will help the island to develop in a positive way. They hope the island will become more modern, without losing its traditional culture.

The Tribe Keeps Growing

Today, Tribewanted continues to use social networking as a tool to connect in a real environment. Anyone can go to the website to join the online tribe, donate money, or plan a visit to Vorovoro. I Members can also visit a new location in Sierra Leone. In the next ten years, the creators of the site hope to create more communities across the globe, bringing people and cultures together in a global Internet tribe.

A | **Understanding the Gist.** Look back at your answer to exercise **C** on page 51. Was your prediction correct?

B | **Identifying Main Ideas.** Write the main idea for each of the paragraphs listed below.

1. Paragraph A: _____

_____

2. Paragraph B: _____

_____

3. Paragraph E: _____

_____

4. Paragraph G: _____

_____

Strategy

When you **scan for key details**, first consider what *kind* of information you need to scan for.

C | **Identifying Key Details.** Read the sentences below. What kind of information is missing in each one? Match the kinds of information (a–h) with the sentences (1–8). Then read the passage to complete each sentence.

| a. a country name | b. a person's name | c. a type of food | d. a website name |
| e. a year | f. an adjective | g. an amount of money | h. an island name |

_____ 1. _____ sent a message to his friend Ben Keene about starting a tribe.

_____ 2. James and Ben named their online site _____.

_____ 3. They found a small island for their tribe. It's called _____.

_____ 4. They paid _____ to lease the island for three years.

_____ 5. In September _____, Keene went to the island with 13 other people.

_____ 6. The members of the new tribe ate _____ while they lived on the island.

_____ 7. Keene and the tribal leader hope the island will become more _____, but still keep its traditions.

_____ 8. James and Keene started another tribe in _____ in West Africa.

D | **Critical Thinking: Making Inferences.** Write your answers to the questions. Underline the parts of the text that help you answer the questions. Then share your answers with a partner.

1. What kind of people do you think join Tribewanted?

_____

2. What do you think Tribewanted members can learn from the experience of going to Vorovoro? _____

_____

3. How do you think Tribewanted has changed Tui Mali and his tribe members?

_____

GOAL: In this lesson, you are going to plan, write, revise, and edit a paragraph on the following topic: ***Do you think online media such as social networks and blogs have mainly improved our lives, or have they changed our lives in a negative way?***

A | Read the information in the box. Use the present perfect tense of the verbs in parentheses to complete the sentences (1–4).

Language for Writing: The Present Perfect Tense

Use the present perfect tense to talk about something that happened several times in the past, something that happened at an unspecified time in the past, something that began in the past and continues to the present, or when the time in the past is not important. To form the present perfect, use *have* or *has* and the past participle of a main verb.

> I think online media **have improved** our lives.
> Thousands of people **have created** blogs in the past few years.
> We **have used** several different kinds of social networks recently.
> She **has posted** videos on YouTube three times.

Remember to use the simple past to talk about something that happened at a *specific* time in the past (see page 35).

For more explanation and examples, see page 216.

Example: I __have contacted__ (*contact*) all of my classmates on Facebook.

1. Social media _____ (*change*) our lives in many ways.

2. Michael Wesch _____ (*use*) social media in several of his classes.

3. My friend _____ (*meet*) a lot of great people on social networking sites.

4. A lot of old friends _____ (*find*) me online.

B | Write five sentences using the present perfect tense. Write about ways that social media have changed your life, and ways that you have used social media.

C | **Brainstorming.** Brainstorm a list of things that people do with online media.

_____

_____

_____

_____

D | **Journal Writing.** Use your ideas from exercise **C** to write a response in your journal to the following question. Write for three minutes.

How have online media changed the way people communicate with each other?

Writing Skill: *Writing a Concluding Sentence*

Formal paragraphs often have concluding sentences. A concluding sentence is the last sentence of a paragraph. It ties the paragraph together.

Concluding sentences can state an opinion (either the author's, or a person mentioned in the paragraph), make a prediction, or ask a question for the reader to think about. They can also restate, or summarize, the main idea of a long or complex paragraph.

E | Critical Thinking: Analyzing. Find and underline these concluding sentences in the reading passages in this unit. What does each sentence do? Write **Q** (asks a question), **P** (makes a prediction), **O** (gives an opinion), or **R** (restates the main idea).
(Note that sentences may have more than one correct answer.)

Reading A:

_____ 1. In fact, Wesch says, "the Web is us."

_____ 2. "And yet do any of us really use it for all the potential that's there?"

Reading B:

_____ 3. We will build an environmentally friendly community and share it with the world.

_____ 4. In James's opinion, these sites could be used for so much more.

_____ 5. In the next 10 years, the creators of the site hope to create more communities across the globe…

F | Write a concluding sentence for each paragraph below.

1.   Everywhere you look these days, people are on their phones, tablets, or computers. Some are talking, some are texting, and some are surfing the Web. It seems like people communicate with each other on social networks and by email more than they do in person. According to Dan Buettner, in his book *Thrive*, people should spend six to seven hours a day socializing with friends and family in order to increase their happiness. Socializing online probably doesn't have the same effect as socializing in person does.

(Write a prediction.) _____

_____

_____

2.   In my opinion, reading the news online is better than reading a newspaper or watching the news on TV. One way that it is better is that readers can comment on articles that they read online. They can have conversations with other readers, and sometimes even with the writer. Also, online articles provide links to additional information. For example, if an article mentions a name, the name is often linked to another article with more information about that person. Finally, online news articles can be updated if something changes during the day. For example, an online news site might post an article about a dangerous storm in the morning. If more information about the storm becomes available later that day, it can be added to the article.

(Restate the main idea.) _____

_____

_____

A | Planning. Follow the steps to make notes for your paragraph. Don't worry about grammar or spelling. Don't write complete sentences.

Step 1: Look at your journal entry from page 55. Underline the positive ways that social networking has changed communication. Circle the negative ways.

Step 2: Decide whether you think online social networking has improved our lives more or harmed us more. Write a topic sentence that states your main idea.

Step 3: Look at your brainstorming notes and journal entry again. Complete the chart.

Outline

Topic: Has online social networking helped us or harmed us?

Topic sentence _____

_____

Supporting Idea
(one way social
networking has helped
or harmed us)
_____

_____

Details: _____

Supporting Idea
(another way social
networking has helped
or harmed us)
_____

_____

Details _____

_____

Concluding sentence _____

_____

B | Draft 1. Use your notes to write a first draft of your paragraph.

Strategy

For an opinion paragraph, you can use these phrases in your topic sentence:

I think . . . I believe . . . In my opinion . . .

You can also use one of them in your concluding sentence if you end the paragraph with a statement of your opinion.

C | Analyzing. The paragraphs below are on the topic of online music sharing.

Which is the first draft? _____   Which is the revision? _____

a There are many views about online music sharing, but in my opinion, people should pay for music instead of getting it free online. I have gotten free music online in the past, and I didn't really think about whether or not it was fair to the musician. Then I thought about how musicians make money. They earn money by giving concerts and selling CDs. I realized that when I get music free online, I'm stealing from the people who made the music. Musicians work hard to write and perform songs. If people want to enjoy those songs, they should pay for them. We don't expect other kinds of professionals to work for free. For example, we don't expect doctors to treat us for free or teachers to teach for free. If musicians don't get paid for their work, they might not be able to continue making music. They might have to find other work in order to make money. Without musicians, where would we get our music?

CT Focus

Make inferences about the paragraph. What can you tell about the writer? Does he or she use the Internet a lot? Do you think this person is generally honest or dishonest?

b There have been a lot of disagreements about online music sharing. I have gotten free music online in the past, and I didn't really think about whether or not it was fair to the musician. Then I thought about how musicians make money. They earn money by giving concerts and selling CDs. I realized that when I get music free online, I'm stealing from the people who made the music. That's when I stopped sharing music online. Now I always pay for music. I feel the same way about sharing movies online. Even though movie studios make millions of dollars, I still don't think it's right to get movies for free. Musicians work hard to write and perform songs. If musicians don't get paid for their work, they might not be able to continue making music. They might have to find other work in order to make money.

D | Analyzing. Work with a partner. Compare the paragraphs above by answering the following questions about each one.

	a		b	
1. Does the paragraph have one main idea?	Y	N	Y	N
2. Does the topic sentence introduce the writer's opinion?	Y	N	Y	N
3. Does the paragraph include 2–3 supporting ideas?	Y	N	Y	N
4. Does the paragraph include 1–2 details for each supporting idea?	Y	N	Y	N
5. Is there any information that doesn't belong?	Y	N	Y	N
6. Does the paragraph have a concluding sentence or question?	Y	N	Y	N

E | Revising. Answer the questions in exercise **D** about your own paragraph.

F | Peer Evaluation. Exchange your draft with a partner and follow these steps:

Step 1: Read your partner's paragraph and tell him or her one thing that you liked about it.

Step 2: Complete the chart below with information from your partner's paragraph.

Main Idea	_____
	_____
Supporting Idea	_____
	_____
Details	_____
	_____
Supporting Idea	_____
	_____
Details	_____
	_____
Concluding sentence	_____
	_____

Step 3: Compare your chart with the chart your partner completed on page 57.

Step 4: The two charts should be similar. If they aren't, discuss how they differ.

G | Draft 2. Write a second draft of your paragraph. Use what you learned from the peer evaluation activity, and your answers to exercise **E**. Make any other necessary changes.

H | Editing Practice. Read the information in the box. Then find and correct one present perfect mistake in each of the sentences (1–5).

> In sentences using the present perfect, remember to:
> • use the correct form of *have*.
> • use the correct form of the past participle of the main verb. (Be careful with irregular past participles, such as *be—been, do—done, have—had, see—seen, take—taken.*)

1. The Internet been in existence for several decades now, but we are still discovering creative ways to use it.

2. I wasn't sure that I would connect with many people when I joined a social network, but several people have contact me in the past few months.

3. Now that it's so easy to share videos, millions of people has posted videos online.

4. I have saw that video a few times, and I still think it's fun to watch.

5. Our class is doing research about blogs, and we has visited over 100 different blogs in the past month.

I | Editing Checklist. Use the checklist to find errors in your second draft.

Editing Checklist	Yes	No
1. Are all the words spelled correctly?		
2. Is the first word of every sentence capitalized?		
3. Does every sentence end with the correct punctuation?		
4. Do your subjects and verbs agree?		
5. Is the use of present perfect and other verb tenses correct?		

J | Final Draft. Now use your Editing Checklist to write a final draft of your paragraph. Make any other necessary changes.

UNIT QUIZ

p.42 1. In 2007, fewer than one in 20 people in Sub-Saharan Africa had
_____.

p.45 2. In the 1950s, the dominant medium was _____.

p.45 3. Michael Wesch believes that if you change the way that people communicate, you change _____ and _____.

p.48 4. Reading quickly to get the general idea of what a passage is about is called _____.

p.52 5. Ben Keene and Mark James created an online tribe. They got the idea from using _____.

p.52 6. After creating their website and gathering online tribe members, Keene and James turned their _____ tribe into a real one.

p.56 7. The final sentence of a paragraph that ties the paragraph's ideas together is called a(n) _____.

p.59 8. The present perfect form of *be* for the subject *I* is _____.

Deep Trouble

Think and Discuss

1. What ocean or sea is nearest your home? When was the last time you saw it?

2. Do you eat seafood? If yes, what types do you eat? If no, why not?

▲ A school of barracuda surrounds a diver off New Hanover Island, Papua New Guinea.

Look at the map and read the information. Then discuss the questions.

1. What do the colors of the map show? What kinds of "activity" does this refer to?

2. Which areas have the highest impact, or effect, of human activities?

3. How is human activity affecting, or changing, the four places described? How are the effects similar and different?

Ocean Impact

Human activities are affecting, in some way, all of the world's oceans. These activities include fishing, farming, manufacturing, and offshore gas and oil drilling.

NORTH AMERICA

EUROPE

ASIA

NORTH PACIFIC OCEAN

NORTH ATLANTIC OCEAN

AFRICA

EQUATOR

SOUTH AMERICA

INDIAN OCEAN

SOUTH PACIFIC OCEAN

SOUTH ATLANTIC OCEAN

ANTARCTICA

Impact of human activity

- Very high
- High
- Medium high
- Medium
- Low
- Very low

Caribbean Sea

Pollution and overfishing are causing some fish species to disappear. The temperature of the water is increasing, too. The rising water temperature makes it more difficult for species to survive.

▶ Garbage washes ashore on the southern edge of Aruba in the Caribbean.

North Sea

Pollution from shipping, farming, and offshore drilling is causing "dead zones"—places without enough oxygen for plants and fish to live. Overfishing adds to the problem.

◄ Pollution from offshore oil and gas drilling is one cause of the North Sea's dead zones.

East China Sea

Several large rivers bring pollution into the sea. It is also a major fishing area and shipping route. Together, these factors cause serious problems for the ocean environment.

◄ Container ships are a common sight on the rivers that flow from several countries into the East China Sea.

NORTH PACIFIC OCEAN

EQUATOR

AUSTRALIA

Coral Sea

The Coral Sea has less impact from human activity than other oceans. However, the water is warming and becoming acidic.[1] Plants and fish cannot live in acidic water.

◄ The humphead wrasse is among thousands of fish species living in the Great Barrier Reef in Australia's Coral Sea.

▲ (Main photo) Waves of sand carpet the ocean floor of Australia's Coral Sea.

[1] If something is **acidic**, it contains acid, a chemical that is harmful to the environment.

A | **Building Vocabulary.** Find the words in **blue** in the reading passage on pages 65–66. Read the words around them and try to guess their meanings. Then write the correct word from the box to complete each sentence (1–10).

diverse	ecosystem	estimate	population	quantity
reduce	restore	species	stable	survive

1. If you _____ something, you make it less.

2. To _____ is to continue to live or exist.

3. If something is _____, it has things that are very different from each other.

4. A(n) _____ is a group of plants or animals whose members are very similar to each other.

5. A(n) _____ is a number or an amount.

6. A(n) _____ is the relationship between all the plants and animals that live together in a particular area.

7. If you _____ something, you make it the way it was before.

8. When you _____ something's size or number, you make a guess based on the information available.

9. The _____ is the number of people or animals that live in a particular place.

10. Something that is _____ is not likely to change.

Word Partners

Use **reduce** with nouns: reduce **costs**, reduce **crime**, reduce **spending**, reduce **the number of** (something), reduce **waste**; you can also use **reduce** with adverbs: **dramatically** reduce, **greatly** reduce, **significantly** reduce.

B | **Using Vocabulary.** Answer the questions. Share your ideas with a classmate.

1. What do fish need to **survive**? What do people need to **survive**?
2. How can we **reduce** pollution?
3. Which countries do you think have the largest **populations**? Which cities have the largest **populations**?

C | **Brainstorming.** Make a list of possible problems in the oceans today.

_____

_____

D | **Predicting.** Read the title of the passage on page 65. Then look at the pictures and the captions. What do you think the reading is mainly about?

a. why there are more fish today

b. why there are fewer fish today

c. why the ocean is polluted today

Where Have All the Fish Gone?

▲ A yellow goby looks through the window of its soda can home in Suruga Bay, Japan.

track 1-10

A **THROUGHOUT HISTORY,** people have thought of the ocean as a diverse and limitless source of food. Yet today there are clear signs that the oceans have a limit. Most of the big fish in our oceans are now gone. One major factor is overfishing. People are taking so many fish from the sea that species cannot replace themselves. How did this problem start? And what is the future for fish?

Source of the Problem

B For centuries, local fishermen caught only enough fish for themselves and their communities. However, in the mid-20th century, people around the world became interested in making protein-rich foods, such as fish, cheaper and more available. In response to this, governments gave money and other help to the fishing industry.

C As a result, the fishing industry grew. Large commercial fishing[1] companies began catching enormous quantities of fish for profit and selling them to worldwide markets. They started using new fishing technologies that made fishing easier. These technologies included sonar[2] to locate fish, and dragging large nets along the ocean floor. Modern technology allows commercial fishermen to catch many more fish than local fishermen can.

▼ A bottom trawler drags along the ocean floor of Baja California.

A thresher shark struggles in a net in the Gulf of California. ▶
An estimated 38 million sharks are caught every year.

[1] **Commercial fishing** is fishing for profit.
[2] **Sonar** technology uses sound waves to locate objects, for example, underwater.

Rise of the Little Fish

D   In 2003, a scientific report estimated that only 10 percent remained of the large ocean fish populations that existed before commercial fishing began. Specifically, commercial fishing has greatly reduced the number of large predatory fish,[3] such as cod and tuna. Today, there are plenty of fish in the sea, but they're mostly just the little ones. Small fish, such as sardines and anchovies, have more than doubled in number—largely because there are not enough big fish to eat them.

E   This trend is a problem because ecosystems need predators to be stable. Predators are necessary to weed out[4] the sick and weak individuals. Without this weeding out, or survival of the fittest, ecosystems become less stable. As a result, fish are less able to survive difficulties such as pollution, environmental change, or changes in the food supply.

WHERE FISH ARE CAUGHT

Early 2000s

Intensity of Ocean Catch — Low ... High

MAP: MARTIN GAMACHE, NGM STAFF
SOURCE: SEA AROUND US PROJECT, UNIVERSITY OF BRITISH COLUMBIA FISHERIES CENTRE

A Future for Fish?

F   A study published in 2006 in the journal *Science* made a prediction: If we continue to overfish the oceans, most of the fish that we catch now—from tuna to sardines—will largely disappear by 2050. However, the researchers say we can prevent this situation if we restore the ocean's biodiversity.[5]

G   Scientists say there are a few ways we can do this. First, commercial fishing companies need to catch fewer fish. This will increase the number of large predatory fish. Another way to improve the biodiversity of the oceans is to develop aquaculture—fish farming. Growing fish on farms means we can rely less on wild-caught fish. This gives species the opportunity to restore themselves. In addition, we can make good choices about what we eat. For example, we can stop eating the fish that are the most in danger. If we are careful today, we can still look forward to a future with fish.

---

[3] **Predatory fish** are fish that kill and eat other fish.
[4] **To weed out** is to remove something because it is not good or strong enough.
[5] **Biodiversity** is the existence of a wide variety of plant and animal species.

A | **Understanding the Gist.** Look back at your answer for exercise **D** on page 64. Was your prediction correct?

B | **Guessing Meaning from Context.** Find the following terms in the reading passage on pages 65–66 and circle them. Note the paragraph letter where you find them. Underline the words or phrases that help you understand their meaning. Then write your own definition.

1. **overfishing:** Paragraph: _____ My definition: _____

2. **survival of the fittest:** Paragraph: _____ My definition: _____

3. **aquaculture:** Paragraph: _____ My definition: _____

C | **Identifying Main Ideas.** Answer the following questions using information from the reading passage.

1. What is the main reason that most of the big fish in the oceans are gone now?

   _____

2. Why can the commercial fishing industry catch more fish than local fishermen can?

   _____

3. Why are large populations of little fish a problem?

   _____

4. What might eventually happen if fishing continues at the current rate?

   _____

D | **Critical Thinking: Analyzing.** Discuss these questions with a partner: What is the main problem described in the reading passage on pages 65–66? What possible solutions are there to this problem? Complete the T-chart.

Main Problem	Solutions
	1.
	2.
	3.

CT Focus

In a **problem-solution passage**, a writer usually describes a problem first and then provides possible solutions. As you read, ask yourself: *Does the writer provide enough information to show why the problem is real? Is it clear how the solutions match the problem(s)?*

E | **Critical Thinking: Evaluating Arguments.** Discuss your answers to the following questions about "Where Have All the Fish Gone?"

1. Does the writer provide enough supporting information to show that the problem of overfishing is real? If so, how does he or she do this?

2. How well do the solutions help to address the problem? Has the writer given enough information so the reader can see how they might work?

F | **Personalizing.** Discuss this question with a partner: After reading the passage, do you plan to change any of your eating choices? Why, or why not?

Reading Skill: *Interpreting Visual Information*

Writers use charts, graphs, and maps to show information **visually**; that is, to make information easier to see.

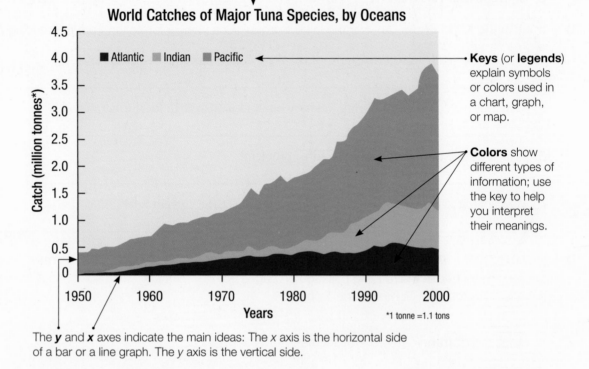

The **title** will help you understand the main idea; that is, what the visual information shows.

World Catches of Major Tuna Species, by Oceans

■ Atlantic ■ Indian ■ Pacific

Catch (million tonnes*)

Years

*1 tonne =1.1 tons

Keys (or **legends**) explain symbols or colors used in a chart, graph, or map.

Colors show different types of information; use the key to help you interpret their meanings.

The **y** and **x** axes indicate the main ideas: The *x* axis is the horizontal side of a bar or a line graph. The *y* axis is the vertical side.

Source: United Nations Fisheries and Agricultural Organization (FAO)

A | **Interpreting a Graph.** Look at the line graph above and discuss your answers to the questions.

1. What does the line graph show?

2. What does the dark blue color represent?

3. Approximately how many tonnes of tuna were caught in the Indian Ocean in 2000?

B | **Interpreting Maps.** Look at the map on page 66 and answer the questions.

1. What does the map show? What do the colors show?

2. How is the map similar to, and different from, the map on pages 62–63?

C | **Critical Thinking: Synthesizing.** Use the map on page 66 and the graph above to answer the following question: In which parts of the world was overfishing a major problem at the end of the 20th century?

Saving Bluefin Tuna

◀ A diver in Tokyo's Sea Life Park reaches out to a passing bluefin tuna, one of the largest and fastest species of fish in the world.

A 1,000 pound (450 kilogram) bluefin ▶ tuna is loaded onto a fishing boat.

Before Viewing

A | **Using a Dictionary.** Here are some words you will hear in the video. Write each word or phrase next to its definition (1–4). Use your dictionary to help you.

breed	hatchlings
in captivity	the wild

1. _hatchlings_: baby fish
2. _in captivity_: not free; unable to go where you want
3. _breed_: have babies
4. _the wild_: a natural environment

B | **Brainstorming.** Look at the video title and read the photo captions. Why might people want to save bluefin tuna? Brainstorm ideas with a partner.

smaller and illegal fisher do mass fishing

While Viewing

A | Watch the video about saving bluefin tuna. Does it mention any of the things that you brainstormed in exercise **B** above?

B | As you view the video, think about the answers to these questions.

1. How is Shukei Masuma helping the bluefin tuna population grow?
2. Why is Masuma's job difficult?
3. How much has the population of bluefin tuna declined since the 1970s? Where?
4. What other solution is there to help save the bluefin tuna?

After Viewing

A | Discuss answers to the questions 1–4 above with a partner.

B | **Critical Thinking: Synthesizing.** According to the reading on pages 65–66, what else could people do to help solve the bluefin tuna problem?

A | **Building Vocabulary.** Read the definitions below of the words in **blue** in the reading on pages 72–73. Then complete each sentence with the correct word or phrase.

advice (*n.*): an opinion about what someone should do

avoid (*v.*): choose not to do something

declining (*v.*): becoming less

definitely (*adv.*): for sure

essential (*adj.*): extremely important or absolutely necessary

impact (*n.*): an effect

individual (*n.*): a person

informed (*adj.*): based on knowledge or information

minimal (*adj.*): very small

rely on (*v.*): need or depend on someone or something in order to live or exist

Word Link

mini = very small:
minimal, **mini**mum,
minimize, **mini**ature,
minibus

1. Commercial fishing has had a big _____impact_____ on the populations of large fish. The numbers of certain fish are declining as a result of this overfishing.

2. A(n) _____ who eats seafood needs to know which fish are disappearing in order to make responsible eating choices.

3. You should _____avoid_____ doing things that are harmful to the environment.

4. People who catch just enough fish for their own families have only a _____ effect on the ocean's ecosystem.

5. Overfishing has led to _____ populations of predator fish.

6. Protection of declining fish populations is _____ for the health of the oceans. If certain species die out, the ocean's ecosystem will be unbalanced.

7. Larger fish _____ smaller fish to survive. They need the smaller fish for food.

Word Partners

Use the adjective **informed** with nouns: informed **choice**, informed **decision**. Use the verb **inform** with nouns: inform **parents**, inform the **police**, inform **readers**, inform **someone** in writing, inform **someone of something**.

8. If you want to make _____ choices about seafood, you can do research online to find out which fish you should eat and which ones you shouldn't.

9. A lot of people want to continue to eat fish, but also protect the ocean, so they need _____ on how to buy and eat fish responsibly.

10. Overfishing is _____ having a negative effect on the ocean's ecosystem. It is destroying some species of fish.

B | Using Vocabulary. Answer the questions in complete sentences. Then share your sentences with a partner.

1. What are three things you think are **essential** for the health of the planet?

2. How do you stay **informed** about environmental issues?

3. Are there any kinds of food that you **avoid**? Why?

4. Does anyone **rely on** you for anything? What do people rely on you for?

C | Brainstorming. Note some ideas about things you can do to help keep the oceans healthy.

stop eating fish with declining populations,

_____

_____

Strategy

Use titles and visuals, such as charts and maps, to predict what a passage will be about.

D | Predicting. Look at the titles and visuals on pages 72–73. Then complete the sentences.

1. I think the interview is about a person who _____.

2. I think the illustration and chart show _____.

track 1-11

An Interview with Barton Seaver

A
Barton Seaver is a chef and conservationist[1] who wants our help to save the oceans. He believes that the choices we make for dinner have a direct impact on the ocean's health. According to Seaver, individuals can make a big difference by making informed choices.

Q. Should people stop eating seafood?

B
People should definitely not stop eating seafood altogether. There are certain species that have been severely overfished and that people should avoid for environmental reasons. But I believe that we can save the oceans while continuing to enjoy seafood. For example, some types of seafood, such as Alaskan salmon, come from well-managed fisheries. And others, such as farmed mussels and oysters, actually help to restore declining wild populations and clean up polluted waters.

Q. What kind of seafood should people eat? What should they not eat?

C
My general advice is to eat fish and shellfish that are low on the food chain and that can be harvested[2] with minimal impact on the environment. Some examples include farmed mussels, clams and oysters, anchovies, sardines, and herring. People should not eat the bigger fish of the sea, like tuna, orange roughy, shark, sturgeon, and swordfish.

Q. Why did you choose to dedicate[3] your life to the ocean?

D
I believe that the next great advance in human knowledge will come not from new discoveries, but rather from learning how we relate to our natural world. Humans are an essential part of nature, yet humans do not have a very strong relationship with the world around them. I have dedicated myself to helping people to understand our place on this planet through the foods that we eat.

Q. Why do you believe people should care about the health of the oceans?

E
The health of the oceans is directly linked to the health of people. The ocean provides most of the air we breathe. It has a big effect on the weather that we rely on for crops and food production. It also provides a necessary and vital[4] diet for billions of people on the planet. So I don't usually say that I am trying to save the oceans. I prefer to say that I am trying to save the vital things that we rely on the ocean for.

[1] A **conservationist** is someone who works to protect the environment.
[2] When you **harvest** something, such as a crop or other type of food, you gather it in.
[3] When you **dedicate** yourself to something, you give it a lot of time and effort because you think it is important.
[4] Something that is **vital** is very important.

LEVEL 4   TOP PREDATOR
When you eat
1 pound
of a level 4 fish,
it's like eating …

What We Eat Makes a Difference

LEVEL 4   TOP PREDATORS

ATLANTIC BLUEFIN TUNA

The ocean's top predators are the biggest, fastest animals. Some examples are sharks, tuna, orange roughy, and seals. They mostly eat smaller carnivores.

ORANGE ROUGHY

ATLANTIC SALMON

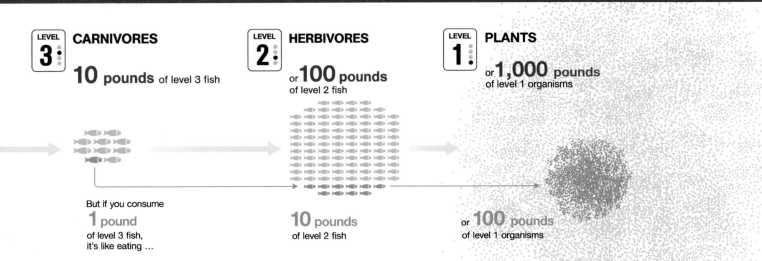

LEVEL 3 : **CARNIVORES**

10 pounds of level 3 fish

LEVEL 2 : **HERBIVORES**

or **100** pounds of level 2 fish

LEVEL 1 : **PLANTS**

or **1,000** pounds of level 1 organisms

But if you consume
1 pound
of level 3 fish,
it's like eating …

10 pounds
of level 2 fish

or **100** pounds
of level 1 organisms

A top predator needs much more food to survive than fish at lower levels of the food chain do. When we catch or eat top predators, we increase our impact on the ocean.

LEVEL 3 : **CARNIVORES**

ALASKA POLLOCK

LEVEL 2 : **HERBIVORES**

ZOOPLANKTON

LEVEL 1 : **PLANTS**

PHYTOPLANKTON

PERUVIAN ANCHOVETA

These fish eat smaller carnivores and herbivores such as zooplankton. Examples of carnivores include squid and sardines. They are eaten by top predators.

These are animals that eat plants. They include tiny animals, known as zooplankton, and small fish such as shrimp and clams. They are eaten by carnivores.

Plants, such as seaweed, sea grasses, and phytoplankton, are eaten by herbivores. They produce all the oxygen in the ocean, just as plants on land do.

JAPANESE FLYING SQUID

ALGAE

AMERICAN LOBSTER

A | Understanding the Gist. What is Barton Seaver's main message in the interview on page 72? Choose the best answer.

a. People should stop eating seafood so the ocean's ecosystem can be restored again.
b. The ocean provides most of the air we breathe and the food we eat.
c. Individuals can have a positive impact on the ocean by making good food choices.

B | Identifying Purpose. Choose the correct answer for each question.

1. What is the purpose of the chart at the top of pages 72–73?
   a. to show how many fish are eaten in one year
   b. to show how our seafood choices impact the ocean's ecosystem

2. What is the purpose of the illustration on pages 72–73?
   a. to illustrate the levels of the ocean food chain, from largest to smallest
   b. to illustrate how some sea animals have become extremely large

C | Identifying Key Details. Use information from pages 72–73 to complete the following sentences.

1. Some examples of herbivores are _Zooplangthon , shrimp_.

2. Plants are important for the ocean's ecosystem because _because herbivores eat plants and produce all oxygen in ocea_

3. Eating a pound of orange roughy is like eating _100 pounds_ of shrimp.

4. Barton Seaver says he works to protect the oceans because _to serve vital things that we rely on the ocea for_.

D | Critical Thinking: Analyzing Problems and Solutions. For each problem below, write one or two of Barton Seaver's suggestions that might help solve it.

CT Focus

Examine the problems and solutions in exercise **D**. Do you think each suggestion is an effective solution to each problem? Are the suggestions realistic?

Problems	Suggestions
Some wild fish populations are declining.	care about what type of. seafood you eating. stop eating ...
People don't have a strong relationship with the world around them.	to help people to understand how we related to our natural world

E | Critical Thinking: Synthesizing. Discuss the questions in small groups.

1. Barton Seaver recommends that people eat smaller fish. How can this help the ocean's ecosystem? _they have largest population and make minimal impact_

2. Do you agree with Seaver that "humans do not have a very strong relationship with the world around them"? What are some examples in this unit for or against this idea? _Yes, bluefin tuna_

GOAL: In this lesson, you are going to plan, write, revise, and edit an explanatory paragraph. Your topic is: **Explain a chart or graph.**

A | **Brainstorming.** Brainstorm a list of charts and graphs that you see in your daily life.

_____

_____

B | **Journal Writing.** Write an answer in your journal to the following question. Write for three minutes.

What kinds of information can charts and graphs show?

C | **Analyzing.** Read the information in the box. Use the language in the box and the graph below to complete the sentences (1–4).

Language for Writing: Describing Charts and Graphs

We use certain words to describe information in charts and graphs.

Phrases to introduce a description of a chart or graph:
According to the graph, . . . As the chart shows, . . . We can see from the chart that . . .

Common verbs (usually in simple past)
↑ *rose to / by, increased to / by, doubled (= x2), tripled (= x3), quadrupled (= x4), reached (a low point of / a high point of)*
↓ *declined, decreased, dipped, dropped, fell*
→ *remained stable/steady, stayed (about) the same*

Prepositions

Use *to* with most verbs to talk about a number or amount that something reached.

Use *by* with most verbs to talk about how much something changed.

Use these words to talk about time: *over*—a period of time; *between*—a period from one year to another; *by*—at a certain time; *in*—during a number of years.

As the graph shows, sales **rose to** $50 million **by** 2010.

According to the graph, seafood sales **fell by** 20 percent over two years.

As the chart shows, sales of orange roughy **doubled in** five years.

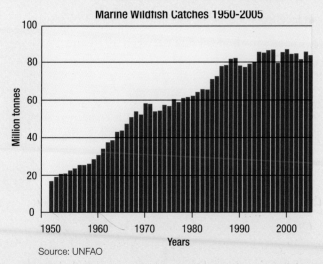

Marine Wildfish Catches 1950-2005

Million tonnes

Source: UNFAO

Example: According to the graph, the amount of fish caught ___doubled___ from about 17 million tons (metric tons) in 1950 to about 35 million tons in 1962.

1. The amount of fish caught more than ___quadrupled / x4___ between 1950 and 2005.

2. The amount of fish caught ___increased___ by about 20 million tons between 1980 and 1990.

3. The amount of fish caught ___dropped___ slightly between 1970 and 1972.

4. The amount of fish caught ___stayed the same___ between 1994 and 2004.

D | **Applying.** Write five more sentences about the chart above.

Writing Skill: *Explaining a Chart or Graph*

We usually begin a description of a chart or graph* by explaining its main idea or purpose.

> *According to the chart, eating top predators has a great impact on the ocean's ecosystem.*

> *As the graph shows, the quantity of fish caught has steadily increased since 1950.*

We then provide supporting details—specific data that support the main idea.

> *Eating one pound of a top predator, such as orange roughy, is like eating 10 pounds of a smaller fish, such as herring.*

> *The amount of fish caught between 1950 and 2006 increased from about 17 million metric tons to more than 80 million in 2006.*

*A **graph** usually shows changes over time; a **chart** usually shows numbers or amounts from a single period.

E | Critical Thinking: Analyzing.
Read the sentences about this chart. Check the sentences that are correct. Correct the remaining sentences. Put the five sentences in order to write a paragraph.

Recent Sea Level Rise

23 Annual Tide Gauge Records

Sea Level Change (cm)

Years

Source: PSMSL, National Oceanography Center, Liverpool, England

Strategy

One way to **conclude a paragraph about a chart or graph** is to describe the most recent piece of data.

☒ 1. According to the graph, sea level rose about 20 centimeters over 120 years. ①

☑ 2. Sea level rose about 10 centimeters in the 50 years between 1910 and 1960. ④

☐ 3. After 1910, it began to fall steadily. ③

☐ 4. By the year 2000, sea level reached almost 30 centimeters. ⑤

☒ 5. Between 1880 and 1910, it went up and down slightly, but it remained fairly stable. ②

According to the graph, sea level rose about 20cm over 120y
Between 1880 and 1910, It went up and down slightly, but it remained fairly stable.
After 1910, It began to fall steadily.
Sea level rose about 10cm in the 60y between 1910 and 1960
by the year 2000, sea level reached Almost 30 centimeters.

A | Planning. Follow the steps to make notes for your paragraph.

Step 1 Study the graph on page 68. Decide what the purpose of the graph is.

Step 2 Complete the chart below.

Outline

Topic: Describing a Graph

What is the main idea of the graph?

world cutches of major Tuna speaes by oceans

What is one detail that supports the main idea of the graph?

Tuna fishing occurs mostly in the Atlantic, Pacific and indian Oceans

What is another detail that supports the main idea of the graph?

the number of fish catch has dramiticly increased in the past 50 years.

What is another detail that supports the main idea of the graph?

the Pacific ocean is the most place to catche Tuna fish.

What is the most recent piece of data in the graph?

in 2000, approximately 4 million tons of tuna fish were caught in the pacific Ocean.

B | Draft 1. Use your notes to write a first draft of your paragraph.

The chart show us major Tuna species catches by oceans. according to the chart Tuna fishing occurs mostly in the Atlantic Pacific.. the number of fish catch has dramiticly increased in the past 50 years, in 2000, approximately 4 millions Tons of Tuna fish were caught in the Pacific ocean. the Pacific ocean is the most place to catche Tuna fish.

C | Analyzing. The paragraphs below describe this graph.

Which is the first draft? _a_

Which is the revision? _b_

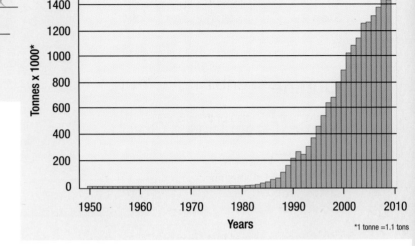

Global Aquaculture Production of Atlantic Salmon 1950–2009

Tonnes x 1000*

*1 tonne =1.1 tons

Years

a According to the graph, farming of Atlantic salmon began in the 1950s and grew quickly in the next 50 years. Between 1980 and 1985, production of Atlantic salmon rose. But around 1985, production began to increase significantly. It rose from about 40 metric tons in 1985 to over 200 in just five years. In the early 1990s, production fell slightly. But then it rose again in 1995. It continued to rise to the year 2000 and beyond. By 2009, production of Atlantic salmon reached almost 1.5 million metric tons. Some people believe that it's better to eat wild salmon, but in my opinion, it's better for the ocean for people to eat farmed salmon.

b According to the graph, farming of Atlantic salmon started to become popular in the 1980s, and after a slow start, it grew quickly. Between 1980 and 1985, production of Atlantic salmon rose slightly. Around 1985, production began to increase more significantly. It rose from about 40,000 metric tons in 1985 to over 200,000 in just five years. Production fell slightly between 1991 and 1992, but then it rose again in 1993. It continued to rise to the year 2000 and beyond. By 2009, production of Atlantic salmon reached almost 1.5 million metric tons.

D | Critical Thinking: Analysis. Work with a partner. Compare the paragraphs above by answering the following questions about each one.

	a		b	
1. Does the paragraph have one main idea?	Y	N	Y	N
2. Does the topic sentence introduce the purpose of the graph?	Y	N	Y	N
3. Does the paragraph include at least three details that support the main idea of the graph?	Y	N	Y	N
4. Is there any information that is incorrect or doesn't belong?	Y	N	Y	N
5. Does the paragraph include correct phrases, verbs, and prepositions to explain charts and graphs?	Y	N	Y	N
6. Does the concluding sentence give information about the most recent data in the graph?	Y	N	Y	N

E | Revising. Answer the questions above about your own paragraph.

F | Peer Evaluation. Exchange your first draft with a partner and follow these steps.

Step 1 Read your partner's paragraph and tell him or her one thing that you liked about it.

Step 2 Complete the chart below with information from your partner's paragraph.

Outline

Topic: Describing a Graph

What is the main idea of the graph?

the word Tuna fishing increased in the past 50 years.

What is one detail that supports the main idea?

Tuna fishing occurs mostly in the Atlantic, Pacific and Indian ocean.

What is another detail that supports the main idea?

the most quantity of Tuna caught in the Pacific ocean.

What is another detail that supports the main idea?

while the number of amount (of fishing) grow slowly in the Atlantic the number in pacific grew massivly.

What is the most recent piece of data in the graph?

in 2000 approximatly 4 millions tons of tuna fish were caught in Pacific ocean

Step 3 Compare your chart with the chart your partner completed on page 77.

Step 4 The two charts should be similar. If they aren't, discuss how they differ.

G | Draft 2. Write a second draft of your paragraph. Use what you learned from the peer evaluation activity, and your answers to exercise **E**. Make any necessary changes.

H | Editing Practice. Read the information in the box. Then find and correct the language mistakes in the sentences below (1–4) that describe the graph on page 78. One of the sentences does not have a mistake.

> In sentences describing a chart or graph, remember to:
> - use the correct prepositions, for example, *between*, *by*, and *in*.
> - use the simple past tense when you are describing data from the past.

1. Between 1991 and 1992, production of Atlantic salmon decline slightly.

2. Production of Atlantic salmon doubled by 1990 and 1995.

3. Production of Atlantic salmon rose steadily between 2000 and 2005.

4. Production of Atlantic salmon increased by about 1.4 million tonnes by 30 years.

I | Editing Checklist. Use the checklist to find errors in your second draft.

Editing Checklist	Yes	No
1. Are all the words spelled correctly?	✓	
2. Is the first word of every sentence capitalized?	✓	
3. Does every sentence end with the correct punctuation?		
4. Do your subjects and verbs agree?		
5. Did you use the past tense to describe changes in the past?		
6. Did you use the correct prepositions and language for describing a graph?		

J | Final Draft. Now use your Editing Checklist to write a third draft of your paragraph. Make any other necessary changes.

UNIT QUIZ

p.62
1. Fishing and offshore drilling are examples of _____Human activites_____ that are affecting the world's oceans.

p.64
2. All the living plants and living creatures in a particular area together make up a(n) _____ecosystem_____.

p.65
3. Most of the big fish in the ocean are gone because of _____overfishing_____.

p.68
4. The horizontal and vertical lines on a graph are called the _____axies_____.

p.72
5. According to Barton Seaver, the health of the oceans is linked to the health of _____the people_____.

p.73
6. Plants in the ocean are important because they produce all the _____oxygen_____ in the sea.

p.75
7. Another way to say something stayed about the same is to say it remained _____stable_____ or _____stady_____.

p.76
8. When we write paragraphs about charts and graphs, the topic sentence usually tells the _____main idea_____ or _____purpose_____ of the chart or graph.

Memory and Learning

ACADEMIC PATHWAYS
Lesson A: Identifying cause and effect in an expository text
Lesson B: Synthesizing information from multiple texts
Lesson C: Using an outline to plan a paragraph
Writing a paragraph with supporting information

Think and Discuss

1. Do you remember what you did on your last birthday? How about your birthday five years ago? Ten years ago?
2. Do you know anyone with a good memory? Why do you think some people can remember things better than others?

As memories fade with age, photographs provide a continuing link with a person's past.

▲ A variety of offerings are left each year by visitors to a war memorial in Maryland, USA.

A. Look at the photo for 30 seconds and answer the questions.

1. How many items can you remember? Close your book and make a list.
2. Compare lists with a classmate. Were some items easier to remember than others?

B. Read the information on this page and discuss these questions with a partner.

1. What are some examples of short-term and long-term memories? What are your earliest long-term memories?
2. What does the chart show about how memory changes with age?

How We Remember

Memory is how the brain stores and recalls information. We make memories when connections are made in the brain's nerve cells, or neurons. Each neuron sends and receives messages. As your eyes scan these pages, billions of **neurons** are working, forming new connections and new memories.

Memories about childhood and things that happened long ago are called **long-term memories**. Telephone numbers and the names of people that we just met are stored in our brains as **short-term memories**.

▲ There are one hundred billion (**100,000,000,000**) nerve cells, or neurons, in the human brain.

Why We Forget

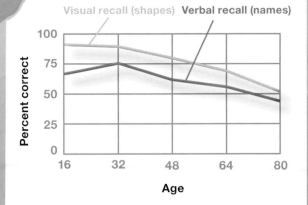

Adult Ability To Recall

Visual recall (shapes)   Verbal recall (names)

Percent correct

100
75
50
25
0

16   32   48   64   80

Age

Most people have no memory of their childhood before the age of three or four (this is called *childhood amnesia*). We still don't know exactly why—it may be because our brains are not yet fully developed at such a young age. From our teenage years, our ability to remember—or recall—things declines over time, as connections between neurons weaken.

A | **Building Vocabulary.** Find the words in **blue** in the reading on pages 85–86.
Read the words around them and try to guess their meanings. Then write the correct form of each word or phrase next to its definition.

1. _____ (*noun*) a special way of doing a particular thing

2. _____ (*noun*) someone with a very high level of intelligence

3. _____ (*noun*) knowledge that all members of a group share

4. _____ (*verb*) to form a picture in your mind of someone
or something

5. _____ (*verb*) to learn something so you remember it exactly

6. _____ (*adj.*) inside of something

7. _____ (*adj.*) outside of something

8. _____ (*adj.*) having many different parts; difficult to understand

9. _____ (*noun*) something that is done successfully

10. _____ (*noun*) a book or other written or printed work

Word Link

The suffix –**ize** forms verbs that mean to cause or become something, e.g., visual**ize**, memor**ize**, internal**ize**, minim**ize**.

B | **Using Vocabulary.** Answer the questions. Share your ideas with a partner.

1. What is an example of **collective knowledge**? _____

2. Name one person who you think is a **genius**. _____

3. What **external** conditions can make it difficult to study? _____

C | **Classifying.** Do you ever make lists to remember things? Do you ever try to *memorize* things? Complete the T-chart below. Compare your answers with a partner's.

Things I make lists for	Things I try to memorize

Strategy

Scanning for repeated words can help you predict what a passage is about.

D | **Predicting.** Scan the reading passage on pages 85–86 quickly. List two other nouns or verbs that appear two or more times.

_____memory_____   _____   _____

Now look at the words you wrote. What do you think the passage is about?

I think the passage is about _____

_____

The Art of Memory

track 1-12

WE ALL TRY TO REMEMBER certain things in our daily lives: telephone numbers, email addresses, facts that we learn in class, important tasks. But did you know that people once had great respect[1] for memory?

People began to value memory as a skill about 2,500 years ago. That's when the poet Simonides of Ceos discovered a powerful technique known as the loci[2] method. Simonides realized that it's easier to remember places and locations than it is to remember lists of names, for example. According to the loci method, if you think of a very familiar place, and visualize certain things in that place, you can keep those things in your memory for a long time.

▲ A young Ukrainian man attends a service to remember soldiers who died in World War II. Remembrance services play an important role in shaping a society's collective knowledge of the past.

Simonides called this imagined place a "memory palace." Your memory palace can be any place that you know well, such as your home or your school. To use the loci method to remember a list of tasks, for example, visualize yourself walking through your house. Imagine yourself doing each task in a different room. Later, when you want to remember your list of tasks, visualize yourself walking through your house again. You will remember your list of tasks as you see yourself performing each one.

Nearly 2,000 years later, a man in 15th-century Italy named Peter of Ravenna used the loci method to memorize books and poems. He memorized religious texts, all of the laws of the time, 200 speeches, and 1,000 poems. By using the loci method, he was able to reread books stored in the "memory palaces" of his mind. "When I [travel] I can truly say I carry everything I own with me," he wrote.

Peter of Ravenna (c. 1448–1508) ▶

[1] If you **respect**, or **have respect for**, something or someone, you have a very high opinion of it or them.
[2] **Loci** is the plural form of the Latin noun *locus*, meaning "place."

When Simonides and Peter of Ravenna were alive, books and pens were not widely available for people to write notes with, so people had to remember what they learned. Mary Carruthers is the author of *The Book of Memory*, a study of the role of memory techniques in the past. She writes, "Ancient and medieval[3] people reserved their awe for memory." In other words, these people thought that a genius was a person with excellent memory. They considered memory to be an art and a great virtue[4] because a person with a good memory could turn external knowledge into internal knowledge.

After Simonides' discovery of the loci method, others continued to develop the art of memory. Memorization gained a complex set of rules and instructions. Students of memory learned what to remember and techniques for how to remember it. In fact, there are long traditions of memory training in many parts of the world. In some cultures, memorization of religious texts is considered a great achievement; many other societies value storytellers who can retell myths and folktales from the past.

But over the past millennium,[5] many things have changed. We've gradually replaced our internal memory with external memory. We've invented technological crutches[6] so we don't have to store information in our brains. We have photographs to record our experiences, calendars to keep track of our schedules, books (and now the Internet) to store our collective knowledge, and note pads—or iPads—for our ideas. By using these crutches, we don't have to remember anything anymore. When we want to know something, we look it up. We've gone from remembering everything to remembering very little. How does this affect us and our society? Did we lose an important skill?

Adapted from "Remember This" by Joshua Foer, *National Geographic Magazine*, Nov 2007

▲ Roman philosopher Seneca the Elder could repeat up to 2,000 names in the order that he heard them.

▼ In Senegal and other parts of West Africa, historians known as *griots* memorize and pass on long stories through poetry, song, and music.

[3] **Medieval** refers to the period of European history between approximately AD 500 and 1500.
[4] A **virtue** is a very good personal quality.
[5] A **millennium** is a period of one thousand years.
[6] A **crutch** is something that someone depends on for support or help

A | **Understanding the Gist.** Look back at your answer for exercise **D** on page 84. Was your prediction correct?

B | **Identifying Key Details.** Write answers to the questions.

1. Why did ancient and medieval people think memory was an art?

_____

_____

2. How does the loci method work? Explain the method in your own words.

_____

_____

C | **Critical Thinking: Applying a Method.** Imagine you have these problems. How might you solve them by using the loci method?

1. You are learning a foreign language. You are having trouble remembering new words.
2. You are taking a history class. It's hard for you to remember when important events happened.

> ### CT Focus
>
> **Applying information** in a new way can help you internalize it more easily. For example, using the loci method yourself will help you understand and remember how it works.

D | **Classifying.** Complete the T-chart using information from the reading on pages 85–86. Write techniques, uses, or names related to internal and external memory.

Internal Memory	External Memory
loci method	

E | **Critical Thinking: Inferring Opinion.** Look at the final paragraph of the reading passage. How might the author answer the question "Did we lose an important skill?" Why do you think so? Discuss your ideas with a partner.

F | **Personalizing.** Complete the sentences with your own ideas.

1. I think internal memory is better for remembering _____.
2. I think external memory is better for remembering _____.
3. I (think / don't think) we lost an important skill. I think _____

_____.

Reading Skill: *Identifying Cause and Effect*

A **cause** is something that makes another event happen. The resulting event is the **effect**. Recognizing causes and effects can help you better understand a reading passage. Look at the sentence from the reading. Does the underlined portion show a cause or an effect?

> *If you think of a very familiar place, and visualize certain things in that place,* <u>*you can keep those things in your memory for a long time*</u>.

The underlined portion shows the effect. Visualizing things within a familiar place is the cause. Keeping memories for a long time is the effect.

You can sometimes identify cause and effect relationships by finding certain connecting or signal words. These include *because, so, if, then, therefore, as a result,* and *by* verb + *-ing*.

> *We don't have to remember phone numbers now* **because** *we can store them on smartphones.*

> *I enter my email password three times a day,* **so** *I remember it easily.*

See page 110 for more explanation and examples.

A | **Analyzing.** Read the information about memory techniques. How many cause-effect relationships can you find? Circle the causes and underline their effects.

MEMORY TRICKS

track 1-13

Techniques for remembering things like lists, numbers, and facts, are called mnemonic devices. For example, people often use things like poems, pictures, or movements because it is easier to remember rhymes, images, or actions than plain facts and lists.

Acronyms are one type of mnemonic. For example, it may be hard to remember the colors of the rainbow in the order that they appear. Someone therefore made an acronym for this: ROY G BIV. The first letters in the acronym are the first letters in the names for the colors: red, orange, yellow, green, blue, indigo, and violet. The name Roy G. Biv is meaningless, but it's short, so it is easier to remember than the list.

English spelling rules can also be difficult to learn, so some students use rhymes to help them remember the rules. By learning "*i* before *e* except after *c* (where you hear *ee*)," students of English remember the spelling of words like *niece* and *receipt*.

▲ Rainbow over Snares Island, New Zealand

CT Focus

Apply this information to words you know. Think of other words that have *ie* or *ei*. Do those words follow the spelling rule?

B | **Analyzing.** Look back at the reading on pages 85–86. Circle three causes and underline their effects.

Memory School

▲ A taxi cab reflects London's famous landmark Westminster Abbey.

Before Viewing

A | **Meaning from Context.** You will hear these phrases in the video. Discuss the meaning of each one with a partner. Write definitions for the words in **bold**.

1. ". . . scientists are studying how the brain is able to **adapt** when it has to **retain** large amounts of information"
2. ". . . **visual processing** takes up more space in the brain than all the other senses combined"
3. ". . . drivers **navigate** the streets of London using a complex **mental map** with thousands of **landmarks** and other locations"

B | **Brainstorming.** When you arrive in a new city, what do you do to become familiar with the streets and find your way around? Make a list with a partner.

___use a GPS___   _____   _____   _____

While Viewing

A | Watch the video about a London driving school. Does it mention any of the things that you listed in exercise **B** above? Circle any items that are mentioned.

B | As you watch the video, think about the answers to these questions.

1. What kinds of things do the taxi drivers do to memorize locations in London?
2. According to the video, what is an important part of preparing for the exam? Why?
3. How do scientists think studying taxi drivers' brains can help other people?
4. What other activities like the London taxi training might enlarge the hippocampus?

After Viewing

A | Discuss answers to the questions 1–4 above with a partner.

B | **Critical Thinking: Synthesizing.** The London taxi drivers' technique and the loci method both involve locations. Discuss with a partner how each technique uses locations.

A | **Building Vocabulary.** Read the sentences below. Look at the words around the **bold** words to guess their meanings. Then circle the best definition.

1. Exercise can **affect** the body in a good way: it can make you healthier.

   a. to make something change in a certain way

   b. to make something bigger

2. People change their **diet** in order to gain or lose weight.

   a. the kinds of food a person normally eats

   b. the times at which a person normally eats

3. Scientists often give a rat a **drug** to make it go to sleep or wake up.

   a. a chemical

   b. an exercise

4. Using the brain in a **mental activity**—such as reading or doing puzzles—can improve memory.

   a. an activity that uses and exercises the mind

   b. an activity that is extremely difficult

5. You need to be in good **physical** condition in order to be a long-distance runner.

   a. relating to the body

   b. relating to money

6. Because of a recent study, we now have **proof** that sleep is important for memory.

   a. information that causes people to disagree

   b. information that shows that something is true

7. A rat learned how to get from one place to another. However, the next day, it got lost because it completely forgot the **route**.

   a. a game

   b. a path

8. If someone is in a **state** of confusion, they are not sure what is happening.

   a. a person's condition at a certain time

   b. a person's hope for the future

Word Partners

Use **stress** with: (*n.*) **effects of** stress, **work-related** stress; (*adj.*) **emotional** stress, **mental** stress, **physical** stress; (*v.*) **cause** stress, **cope with** stress, **deal with** stress, **experience** stress, **reduce** stress.

9. If a student has a lot of **stress** in his or her life, for example, because of problems at school, it might make learning much harder.

    a. a feeling of worry that is caused by difficulties in your life

    b. an illness or a disease that makes it difficult to remember things

10. Taking notes helps you **transfer** information from internal to external memory. This can help you to remember it better.

    a. to move something from one place to another

    b. a study of something that helps people learn about it

Word Link

The prefix **trans-** means "moving across or changing from one thing to another," e.g., **trans**fer, **trans**ition, **trans**late, **trans**form.

B | Using Vocabulary. Answer the questions in complete sentences. Then share your sentences with a partner.

1. What are some ways that you deal with **stress** in your life?

_____

_____

2. What **routes** do you remember best?

_____

_____

> **Top 5 Causes of Stress for College Students**
>
> 1. Finances
> 2. Academic pressure
> 3. Time management
> 4. Roommate conflicts
> 5. Relationships
>
> Source: www.collegeandfinance.com

3. Do you ever stay up all night to study for a test? How do you think this might **affect** your memory?

_____

C | Predicting. Underline the key words in the titles and the subheads of the reading passages on pages 92–93. Use the words to help you complete the sentences.

1. I think the reading passage on page 92 is about how _____

_____

2. I think the reading passage on page 93 is about how _____

_____

Strategy

Use key words in titles and subheads to help you predict what a passage is about.

track 1-14

NEWSWATCH

Train Your Brain!

A
Is there anything you can do to have a better memory? Research shows that mental and physical exercise and lifestyle choices can affect memory. In fact, many experts agree it is possible to improve your memory. Here are some tips:

Avoid stress

B
Recent research shows that stress is bad for the brain. In fact, one study connects worrying with memory loss. Therefore, if you can avoid stress in your life, you may also improve your memory. Relaxation techniques like yoga are one way to reduce stress.

Play games

C
Can brainteasers[1] like sudoku puzzles improve memory? Some scientists say that mental activity might help memory. Puzzles, math problems, even reading and writing, can probably all benefit the brain.

Get some rest

D
"Poor sleep before or after learning makes it hard to encode[2] new memories," says Harvard University scientist Robert Stickgold. One study shows that by getting a good night's sleep, people remember a motor skill (such as piano playing) 30 percent better.

Read more about the connection between sleep and memory.

Eat right

E
Your brain can benefit from a healthy diet, just like the rest of your body. Foods that have antioxidants,[3] such as blueberries, are good for brain cells. This helps memory.

---

[1] **Brainteasers** are activities that exercise the mind, such as puzzles.

[2] If you **encode** information, you put it into a different form or system of language.

[3] **Antioxidants** are chemicals that can reduce the effect of harmful substances in your body.

Sleep and Memory

Many people think that sleep must be important for learning and memory, but until recently there was no proof. Scientists also believe the hippocampus plays a role in making long-term memories, but they weren't sure how. Now they understand how the process happens—and why sleep is so important.

▲ During sleep, ripples travel from the hippocampus (dark purple in this scan) to outer parts of the brain, such as the prefrontal cortex (red).

Memories in Motion

A research team at Rutgers University recently discovered a type of brain activity that happens during sleep. The activity transfers new information from the hippocampus to the neocortex. The neocortex stores long-term memories. The researchers call the transferring activity "sharp wave ripples," because the transferring activity looks like powerful, short waves. The brain creates these waves in the hippocampus during the deepest levels of sleep.

The Rutgers scientists discovered the wave activity in a 2009 study using rats. They trained the rats to learn a route in a maze. Then they let the rats sleep after the training session. They gave one group of sleeping rats a drug. The drug stopped the rats' wave activity. As a result, this group of rats had trouble remembering the route. The reason? The new information didn't have a chance to leave the hippocampus and go to the neocortex.

▼ At night we cycle through different levels, or stages, of sleep. Scientists believe long-term memories are formed during the deepest levels.

Adult Sleep

Lifelong Memories

The experiment explains how we create long-term memories. The wave activity transfers short-term memories from the hippocampus to the neocortex. Then the neocortex turns the sharp wave ripples into long-term memories. Researcher György Buzsaki says this is "why certain events may only take place once in the waking state and yet can be remembered for a lifetime."

The Rutgers study is important because it proves the importance of sleep for learning and memory. It also finally explains how the brain makes long-term memories.

A | **Understanding the Gist.** Look back at your answers for exercise **C** on page 91. Were your predictions about the two reading passages correct?

B | **Identifying Key Ideas.** Work with a partner. Check the things that can improve memory, according to the first reading "Train Your Brain!"

_____ antioxidants _____ exercise _____ fatty foods _____ puzzles

_____ sleep _____ stress

C | **Understanding the Main Idea.** What did you learn from the second reading "Sleep and Memory"? Work with a partner to complete this sentence:

The main idea of "Sleep and Memory" is _____

_____

Strategy

Use key words in questions, especially nouns and noun phrases, to help you scan for the most relevant parts of a text.

D | **Restating Key Details.** Complete the following sentences about "Sleep and Memory."

1. A team from Rutgers University found _____

_____.

2. Sharp wave ripples transfer information from the _____

to the _____.

3. Some rats had trouble remembering a route because _____

_____.

E | **Matching Cause and Effect.** Match the cause with the effect (**a–c**) mentioned in the first reading.

Cause   **Effect**

stress _____   a. forgetting things   b. getting too much sleep   c. avoiding exercise

Now find two cause-effect relationships in the second reading. Circle the causes and underline their effects.

F | **Critical Thinking: Synthesizing.** Discuss these questions in small groups:

1. List all the methods and tips for improving memory that you learned about in this unit. Circle ones you think you are most likely to use.

the loci method _____ _____

_____ _____ _____

2. What do people know now about memory that people in the past did not know?

GOAL: In this lesson, you are going to plan, write, revise, and edit a paragraph on the following topic: **What can a person do to improve his or her memory?**

A | **Brainstorming.** Look back at your list for exercise **F** on page 94. Work with a partner. Can you think of any other ways a person could improve their memory? Add ideas to your list.

B | **Journal Writing.** Write an answer in your journal to the following question. Write for three minutes. *What are some ways to improve your memory?*

C | Read the information in the box. Use *by* + gerund to combine the sentence parts (1–3).

Language for Writing: Using *By* + Gerund

Use *by* with a gerund to say how to do something. *By* + gerund forms can appear at the beginning or at the end of a sentence. Use a comma when they appear at the beginning of a sentence.

You can improve your memory   ***By getting*** *enough sleep, you can*
by getting *enough sleep.*   *improve your memory.*

By + gerund expresses how to reach a result:

By eating right, *you can improve your memory.*

    cause   effect

For more explanation and examples, see page 217.

Example: get a good night's sleep / you help your brain form memories

> By getting a good night's sleep, you help your brain form memories.

1. write new words on cards / a person can retain them better

   _____

2. give rats drugs / the scientists stopped their brain waves

   _____

3. you can improve your memory / do puzzles

   _____

D | Write five more sentences using *by* + gerund.

Writing Skill: *Using an Outline*

Using an outline helps you to organize your main idea, supporting ideas, and examples and/or details. The examples might be a list of reasons, or steps in a process. An outline is like a map because it gives you something to follow. For example, you can use an outline to develop your ideas in a descriptive paragraph.

Don't write complete sentences in an outline, except for your topic sentence.

E | Matching. Look at the outline below and read the paragraph that follows. Match sentences in the paragraph (a–i) to the parts of the outline. (Two sentences are extra.)

Topic	**How to Memorize a Route**
Topic sentence	_____
Supporting Idea 1	memorize as steps _____
Details	write names, directions _____
	repeat _____
Supporting Idea 2	create mental picture _____
Details	study a map _____
	imagine following route _____

a. When you have to memorize a route, you should use a technique that works well for you. b. One way is to memorize the directions as a set of steps. c. To do this, write the street names and directions in the correct order on a piece of paper. For example, Step 1 might be: "Drive three miles down Main Street." Step 2 might be: "Turn right on Oak Street." d. If you repeat the steps several times, you won't have to look at the list anymore. e. You can also memorize a route by creating a mental picture of it. f. That is, see the streets and the places on the streets in your mind. g. To do this, study the route as it appears on a map. h. Then imagine yourself following the route. See the buildings and other places along the route in your mind. Turn your body to the right and to the left as you make the turns. By seeing the route in your mind, you will learn it faster. i. There are other ways to learn routes; use the method that works best for you.

F | Critical Thinking: Analyzing. Look again at the two sentences that didn't match the outline. What functions do they have in the paragraph? Match each one to a description:

_____ uses paraphrasing to explain an idea   _____ provides a concluding statement

G | Find and underline two cause-effect relationships in the paragraph.

A | Planning. Follow the steps to complete an outline for your paragraph.

Step 1 From your brainstorming notes on page 95, choose your best two or three supporting ideas and write them in the outline below. Don't write complete sentences.

Step 2 Write a topic sentence that introduces your supporting ideas.

Step 3 Now write two examples or details for each supporting idea.

Outline

Topic: How to Improve Your Memory

Topic Sentence   _____

Supporting Idea 1   _____

       A. _____

       B. _____

Supporting Idea 2   _____

       A. _____

       B. _____

Supporting Idea 3   _____

       A. _____

       B. _____

B | Draft 1. Use your outline to write a first draft. Think about the following questions as you write:

1. Does your paragraph have one main idea?
2. Does your topic sentence introduce your main idea?
3. Do you have 2–3 different supporting ideas?
4. Do you have at least two examples or details for each supporting idea?
5. Is there any information that doesn't belong?
6. Do you have sentences that show cause and effect? Are you using *by* + gerund forms?
7. Are you able to include new vocabulary you have learned in this unit?

C | Analyzing. The paragraphs below are on the topic of how people can keep lasting memories.

Which is the first draft? _____   Which is the revision? _____

a One way to record important events in life is to keep a journal. A journal is a written record of events, activities, and thoughts. You can keep a daily journal or an occasional journal. You can write it by hand in a notebook, or type it on a computer. You can also include pictures. Another way to create lasting memories is to use a video journal. With a video journal, you can record activities and events as they are happening. You can make additional recordings afterwards of yourself talking about your thoughts on the events or activities. My phone has a video recorder, but sometimes it doesn't work very well.

b There are two main ways to record the important events in life so that they will become lasting memories. One way is to keep a written journal. This is a written record of events, activities, and thoughts. You can keep a daily journal or an occasional journal. You can write it by hand in a notebook, or type it on a computer. You can also include pictures in your journal. It's a good idea to add text to your photos as a reminder of the places and the people in the photos. Another way to create lasting memories is to use a video journal. With a video journal, you can record activities and events as they are happening. You can also make recordings afterwards of yourself talking about your thoughts on the events or activities. These are just a few of the ways to create lasting memories that you will enjoy for many years.

D | Critical Thinking: Analysis. Work with a partner. Compare the paragraphs above by answering the following questions about each one.

	a		b	
1. Does the paragraph have one main idea?	Y	N	Y	N
2. Does the topic sentence introduce the main idea?	Y	N	Y	N
3. Are there two different supporting ideas?	Y	N	Y	N
4. Are there at least two examples for each supporting idea?	Y	N	Y	N
5. Is there any information that doesn't belong?	Y	N	Y	N
6. Is there a concluding sentence?	Y	N	Y	N

CT Focus

Apply these criteria to another paragraph in this Unit, e.g. the final paragraph on p. 86.

E | Revising. Answer the questions above about your own paragraph.

F | **Peer Evaluation.** Exchange your first draft with a partner and follow these steps:

Step 1 Read your partner's paragraph and tell him or her one thing that you liked about it.

Step 2 Write an outline of your partner's paragraph in the space below.

Outline

Topic: How to Improve Your Memory

Topic Sentence _____

Supporting Idea 1 _____

        A. _____

        B. _____

Supporting Idea 2 _____

        A. _____

        B. _____

Supporting Idea 3 _____

        A. _____

        B. _____

Step 3: Compare your outline with the outline that your partner completed on page 97.

Step 4: The two outlines should be similar. If they aren't, discuss how they differ.

G | **Draft 2.** Write a second draft of your paragraph. Use what you learned from the peer evaluation activity, and your answers to exercise **E**. Make any other necessary changes.

H | **Editing Practice.** Read the information in the box. Then find and correct one *by* + gerund mistake in each of the sentences (1–4).

When you look for mistakes with *by* + gerund, remember to:

- use the *-ing* form of the verb.
- use a comma when the *by* + gerund form appears at the beginning of a sentence.

---

1. You can't remember all of the information by just listen to a lecture.
2. By take notes while you listen, you can remember information better.
3. By doing a motor activity while you listen you can improve your memory.
4. By write a summary of your notes after a lecture, you will remember the information more easily.

I | Editing Checklist. Use the checklist to find errors in your second draft.

Editing Checklist	Yes	No
1. Are all the words spelled correctly?		
2. Is the first word of every sentence capitalized?		
3. Does every sentence end with the correct punctuation?		
4. Do your subjects and verbs agree?		
5. Are the verb tenses correct?		
6. Did you use *by* + gerund correctly?		

J | Final Draft. Now use your Editing Checklist to write a third draft of your paragraph. Make any other necessary changes.

UNIT QUIZ

p.83   1. We create memories when connections happen in the brain's
_____, called neurons.

p.83   2. When you try to remember the name of someone you've just met, you use your
_____ memory.

p.84   3. A special way of doing something is called a(n) _____.

p.85   4. Visualizing things arranged in an imagined space is called the
_____.

p.86   5. Taking a picture to remember someone is an
example of _____ memory.

p.88   6. The underlined part of the sentence below shows the **cause / effect**.

Because they learned a rhyme, <u>the students were able to remember a new grammar rule</u>.

p.88   7. ROY G BIV is a type of mnemonic
called a(n) _____.

p.93   8. The brain creates and stores _____
memories while we are asleep.

Dangerous Cures

Think and Discuss

1. Have you ever been bitten or stung by an animal?

2. How might animals that sting or bite be useful to humans?

A tarantula's venom is collected in a test tube. ▲

Look at the photos, read the information, and discuss the questions.

1. How would you describe each animal? How do you feel about each one?
2. Which animals are deadly to humans?
3. How are the animals similar? How are they different?

Deadly, Deadlier, Deadliest

Some animals and plants produce poisonous chemicals called **toxins**. Animals such as snakes and spiders use toxins to attack other animals by biting or stinging. This kind of toxin is called **venom**. Other animals, like poisonous frogs, use toxins to protect themselves from predators. Some animal toxins are deadly to humans; others may just cause pain.

Poison Dart Frog

Location: Pacific coastal rainforest of Colombia

How deadly? One of the most toxic of all animals on Earth, the poison dart frog is coated in poison. A single frog—just two inches (five centimeters) long— has enough venom on its skin to kill 10 human adults.

Fact: The frog's name comes from the blowgun darts of the Emberá people of Colombia. The Emberá traditionally add the venom to their darts before hunting.

Nudibranch

Location: Oceans all over the world

How deadly? Although not toxic to humans, the nudibranch is poisonous to most creatures underwater.

Fact: The nudibranch produces toxin in its skin for protection. The bright skin colors tell predators that it is poisonous.

Taipan

Location: Australia

How deadly? The inland taipan is probably the world's most venomous land snake. Its venom carries more than 50 toxins. Others, such as the coastal taipan (pictured), are less deadly—but still highly dangerous.

Fact: The inland taipan changes color with the seasons. It is darker in the winter and lighter in the summer. This allows it to take in more heat during winter and less in hot summer months.

Centipede

Location: In dirt, under stones, and inside logs all over the world

How deadly? Their venom can kill insects, spiders, and small animals. Although painful to humans, it is not normally deadly.

Fact: The name *centipede* means "100 legs." However, some species have fewer than 20; others have more than 300.

Black Widow

Location: Every continent except Antarctica

How deadly? Black widow bites are not usually strong enough to kill a human adult, but they can be deadly for small children.

Fact: Female black widow spiders sometimes kill male spiders after mating. This is how the spider got its name.

A | **Building Vocabulary.** Find the words in **blue** in the reading passage on pages 105–106. Read the words around them and try to guess their meanings. Then write the correct word or phrase from the box to complete each sentence (1–10).

colleague	cure	disease	encounter	endangered
model	resources	side effects	specific	target

1. If you talk about a(n) _____Specific_____ thing, you talk about one particular thing.

2. A(n) _____target_____ is something that you aim at and try to hit.

3. If you have a(n) _____disease_____, you have a serious illness.

4. Your _____colleague_____ is someone that you work with, especially in a professional job.

5. A(n) _____endangered_____ animal is one that may not exist in the future.

6. If you _____encounter_____ problems or difficulties, you experience them.

7. A(n) _____cure_____ is a medicine or a treatment that makes an illness go away.

8. If you create something based on a(n) _____model_____, you copy the design of something.

9. If you have _____resources_____, you have materials, money, and other things that you need in order to do something.

10. As well as making an illness go away, some drugs also cause bad, unwanted _____side effects_____.

B | **Using Vocabulary.** Answer the questions. Share your ideas with a classmate.

1. What are some examples of **endangered** species?

2. What **diseases** do you know that do not have **cures**? HSV – nebula –

3. What are some examples of **resources** that you might need to find a new job?
certificate – books – time.

C | **Brainstorming.** What are some ways to fight or cure diseases? Make a list of your ideas.
restrict the peoples that already have,
go to doctor – get prescription – follow the rulls.

D | **Predicting.** Skim the reading on pages 105–106 quickly. What do you think the reading is mainly about? Circle your answer.

a recent event   a person's job   an unusual place

a serious disease   an endangered animal

The Snake Chaser

A **AS A BOY,** Zoltan Takacs caught snakes and kept them in his room. Now he hunts them for a living.[1]

B Zoltan Takacs collects snake venom so that he can study it. He wants to find out if the venom can be used as medicine to cure people. Usually, he travels alone with only a backpack, a camera bag, and equipment for collecting the venom. He often flies small planes to reach faraway places, and has traveled to 134 countries. His trips are often dangerous: he has encountered pirates,[2] wars, and angry elephants. He has also survived six venomous snake bites. Takacs's adventures are like action movies, but his goal is pure science: "Animal venoms," Takacs explains, "are the source of over a dozen medications."[3]

Why do toxins make good medications?

C Many drugs produce side effects. These side effects happen because the drugs affect more than one target. For example, most cancer drugs can't tell the difference between cancer cells and healthy cells. So the drugs kill cancer cells, but they also kill other healthy cells in the body. Toxins are a good model for medications because they can hit a single target. But finding the right toxin to fight a specific disease can take years of work. That's why Takacs and his colleagues have developed a new technology. It allows the creation of "toxin libraries."

[1] If you do something **for a living**, you do it as your main job.
[2] **Pirates** are people who attack ships to rob them.
[3] **Medications** are medicines that are used to treat and cure illnesses.

How does the technology work?

The new toxin libraries help researchers identify which toxin might cure a specific disease. With the new technology, testing can happen much more quickly and efficiently than before. A researcher can test many different toxins at once to see if any of them have an effect on a specific disease. Takacs thinks the technology will help researchers develop new toxin-based drugs for a lot of different diseases. But Takacs is also worried that a lot of possible toxin-based drugs are being lost.

Why are we losing potential drugs?

According to Takacs, "Scientists have studied fewer than a thousand animal toxins. … But some 20 million more exist." Some of these animal toxins come from endangered species. So every time an animal becomes extinct, it's possible that a new drug is lost, too. For example, the venom of an endangered snake could potentially lead to a medicine that saves human lives.

▲ "Scientists have studied fewer than a thousand animal toxins," says Takacs. "But some 20 million more exist."

Takacs explains, "Once we've allowed something to become extinct . . . , there's no way back. . . . For me, losing biodiversity means losing beauty, . . . knowledge, and resources, including possibilities for treating diseases." Losing species, he says, is "like peeling[4] out pages from a book we've never read, then burning them."

Why do snakes not poison themselves?

A snake's venom aims only at a specific part of the body. However, if contact with the target is blocked, the toxin has no effect. For example, when researchers inject[5] a cobra with its own venom, nothing happens. This is because cobras have a molecule[6] that blocks the toxin from making contact with its target.

[4] If you **peel** something, you remove layers from it one at a time.
[5] If you **inject** something, such as medicine, you put it into a person or animal using a needle.
[6] A **molecule** is the smallest amount of a chemical that can exist by itself.

A | Understanding the Gist. What is the gist of the reading on pages 105–106? Circle the correct answer.

   a. Zoltan Takacs is one of the few people in the world who works as a snake chaser.

   (b.) Zoltan Takacs collects snake venom because it can be used to create important medicines.

   c. Zoltan Takacs believes there are many toxin-based drugs that have not been properly tested.

B | Identifying Key Details. Use information from the reading to complete each sentence with a reason.

Reasons
1. Zoltan Takacs studies snakes because . . .
2. Toxins are a good model for medications because . . . *dont have side effects and hit single target*
3. Takacs and his colleagues developed "toxin libraries" because . . . *this libraries help researchers identify which toxin might cure septic disease*
4. Toxin libraries are very useful for testing venoms because . . . *researcher can test many of them at once to see if any*
5. Takacs believes it's important to protect endangered species because . . . *everytime an animal became extinct, its possible that a new drug is lost, too.*
6. Cobras are not affected by their own venom because . . . *Cobra have a molecule that block the toxin from making contact with its target.*

C | Critical Thinking: Identifying Figurative Language. What is the writer's or speaker's meaning in each sentence? Circle **a** or **b**.

1. *Takacs's adventures are like action movies.*

   a. Takacs's life is similar to the life of a famous movie actor.
   (b.) Takacs's job is sometimes like the events in a movie.

2. *Takacs and his colleagues have developed a new technology. It allows the creation of "toxin libraries."*

   a. In a toxin library, toxins are arranged in order on shelves, like books in a library.
   (b.) In a toxin library, a lot of information is stored in a way that's easy to search.

3. *"(Biodiversity loss is) like peeling out pages from a book we've never read, then burning them."*

   a. Biodiversity loss can be very dangerous, as it often results from burning large areas of forest.
   (b.) Biodiversity loss is a problem because we lose species before we understand them.

> **CT Focus**
>
> **Figurative language** allows a writer to compare one thing to another. When you read, it's important to understand how the two things being compared are similar.

D | Personalizing. Write answers to the questions.

1. Would you like to have a job like Zoltan Takacs's? Why, or why not? *Yes, I like to work with animals, I like Adwancher*
2. Have any of your opinions changed after reading the article (*e.g., about toxins or snakes*)? If so, in what way?
   no

Reading Skill: *Identifying Pros and Cons*

Pros are advantages (positive effects) of something, and *cons* are disadvantages (negative effects) of something. Writers often provide the pros and cons of an issue in order to make a more balanced argument. Identifying the pros and cons of an issue will help you evaluate the strength of a writer's arguments. It will also help you decide your own opinion on the issue.

Look at the facts below about the reading on pages 105–106. Is each fact a pro or a con for studying snake venom?

> *It can be very dangerous.*
> *A snake's venom might be used to cure a serious disease.*
> *Snake venom is a good model for medications.*

The first fact is a con (a disadvantage of studying snake venom), and the other two are pros.

A | **Identifying Pros and Cons.** Read the passage below about the study of viruses. Then take notes in the chart.

Should Dead Viruses Be Given New Life?

track 2-02

Scientists called virologists study viruses[1] to discover how they work and how to stop people from getting them. Of course, working with viruses is very dangerous. Some viruses can infect large numbers of people very quickly. Other viruses, such as HIV, still have no widely available vaccine[2] or cure. In the past few years, some virologists have begun studying extinct viruses—ones that died out long ago. They discovered that all humans have pieces of very old viruses in their bodies. Some of these viruses are hundreds of thousands of years old. The virologists were able to rebuild some of the viruses and bring them back to life.

Although some people think that rebuilding viruses is potentially very dangerous, the virologists argue that studying these extinct viruses can teach us more about how viruses cause disease. They also believe that these viruses can tell us a lot about how our human species developed in the past. In addition, the scientists can develop vaccines for these diseases in case they reappear one day and begin infecting people again.

Pros of Studying Extinct Viruses	
Cons of Studying Extinct Viruses	

[1] A **virus** is a germ that can cause disease, such as smallpox, polio, and HIV.
[2] A **vaccine** is a substance that doctors put in people's bodies so that they won't get particular diseases.

B | **Evaluating Arguments.** Now look at your list of pros and cons. What is your opinion of studying extinct viruses? Write your ideas.

I think virologists ***should / shouldn't*** study extinct viruses because . . .

when we know more about past we can defeat more in the future

The Frog Licker

Madagascar

▲ Scientist Valerie Clark is an expert on frogs, including the colorful Mantella poison frog.

Before Viewing

A | **Meaning from Context.** The words and phrases in **bold** are used in the video. Match each phrase with the correct definition. What do you think the sentence means?

"The more **[A] primary forest** that we have, the **[B] better chance** we have of finding new drug **[C] leads**."

1. _____ clues that help you find something
2. _____ greater possibility
3. _____ area of old land with many trees, not changed by human activity

B | **Predicting.** What do you think scientists such as Valerie Clark (above) hope to learn from frogs? List your ideas.

_____

_____

While Viewing

A | Watch the video about Valerie Clark. Does it mention any of the things that you listed in exercise **B** above?

B | As you view the video, think about the answers to these questions.

1. What makes the Mantella poison frog poisonous?
2. What are the two ways that Clark tests the toxins in a frog's skin?
3. Why doesn't the frog's poison harm Clark?
4. What might happen if the diversity of insects in the rainforest decreases?

▲ Madagascar's Mantella frogs come in a wide range of colors— from golden to orange, green, and black.

After Viewing

A | Discuss answers to the questions 1–4 above with a partner.

B | **Critical Thinking: Synthesizing.** How are Zoltan Takacs's and Valerie Clark's jobs similar? How are they different? Discuss with a partner.

A | **Building Vocabulary.** Read the sentences below. Use the context to help you identify the part of speech and meaning of each **bold** word. Write your answers. Check your answers in a dictionary.

1. If you study biology, you can have a **career** in science. For example, you can become a biologist or a virologist.

   Part of speech: _____

   Meaning: _____ job _____

2. A researcher named Jonas Salk made one of the biggest **contributions** to science. He developed the polio vaccine.

   Part of speech: _____ none _____

   Meaning: _____ help, assistance, part, assistance _____

3. When you have a fever, it's important to try to keep **control** of your temperature. It's dangerous to let your fever get too high.

   Part of speech: _____ none _____

   Meaning: _____ monitor - take care _____

4. One main thing **differentiates** venomous animals and poisonous animals. Venomous animals inject toxins into their victims; poisonous animals usually have toxins on their skin.

   Part of speech: _____

   Meaning: _____ seperates, dedicates _____

5. When you take medicine, it's important to take the correct **dose**. Too much can harm you, and too little may not have an effect.

   Part of speech: _____ none _____

   Meaning: _____ Volume - size of _____

6. Zoltan Takacs is an **expert** in snake venoms. He knows a lot about how they work.

   Part of speech: _____ none _____

   Meaning: _____ professor - junior _____

7. People who want to become doctors have to spend several years in **medical** school.

   Part of speech: _____ adj _____

   Meaning: _____ cure - _____

Word Partners

Use **relief** with: (*n.*) **pain** relief, **sense of** relief; (*v.*) **express** relief, **feel** relief, **bring** relief, **get** relief (from), **provide** relief (for).

8. For minor headaches, you can get **relief** from medicines that you can buy at a drugstore. For more severe headaches, you should see a doctor.

Part of speech: _____

Meaning: _____ *pill* _____

9. There is no cure for colds. When you have a cold, sleep is probably the most important **remedy**.

Part of speech: _____ *none* _____

Meaning: _____ *why* _____ *part* _____

10. Some scientists **risk** their health, or even their lives, when they study dangerous toxins.

Part of speech: _____ *verb* _____

Meaning: _____ *Put in danger* _____

B | Using Vocabulary. Answer the questions in complete sentences. Then share your sentences with a partner.

1. What **career** do you hope to have?

_____ *I hope to be Part of red Team in cert for cybersecurity.* _____

_____

2. In what kinds of jobs do people **risk** their lives to help others?

_____ *most of them in general security and incidence response Jobs* _____

_____ *like Police, firemans* _____

3. What are some common cold **remedies**?

_____

_____

4. What are you an **expert** in? Or what would you like to be an **expert** in?

_____

_____

5. In your opinion, what **differentiates** someone like Zoltan Takacs from most people?

_____

_____

C | Predicting. Skim the reading passages on pages 112–113. What careers do you think Leon Fleisher and Karen Wetterhahn had? What do you think happened to each one?

Leon Fleisher: _____.

Karen Wetterhahn: _____.

Poison and the Piano Player

track 2-03

A In the 1950s and '60s, Leon Fleisher was one of the world's greatest piano players. But one day in 1964, his career suddenly ended. While he was practicing, he started to lose control of the fourth and fifth fingers on his right hand. "Wow," he thought, "I'd better practice harder." But his problem got worse.

B Fleisher saw several different doctors. He had injections and medications and other treatments, but nothing worked. "It was as if my hand had been taken over by aliens," he says. "It was not under my control." His career was finished.

"It was as if my hand had been taken over by aliens. It was not under my control."

C Finally, after more than 30 years, Fleisher found out what was wrong. He had focal dystonia, a disease that makes muscles move in strange, and sometimes painful, ways. At last relief seemed possible. He went to the U.S. National Institutes of Health, where researchers were testing botulinum toxin as a cure for the disease.

D Botulinum toxin is one of the most poisonous toxins in the world: One gram of it could kill 20 million people. But scientists have used it to create the drug Botox. This drug is now safely used in small doses to treat many different problems. It's used to make skin look younger, to stop headaches, and even to cure some serious diseases.

▲ A woman prepares for an injection of Botox, a treatment for aging skin.

E The botulinum toxin cured Fleisher, and he got his career back. He began performing again, and he made his first recording in 40 years. Recently, he received a Kennedy Center Award, which is given for important contributions to the arts in America.

A Dangerous Job

On August 14, 1996, a tiny drop of a very toxic chemical called dimethylmercury fell onto the left hand of Karen Wetterhahn, a toxicologist[1] and professor of chemistry at Dartmouth College. Wetterhahn was an expert on how toxic metals cause cancer. When the poisonous drop fell onto her hand, she wasn't worried; she was wearing protective gloves.

Unfortunately, the dimethylmercury went through her glove. After a while, Wetterhahn had difficulty walking and speaking. After three weeks, she was in a coma.[2] Karen Wetterhahn died five months later. She was 48 years old, a wife and mother of two.

You might say that a toxicologist studies substances that lead to death. But toxicology is also about saving lives. What can kill, can cure. Medical researchers such as Wetterhahn risk their lives daily for the benefit of others. Their work is dangerous, but it has the potential to save lives. In memory of Wetterhahn's life and work, Dartmouth College created the Karen Wetterhahn Memorial Award. The award is given to female science students who receive money to continue their scientific research.

▲ Toxicologists such as Karen Wetterhahn (above) risk their lives in a search for new medical cures.

Arsenic: Poison or Cure?

Paracelsus, a 16th-century German-Swiss doctor said, "All substances[3] are poisons; there is none which is not a poison. The right dose differentiates a poison and a remedy." In fact, too much of almost anything can be poisonous. Too much vitamin A, too much vitamin D, even too much water can cause problems in different parts of the body. But some things are deadly even in very small amounts.

For example, arsenic is a very strong poison. Take less than a tenth of an ounce (2.83 grams) at once, and you have severe illness, then death. But in the fifth century BC, Hippocrates[4] used arsenic as medicine for stomach problems. Centuries later, people used it for treating illnesses like asthma, a condition that causes difficulty breathing, and types of cancer. In 1890, William Osier found arsenic to be the best drug for leukemia,[5] and it is still used to treat leukemia today.

---

[1] A **toxicologist** is a scientist who studies poisons.
[2] Someone who is **in a coma** is in a state of unconsciousness, usually because of a serious injury or illness.
[3] A **substance** is a type of matter (e.g., a solid or liquid) with a particular chemical content.
[4] **Hippocrates** (c. 460–370 BC) was an ancient Greek physician (doctor), considered to be the father of Western medicine.
[5] **Leukemia** is a disease of the blood in which the body produces too many white blood cells.

A | **Understanding the Gist.** Work with a partner to write the gist of the following readings in a complete sentence.

"Poison and the Piano Player": _____.

"A Dangerous Job": _____.

B | **Identifying Pros and Cons.** Complete the chart below with the poisons that are mentioned in the reading passages on pages 112–113.

Toxin	How it can harm	How it can help
botulinum toxin	One gram can kill 20 million people	
arsenic	tenth of an ounce can make several illnes and bird	treting asma

C | **Identifying Key Details.** Complete the following sentences about the reading passages on pages 112–113.

1. Leon Fleisher had a disease called _____.

2. Because of this disease, he couldn't _____.

3. Karen Wetterhahn wasn't worried when _____.

4. According to Paracelsus, every substance is _____.

5. Over 2000 years ago, people used arsenic to treat _____.

6. Today, people use arsenic to treat _____.

D | **Understanding References.** What does the word *it* refer to in each sentence (1–4) from the first reading passage? Use information in the reading to match items a–f with the sentences. Two items are extra.

a. a headache　　b. Botox　　c. botulinum

d. Fleisher's career　　e. Fleisher's hand　　f. the feeling

Paragraph B:

_____ 1. "**It** was as if my hand had been taken over by aliens."

_____ 2. "**It** was not under my control."

Paragraph D:

_____ 3. One gram of **it** could kill 20 million people.

_____ 4. **It**'s used to make skin look younger . . .

E | **Critical Thinking: Synthesizing.** Discuss these questions in small groups:

1. Which type of work discussed in this unit do you think is the most dangerous? Why?

2. Wetterhahn's college created an award in her name. Do you know other awards that are given in someone's name? What is the purpose of the award?

GOAL: In this lesson, you are going to plan, write, revise, and edit a paragraph on the following topic: **Should scientists study toxins?**

A | **Brainstorming.** Brainstorm a list of the kinds of things that toxicologists do in their jobs.

how tonic metal cause cancer , how to use substances of a toxin for cure

B | **Journal Writing.** Use one of your ideas from exercise **A** to write a response in your journal to the following prompt. Write for three minutes.

What are some pros of studying toxins? What are some cons?

C | **Analyzing.** Read the information in the box. Use *although*, *even though*, and *though* to connect the ideas below (1–3). Then take turns with a partner explaining what the writer of each sentence is saying.

Language for Writing: Making Concessions

Making a concession is saying that *one* idea is true, but *another* idea is stronger or more important, according to the writer. In other words, it is more persuasive. Use *although*, *though*, and *even though* to make concessions:

> **Although** botulinum toxin can be deadly, it can also cure several serious diseases.
> **Even though** botulinum toxin can cure several diseases, it can be deadly.

In each sentence, the idea in the second clause is emphasized—the writer feels it is stronger and more important.

In the first sentence, the writer concedes that botulinum toxin is dangerous. However, the writer believes its ability to cure diseases is more important. (In other words, scientists should continue to work with it.) In the second sentence, the writer concedes that botulinum toxin can cure diseases. However, the writer believes that the fact that it is dangerous is more important. (Scientists should stop working with it.)

Example: more important: *Leon Fleisher was recently able to make a new recording.*
less important: *Leon Fleisher was unable to play the piano for many years.*

Although Fleisher was unable to play the piano for years, he was recently able to make a new recording.

1. more important: *Arsenic is still used to treat leukemia.*
   less important: *Just a small amount of arsenic can be deadly.*
   Although just a small amount of arsenic can be deadly, it is still used to treat leukemia

2. less important: *Snake venom is dangerous to humans.*
   more important: *Snake venom is used in a lot of important medications.*
   Although snake venom is used in a lot of important medications, it is dangerous to humans

3. more important: *Studying extinct viruses might bring back deadly diseases.*
   less important: *Studying extinct viruses can tell us about the human species.*
   Although studying extinct viruses can tell us about the human species, it might bring back deadly diseases

D | **Applying.** Write two sentences for making concessions using *although* and *even though*. Use ideas from this unit, from previous units, or your own ideas.

Writing Skill: *Writing a Persuasive Paragraph*

In a persuasive paragraph, you try to convince the reader that something is true. First, you state the issue. Then you state your argument. Finally, you explain the reasons why you think your argument is valid or true.

Making concessions in a persuasive paragraph can help strengthen your argument. It shows the reader that you have thought about the different arguments, but you believe that your argument is the strongest and most important.

E | **Identifying Concessions.** Read the paragraph about animal testing. Underline the two sentences that make a concession.

    Many cosmetic and drug companies test their products on animals to make sure that they are safe. However, this kind of testing is cruel and unnecessary. Although people who support animal testing say that animals are not harmed during tests, animals usually have to live in small cages in laboratories. In addition, animals are often badly injured during testing, and some are even killed. Even though drug companies need to make their products safe for people, their products don't always have the same effect on animals and humans. So it's possible that these tests don't show how products might affect humans. In fact, according to the Food and Drug Administration, over 90 percent of drugs that are used in testing are safe for animals, but are not safe for humans. Since animal testing harms animals and may not help humans, researchers should stop testing products on animals.

F | **Critical Thinking: Analyzing.** Complete the outline below with information from the paragraph in exercise **E**.

Issue: Companies test products on animals.

Argument _____

Supporting Idea 1 <u>Animals are harmed.</u>

Details _____

_____

Supporting Idea 2 _____

Details _____

_____

A | Planning. Follow the steps to make an outline for your paragraph. Don't worry about grammar or spelling. Don't write complete sentences.

Step 1   Look at your journal entry from page 115. Underline the pros of studying toxins. Circle the cons.

Step 2   Decide whether you think scientists should study toxins.

Step 3   Look at your brainstorming notes and journal entry again. Complete the outline. Include at least two supporting ideas.

Issue: Scientists study toxins

Argument   _____

                             _____

Supporting Idea 1   _____

Details   _____

                             _____

Supporting Idea 2   _____

Details   _____

                             _____

Supporting Idea 3   _____

Details   _____

                             _____

B | Draft 1. Use the information in your outline to write a first draft of your paragraph.

C | Revising. The paragraphs below are on the topic of botulinum toxin.

Which is the first draft? _____   Which is the revision? _____

a   Botox, which comes from a deadly form of bacteria called botulinum toxin, is very popular these days because it gives people smooth, unwrinkled faces. However, scientists should not make beauty products from dangerous toxins. Though the study of toxins can lead to the creation of important medications, dealing with these toxins can be very dangerous. Scientists should not risk their lives, and possibly ours, in order to help people be more beautiful. Although scientists safely created a safe cosmetic product with botulinum toxin, we can't be sure that other toxins will be safe. Perhaps the next toxin that researchers work with will cause an outbreak of disease. Or perhaps a toxin-based product will cause medical problems after you use it for several years. Many people want to be more beautiful, but studying and using toxins in beauty products is not worth the risk.

b   Many celebrities spend a lot of money on expensive beauty products and treatments. Some have dangerous surgeries just to make themselves look more attractive. Scientists should not make beauty products from dangerous toxins. Though Botox is safe, people should be happy with the way they look. They should not inject Botox in their faces. Perhaps the next toxin that researchers work with will cause an outbreak of disease. Or perhaps we will find out a product that is made from toxins actually causes medical problems after you use it for several years. Many people want to be more beautiful, but studying and using toxins in beauty products is not worth the risk.

D | Critical Thinking: Analyzing. Work with a partner. Compare the paragraphs above by answering the following questions about each one.

		a		**b**	
1.	Does the paragraph present the issue?	Y	N	Y	N
2.	Does the paragraph state the main argument?	Y	N	Y	N
3.	Does the paragraph include 2–3 supporting ideas?	Y	N	Y	N
4.	Does the paragraph include 1–2 details for each supporting idea?	Y	N	Y	N
5.	Does the paragraph include concessions?	Y	N	Y	N
6.	Is there any information that doesn't belong?	Y	N	Y	N
7.	Does the paragraph include a concluding sentence?	Y	N	Y	N

E | Revising. Answer the questions above about your own paragraph.

F | Peer Evaluation. Exchange your first draft with a partner and follow the steps below.

Step 1   Read your partner's paragraph and tell him or her one thing that you liked about it.

Step 2   Underline the topic sentence of your partner's paragraph.

Step 3   Circle the supporting ideas. Are there two or three ideas?

Step 4   Double underline the details. Is there at least one detail for each supporting idea? If not, discuss possible reasons with your partner.

G | Draft 2. Write a second draft of your paragraph. Use what you learned from the peer evaluation activity, and your answers to exercise **E**. Make any other necessary changes.

H | Editing Practice. Read the information in the box. Then find and correct one mistake in each of the sentences (1–5).

In sentences for making concession, remember to:

- put the less important idea after *although* or *even though*.
- use a comma after the clause with *although* or *even though*.
- include a subject and a verb in both clauses.

---

1. Even though she's afraid of snakes she wants to study snake venoms.

2. Although golden poison dart frogs are very small, they very deadly.

3. Even though Leon Fleisher had a serious disease, can still play the piano.

4. Although a black widow's venom is deadlier than a rattlesnake's it rarely kills humans.

5. Although there are many thousands of toxins in the wild scientists have studied only a few hundred.

I | Editing Checklist. Use the checklist to find errors in your second draft.

Editing Checklist	Yes	No
1. Are all the words spelled correctly?		
2. Is the first word of every sentence capitalized?		
3. Does every sentence end with the correct punctuation?		
4. Do your subjects and verbs agree?		
5. Are the verb tenses correct?		
6. Did you use *although*, *even though*, and *though* correctly?		
7. Did you include a concluding sentence?		

J | Final Draft. Now use your Editing Checklist to write a third draft of your paragraph. Make any other necessary changes.

UNIT QUIZ

p.102
1. _____Venom_____ is a kind of toxin used by animals that bite or sting.

p.105
2. Toxins are good models for medications because _they can hit the single target._

p.106
3. Zoltan Takacs believes that it is important to protect endangered species because _every time an animal became extinct its posible that a new drug is lost_

p.108
4. The advantages of something are called _____Pros_____, and the disadvantages are called _____Cons_____.

p.108
5. Viruses that died out long ago are called _____extinct viruses_____.

p.112
6. Leon Fleisher had a disease that affected _muscles move in strange_

p.115
7. You can use *although*, *even though*, and *though* to make _____Concessins_____.

p.116
8. A paragraph that is used to convince the reader that something is true is called a(n) _____persuasive_____ paragraph.

Nature's Fury

Think and Discuss

1. What types of extreme natural events can you think of? Do any happen in your area?

2. Which of these natural events are the most dangerous? Why?

▲ A lightning bolt appears next to a waterspout over Lake Okeechobee, Florida, USA.

Lightning

- Lightning strikes somewhere on Earth about 100 times every second.
- Lightning is extremely hot—it can heat the air around it to temperatures five times hotter than the surface of the sun.
- In most cases, lightning is caused by electrical activity in clouds.

A. Look at the photos. Which natural event do you think each sentence describes?

1. This event is always happening somewhere in the world.
2. This event causes the fastest winds on Earth.
3. This event can create its own weather system.

B. Read the information and check your answers to **A**. Then discuss the questions.

1. Which events have natural causes? Which event is normally caused by people?
2. Which events can cause other natural events?

Tornadoes

- Tornadoes, also called twisters, are born from thunderstorms. They occur over land when warm, moist (wet) air meets cool, dry air.

- Moving at up to 250 mph (400 kph), they are the fastest winds on Earth.

- Tornadoes can form at any time of the day and year, but they happen more often in late afternoon, when thunderstorms are common.

- Most tornadoes in the U.S. occur in a region called Tornado Alley, between the Rocky Mountains and the Gulf of Mexico.

Wildfire

- A wildfire moves at speeds of up to 14 mph (23 kph).

- Four out of five wildfires are started by people. A natural event such as lightning can also start a wildfire.

- A strong fire can create its own weather system: Air around the fire gets warmer, the warm air rises, and this process sometimes creates winds.

A | Building Vocabulary. Find the words in **blue** in the reading passage on pages 125–126. Read the words around them and try to guess their meanings. Then match the sentence parts below to make definitions.

1. _____ The **climate** of a place is
2. _____ If things **collide**,
3. _____ A **condition** is
4. _____ **Data** are
5. _____ If something **extends** from one place to another,
6. _____ When things **form**,
7. _____ When events **occur**,
8. _____ A **region** is
9. _____ If an object **strikes** other things,
10. _____ If something is **violent**,

a. they begin to exist and take shape.
b. facts and statistics that you can analyze.
c. the weather conditions that are normal there.
d. they happen.
e. an area of a country or the world.
f. it uses physical force to hurt or kill people.
g. they crash into each other.
h. it covers that area or distance.
i. the state that something is in.
j. it hits them.

B | Using Vocabulary. Answer the questions. Share your ideas with a classmate.

1. What is the **climate** like in your area?
2. What is an example of a **violent** natural event? What causes it to be violent?
3. What extreme natural events **occur** in your **region**?

C | Brainstorming. What are some possible effects of a tornado? Complete the cause-and-effect chart.

Cause	Effects
tornado	*trees fall down,*

D | Predicting. Scan the reading on pages 125–126. Note the dates and names of places you find.

_____

_____

Now look at the information you wrote. What do you think the reading is mainly about?

a. facts about past tornadoes around the world
b. information about recent tornadoes in the United States
c. predictions about future tornadoes in the United States

Word Partners

Use **occur** with (n.): **accidents** occur, **changes** occur, **events** occur; (adv.): **frequently** occur, **naturally** occur, **normally** occur, **often** occur.

When Tornadoes Strike

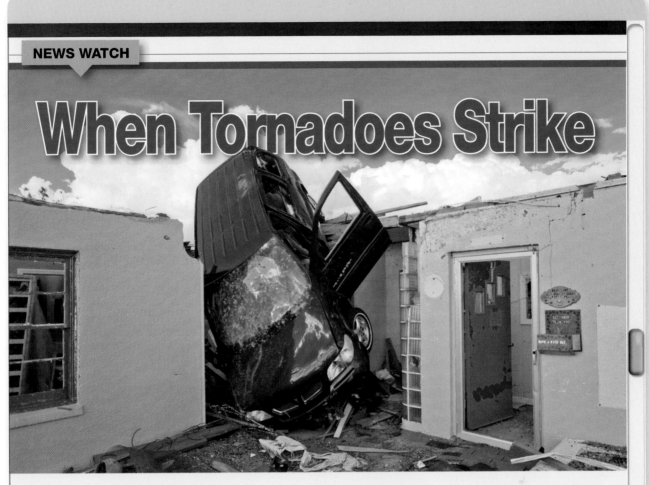

▲ A powerful tornado in Kansas threw this van against a hotel building.

track **2-04**

A The tornado that hit Joplin, Missouri, on April 26, 2011, threw cars into the air as if they were toys. It pulled buildings apart and even broke up pavement[1]—something that only the strongest twisters can do. The Joplin tornado was strong, but it was just one of an amazing number of powerful twisters to strike the United States recently.

B A huge number of intense tornadoes hit several regions of the southern United States in 2011. In fact, more violent tornadoes struck the United States in April 2011 than in any other month on record.[2] In just two days, from April 26 to April 27, there were more than 100 separate twisters. The tornadoes moved through six states and killed at least 283 people.

The "Perfect Storm"

C From April 26 to April 27, "perfect storm" conditions gave birth to a monster twister in Tuscaloosa, Alabama. "Perfect storm" conditions occur when warm, wet air rises and collides with cold, dry air at high altitudes.[3]

---

[1] The **pavement** is the hard surface of a road.

[2] If something is **on record**, it is written down and remembered from the past.

[3] If something is at a particular **altitude**, it is at that height above sea level.

D The Tuscaloosa tornado was 1.0 mile (1.6 kilometers) wide, with winds over 260 mph (400 kph). It stayed on the ground for an unusually long time. Tornadoes usually touch the ground for only a few miles before they die. But experts think the Tuscaloosa tornado stayed on the ground and traveled 300 miles (480 kilometers) across a region extending from Alabama to Georgia. "There were no limitations," said tornado expert Tim Samaras. "It went absolutely crazy. It had nothing but hundreds of miles to grow and develop."

Strong, But Not Surprising?

E What caused the violent tornadoes in 2011? Experts disagree. Some think warmer-than-normal water temperatures in the Gulf of Mexico were the cause. Other people, such as Russell Schneider, director of the U.S. Storm Prediction Center, think it's because of a weather pattern called "La Niña."[4] La Niña can affect the climate in the United States. It makes air drier or wetter and causes temperatures to rise and fall. Some experts, such as Samaras, think we simply don't have enough data to decide.

F Because their cause is unclear, scientists around the world continue to study tornadoes. One day their research will help us to better understand the conditions that cause tornadoes to form. Eventually, we may even be able to predict how strong they will be and where they will hit.

How Twisters Form

● warm air   ● cold air

1

2

3

G ▲ First, warm air and cold air collide and form a tube of rotating air.

H Next, the rotating air turns to become a vertical column. Warm, ▲ moist air rotates upward. Cooler air moves downward and pushes rain to the ground.

I Then, movements of warm and cold air cause the rotating winds ▶ to form a funnel[5] shape. When the funnel touches the ground, it becomes a tornado.

[4] **La Niña** (Spanish for *the girl*) is a weather pattern that occurs when cold water in the Pacific comes to the surface of the ocean off the coast of South America.

[5] A **funnel** is a shape with a wide, circular top and a narrow, short tube at the bottom.

A | **Understanding the Gist.** Look back at your answer for exercise **D** on page 124. Was your prediction correct?

B | **Identifying Main Ideas.** Write answers to the questions.

1. What made the April 2011 tornado season so unusual?

   _____

   _____

2. What was unusual about the Tuscaloosa tornado?

   _____

   _____

C | **Identifying Key Details.** Find in the reading passage the answers to the following questions. Note the paragraphs in which you find the information. Write the answers in your own words. Then share your answers with a partner.

1. What are "perfect storm" conditions for a tornado?

   Paragraph: _____ _____

   _____

2. What may have caused the violent tornadoes of 2011?

   Paragraph: _____ _____

   _____

D | **Critical Thinking: Evaluating Sources.** Find the following quote and paraphrase in "When Tornadoes Strike." Note the paragraphs where you find each one. Then discuss your answers to the questions.

Quote: "*There were no limitations,*" *said tornado expert Tim Samaras.* "*It went absolutely crazy. It had nothing but hundreds of miles to grow and develop.*" Paragraph: _____

Paraphrase: *Other people, such as Russell Schneider, director of the U.S. Storm Prediction Center, think it's because of a weather pattern called "La Niña."* Paragraph: _____

1. Why did the writer quote Samaras? (What idea does it support?)
   Why did the writer paraphrase Schneider? (What idea does it support?)

2. How does the writer describe Samaras and Schneider? For which source do you have more specific information?

E | **Critical Thinking: Analyzing.** Does the article give the cause of the unusual tornado outbreak? Discuss your answer with a partner.

F | **Critical Thinking: Inferring.** According to the reading, tornadoes killed 283 people in April 2011. How else do you think people were affected by these tornadoes?

> **CT Focus**
>
> Writers often **quote or paraphrase** (restate) the ideas of experts to support information in an article. They may introduce these sources with *According to . . .* or [the expert] *thinks / says . . .*

Reading Skill: *Identifying Sequence*

When writers describe processes—how things happen—they use transition words and phrases to show the order, or **sequence**, of the steps or events in the process. Look at these sentences from page 126:

> **First**, warm air and cold air collide and form a tube of rotating air.   **Next**, the rotating air turns to become a vertical column.

The words *first* and *next* tell you that warm and cold air collide and form a tube *before* the rotating air becomes a vertical column.

Other transition words that indicate sequence include *then*, *second*, and *finally*. Time clauses with *before*, *after*, *when*, *as soon as*, *once*, and *during* also show order.

> **Before** you go out, check the weather report.   **After** the storm passes, it's safe to go outside.
> **Once** the storm hits, go inside.

Note: *When*, *as soon as*, and *once* describe an event that happens just before another event. *During* shows a period of time in which an event occurs.

> Keep windows closed **during** the storm.   **As soon as** the storm stops, it's safe to go outside.

A | **Analyzing.** Read the information about what to do if a tornado strikes. Underline the words and phrases that show order.

What to Do When a Tornado Strikes

track 2-05

If you live in a tornado region, it's important to know what to do when tornadoes strike. Follow these steps for what to do before, during, and after a tornado strikes, and you will have the best chance to stay safe. First, always pay attention to weather reports during tornado season. In addition, keep your eye on the sky. Watch for dark, greenish-colored clouds, and clouds that are close to the ground. This may mean that a tornado is coming. As soon as you know a tornado is about to hit, find shelter immediately if you are outdoors. If you are indoors, go to the lowest level you can, for example, to a basement. Once the tornado hits, stay inside for the entire time. During a tornado, stay away from windows, as tornadoes can cause them to break. When the storm is over, make sure family members are safe. Check your home and the area around it for damage. Finally, contact disaster relief organizations such as the American Red Cross for help with cleanup and other assistance, such as food and shelter.

Source: http://www.fema.gov

B | **Identifying Sequence.** Discuss your answers to these questions: What should you do before a tornado? What should you do during a tornado? What should you do when a tornado is over?

C | **Critical Thinking: Evaluating Sources.** Discuss your answers to these questions: What is the source of the paragraph in exercise **A**? Is this a reliable source of information on tornadoes? Why, or why not?

D | **Identifying Sequence.** Look back at "How Twisters Form" on page 126. Underline the words and phrases that show order. Then write an answer to the following question: When does a funnel become a tornado?

Lightning

◀ A lightning storm lights up the night sky over Puyehue-Cordón Caulle Volcano in southern Chile.

Before Viewing

A | Using a Dictionary. Here are some words you will hear in the video. Match each word with the correct definition. Use your dictionary to help you.

> charge
> expand
> flash
> particle
> volt

1. _____: get bigger
2. _____: the type of electricity that something contains (either positive or negative)
3. _____: a measurement unit for electricity
4. _____: a very small piece of matter
5. _____: a sudden burst of light

B | Thinking Ahead. You are going to watch a video about lightning. What do you already know about lightning? Read the sentences. Circle **T** for *true* and **F** for *false*.

1. Lightning is electricity.   **T**   **F**

2. Lightning occurs 1000 times a second worldwide.   **T**   **F**

3. Most lightning occurs in Europe.   **T**   **F**

4. Lightning is usually not as dangerous as a tornado.   **T**   **F**

While Viewing

A | Watch the video about lightning. As you watch, check and correct your answers to exercise **B** above.

B | As you view the video, think about the answers to these questions.

1. Where in the world does lightning strike the most?
2. What does lightning often look like when it strikes the Earth?

3. What causes the loud noise you usually hear with lightning?
4. What should you do to stay safe during a lightning storm?

After Viewing

A | Discuss answers to questions 1–4 above with a partner.

B | Critical Thinking: Synthesizing. Compare lightning and tornadoes. Where in the world do they happen? What causes them? How do they affect people and communities?

A | **Building Vocabulary.** Read the sentences below. Use the context to help you identify the part of speech and meaning of each **bold** word. Write your answers. Check your answers in a dictionary.

1. Putting out a fire is not always the most **appropriate** thing to do. Sometimes it's better to let a fire burn.

   Part of speech: _____

   Meaning: _____

2. Firefighters look for natural objects that can **block** a fire, such as a river.

   Part of speech: _____

   Meaning: _____

3. **Experience** shows that fires are less dangerous when people call the fire department immediately. When firefighters arrive quickly, the fire doesn't have a chance to spread.

   Part of speech: _____

   Meaning: _____

4. **Frequent** lightning storms are dangerous. Many storms in a short period of time can cause fires.

   Part of speech: _____

   Meaning: _____

5. The 2008 Santa Barbara fire was dangerous because there was a lot of **fuel** in its path, such as trees, grass, and homes.

   Part of speech: _____

   Meaning: _____

6. One **method** for preventing dangerous fires is cutting down dead trees.

   Part of speech: _____

   Meaning: _____

7. Many fires are the result of accidents. However, firefighters sometimes set small fires **on purpose** to prevent larger, more dangerous fires.

   Part of speech: _____

   Meaning: _____

> **Word Partners**
>
> Use **experience** with adjectives: **professional** experience, **valuable** experience, **past** experience, **shared** experience, **learning** experience. You can also use **experience** with nouns: **work** experience, **life** experience, experience **danger**.

8. Fires that occur in places where a lot of people live are **particularly** dangerous because many people may be at risk.

Part of speech: _____

Meaning: _____

9. If you want **significant** data on fires in your area, look on your local fire department's website. Other sites may not have the most up-to-date or important information.

Part of speech: _____

Meaning: _____

10. You can avoid fires if you do not build houses near dry, dead plants. This **strategy** saves many lives.

Part of speech: _____

Meaning: _____

B | **Using Vocabulary.** Answer the questions in complete sentences. Then share your sentences with a partner.

1. If there is a fire in a crowded building, what is the **appropriate** thing to do?

_____

_____

2. What weather conditions are **particularly** dangerous, in your opinion?

_____

_____

3. Do fires occur **frequently** in your community? Why, or why not?

_____

_____

4. What are some **strategies** that you use to stay safe in bad weather conditions?

_____

_____

5. Describe something you did recently **on purpose**. Why did you do it?

_____

_____

C | **Predicting.** Skim the reading on pages 132–133. What do you think it is mainly about?

☐ How to escape from a wildfire

☐ How to keep wildfires from starting

☐ How to prevent wildfires from spreading

Wildfires!

track 2-06

◄ A flare is shot onto a burning hillside in Montana to create a backfire.

A Wildfires occur all around the world, but they are most frequent in areas that have wet seasons followed by long, hot, dry seasons. These conditions exist in parts of Australia, South Africa, Southern Europe, and the western regions of the United States.

B Wildfires can move quickly and destroy large areas of land in just a few minutes. Wildfires need three conditions: fuel, oxygen, and a heat source. Fuel is anything in the path of the fire that can burn: trees, grasses, even homes. Air supplies the oxygen. Heat sources include lightning, cigarettes, or just heat from the sun.

C From past experience we know that it is difficult to prevent wildfires, but it is possible to stop them from becoming too big. One strategy is to cut down trees. Another strategy is to start fires on purpose. Both of these strategies limit the amount of fuel available for future fires. In addition, people who live in areas where wildfires occur can build fire-resistant[1] homes, according to fire researcher Jack Cohen. Cohen says that in some recent California fires, "there were significant cases of communities that did not burn . . . because they were fire-resistant."

D However, most experts agree that no single action will reduce fires or their damage. The best method is to consider all these strategies and use each of them when and where they are the most appropriate.

[1] If something is **fire-resistant**, it does not catch fire easily.

[2] A **military campaign** is a planned set of activities for fighting a war.

[3] A **trench** is a long, narrow channel.

[4] **Chemical fire retardant** is a type of chemical that slows down the burning of fire.

[5] **Backburning** is removing fuel, such as plants and trees, in a fire's path, usually by burning it in a controlled way.

Fighting Fire

Fighting fires is similar to a military campaign.[2] Attacks come from the air and from the ground. The firefighters must consider three main factors: the shape of the land, the weather, and the type of fuel in the path of the fire. For example, southern sides of mountains are sunnier and drier, so they are more likely to burn than the northern sides. Between two mountains, in the canyons, strong winds can suddenly change the direction of a fire. **1** These places, therefore, experience particularly dangerous fires.

- To control a wildfire, firefighters on the ground first look for something in the area that can block the fire, such as a river or a road. **2** Then they dig a deep trench.[3] This is a "fire line," a line that fire cannot cross. **3**

- While firefighters on the ground create a fire line, planes and helicopters drop water or chemical fire retardant[4] on the fire. **4** Pilots communicate with firefighters on the ground so they know what areas to hit.

- As soon as the fire line is created, firefighters cut down any dead trees in the area between the fire line and the fire. **5** This helps keep flames from climbing higher into the treetops.

- At the same time, other firefighters on the ground begin backburning[5] in the area between the fire line and the fire. **6**

A | Understanding the Gist. Look back at your answer for exercise **C** on page 131. Was your prediction correct?

B | Identifying Key Ideas. Find answers to questions 1–3 in the reading. Note the paragraphs in which you find the information. With a partner, take turns explaining your answers.

1. Where are wildfires most common?_____
    _____ Paragraph: _____

2. What conditions do wildfires need to burn?_____
    _____ Paragraph: _____

3. What are some ways to prevent wildfires from getting bigger?_____
    _____ Paragraph: _____

CT Focus

Evaluating sources: When you see a quote from an expert in an article, think about why the writer included it and the ideas it supports.

C | Critical Thinking: Evaluating Sources. Discuss your answers to these questions: Why does the writer quote Jack Cohen? What idea does his quote support?

D | Identifying Supporting Examples. According to the two reading passages, what are the main factors that firefighters consider when they are fighting a fire? What are examples of each one? Complete the chart.

Factor	shape of the land		
Examples			dry grass, plants

E | Critical Thinking: Making Comparisons. How is fighting fire similar to a military campaign?

In both military campaigns and fighting fires, _____

_____.

F | Identifying Sequence. Underline the sequencing words and phrases in the reading "Fighting Fire," on page 133. Then number the events below in the correct order. If two events happen at the same time, give them the same number.

a. _____ Firefighters backburn the area between the fire and the fire line.

b. _____ Firefighters look for something in the area to block the fire.

c. _____ Firefighters cut down dead trees in the area between the fire and the fire line.

d. _____ Planes and helicopters drop fire retardant on the fire.

e. _____ Firefighters dig a trench to create a fire line.

G | Critical Thinking: Synthesizing. Discuss the questions in small groups.

1. What is the role of weather in each of the natural events you learned about in this unit?

2. Which events can we predict? Which ones can we control? Which ones can we prevent? Explain your answers.

GOAL: In this lesson, you are going to plan, write, revise, and edit a paragraph on the following topic: ***Explain a process that you know well.***

A | **Brainstorming.** You are going to write a process paragraph. A process can be either an explanation of how to do something or an explanation of how something happens.

Work with a partner. Make a list of processes that you are familiar with. Put a check next to the ones that you can explain. Then take turns explaining them to your partner.

☐ what to do when lightning strikes   ☐ _____

☐ _____   ☐ _____

☐ _____   ☐ _____

☐ _____   ☐ _____

B | **Journal Writing.** Write in your journal about one of the processes that you checked in exercise **A**. Write for three minutes.

C | **Analyzing.** Read the information in the box. Complete the sentences (1–3) with the correct form of the verb in parentheses.

Language for Writing: Verb Forms for Describing a Process

Writers usually use two verb forms when they describe a process—the imperative and the simple present.

If you are explaining how to do something, use the imperative. The imperative is the base form of a verb. You do not use a subject with the imperative. For example:

> First, **remove** fuel in the fire's path.

The subject, *you*, is understood. *Remove* is the base form of the verb.

If you are explaining how something happens, use the simple present. For example:

> Then warm air **moves** upward.
> Then firefighters **look** for something in the area that can block the fire.

Remember to make subjects and verbs agree when you use the simple present.

---

1. _____ (*move*) indoors during a lightning storm, if possible.

2. Firefighters _____ (*dig*) a trench to block the fire.

3. First, warm air _____ (*collide*) with cold air at high altitudes.

D | **Applying.** Write three imperative sentences and three sentences in the simple present. Use the ideas from exercises **A** and **B** above.

Writing Skill: *Organizing a Process Paragraph*

When you write a process paragraph, you explain steps or events in a process in **chronological order**—the first event appears first, then the next event, and so on.

To plan a process paragraph, first list each step or event in the correct order. When you write your paragraph, use transition words and phrases to help the reader follow the order.

> *first, second, third; then, next, in addition; finally*
>
> *before, after, once, when, as soon as, during, while*

Note that *during* and *while* have similar meanings but are used differently in a sentence.

> **During** *the storm, it isn't safe to go outside. (during + noun)*
>
> **While** *the storm is happening, stay indoors. (while + noun + be + verb + -ing)*

As you saw on page 135, writers usually use the simple present or the imperative to describe a process. You can also use the present perfect with *after* and *once*.

> **After / Once** *the storm* <u>*has passed*</u>*, it's safe to go outside.*

Note: A process paragraph is more than a list of steps. It is also important to include details that help the reader understand the steps or events.

E | **Sequencing.** Look at the list of events for a process paragraph. Number them to put them in the best order. Then underline any transition words or phrases that show order.

_____ After that, turn off any of your home energy sources that can act as fuel, such as natural gas

_____ Finally, leave the area as quickly as possible. Do not return home until it is safe.

_____ Then go back inside and close all windows, doors, and other openings. This helps prevent the fire from moving easily through the house.

_____ If a fire is approaching your home, first go outside and move any items that can act as fuel for the fire, such as dead plants.

_____ Then fill large containers such as garbage cans and bathtubs with water. This will slow down the fire.

Source: http://environment.nationalgeographic.com/environment/natural-disasters/wildfire-safety-tips/

Now write the paragraph.

> *Wildfires move quickly and are extremely dangerous, but you can avoid danger if you follow these steps.* _____
>
> _____
>
> _____
>
> _____
>
> _____
>
> _____
>
> _____
>
> *If you follow these steps, you will have the best chances for staying safe if a wildfire occurs.*

A | **Planning.** Follow the steps to plan your process paragraph.

Step 1   Write your topic on the line.
Step 2   List the steps or events for your process in the correct order in the chart below.
                Don't write complete sentences.
Step 3   Write a topic sentence that introduces your process.
Step 4   Now write any details that will help the reader to better understand your steps or events.

Topic: _____

Topic sentence: _____

Steps or events   **Details**

1. _____   _____

2. _____   _____

3. _____   _____

4. _____   _____

5. _____   _____

6. _____   _____

7. _____   _____

8. _____   _____

B | **Draft 1.** Use your chart to write a first draft.

C | Analyzing. The paragraphs below are on the topic of what to do when an earthquake hits.

Which is the first draft? _____   Which is the revision? _____

ⓐ   If you are indoors when an earthquake occurs, there are several things to do to stay safe. First, try to stay in one place. You will be safer if you move as little as possible. Then drop to the ground. Try to find a strong object nearby that you can get under, such as a table or other piece of furniture. If you are not near a piece of furniture that you can get under, stand in a doorway. While the earthquake is happening, hold on to the furniture or the doorframe. As soon as the shaking stops, it's safe to move around. After an earthquake, be careful opening cupboards and closets, as objects may fall out. By following these steps, you will keep yourself as safe as possible when an earthquake hits.

ⓑ   Earthquakes are extremely dangerous. Never go outside during an earthquake. After an earthquake, it can still be dangerous because of aftershocks— smaller earthquakes—and fires caused by the earthquake. If you are indoors when an earthquake occurs, try to stay in one place. Try to find a strong object nearby that you can get under, such as a table or other piece of furniture. If you are not near a piece of furniture that you can get under, stand in a doorway. Hold on to the furniture or the doorframe until the shaking stops. Do not go outside until the shaking stops. By following these steps, you will keep yourself as safe as possible when an earthquake hits.

Source: http://www.fema.gov

D | Critical Thinking: Analyzing. Work with a partner. Compare the paragraphs above by answering the following questions about each one.

	ⓐ		ⓑ	
1. Does the paragraph have one main idea?	Y	N	Y	N
2. Does the topic sentence introduce the main idea?	Y	N	Y	N
3. Are the steps in the correct order?	Y	N	Y	N
4. Are there transition words and phrases to show order?	Y	N	Y	N
5. Are there detail sentences for some of the steps?	Y	N	Y	N
6. Is there a concluding sentence?	Y	N	Y	N

Now discuss your answer to this question: Which paragraph is better? Why?

E | Revising. Answer the questions above about your own paragraph.

F | Peer Evaluation. Exchange your first draft with a partner and follow these steps:

Step 1   Read your partner's paragraph and tell him or her one thing that you liked about it.

Step 2   Write the steps or events of your partner's paragraph in the chart below.

Topic: _____

Topic sentence: _____

Steps or events   **Details**

1. _____   _____

2. _____   _____

3. _____   _____

4. _____   _____

5. _____   _____

6. _____   _____

7. _____   _____

8. _____   _____

Step 3   Compare your list of steps with the steps that your partner wrote in exercise **A** on page 137.

Step 4   The two lists should be similar. If they aren't, discuss how they differ.

G | Draft 2. Write a second draft of your paragraph. Use what you learned from the peer evaluation activity, and your answers to exercise **E**. Make any other necessary changes.

H | Editing Practice. Read the information in the box. Then find and correct one verb form mistake in each of the sentences (1–5).

In sentences using imperatives and the simple present, remember to:

• use the base form of the verb in the imperative   • use verbs that agree with subjects in the simple present

---

1. Most earthquake injuries happens when people go outside before the quake is over.
2. Before a tornado hits, listens carefully to weather reports.
3. When lighting strike, move indoors as quickly as possible.
4. Finding the lowest area in a building when a tornado is about to hit.
5. A firefighter try to remove fuel in the fire's path, such as dead trees and plants.

WRITING TASK: Editing

I | Editing Checklist. Use the checklist to find errors in your second draft.

Editing Checklist	Yes	No
1. Are all the words spelled correctly?		
2. Is the first word of every sentence capitalized?		
3. Does every sentence end with the correct punctuation?		
4. Do your subjects and verbs agree?		
5. Did you use the imperative correctly?		
6. Are other verb tenses correct?		

J | Final Draft. Now use your Editing Checklist to write a third draft of your paragraph. Make any other necessary changes.

UNIT QUIZ

p.123
1. Another word for a tornado is a(n) _____.

p.123
2. The region where tornadoes occur the most in the United States is called _____.

p.125
3. Tornadoes occur when warm air _____ with cold air.

p.128
4. The underlined word below shows that the event in the first sentence happens **before / at the same time as** the event in the second sentence.
Firefighters on the ground dig a trench and cut down dead trees between the trench and the fire. <u>While</u> they are cutting down trees in the fire's path, other firefighters drop fire retardant from the air.

p.129
5. A(n) _____ is a sudden bright light.

p.130
6. _____ is the material that fires burn, such as trees and grasses.

p.130
7. Not all fires are the results of accidents: Firefighters sometimes set fires _____ because it can keep forests healthy.

p.136
8. A process paragraph shows the **order / results** of events.

Building Wonders

ACADEMIC PATHWAYS

Lesson A: Scanning for specific information
Lesson B: Reading a comparison text
Lesson C: Using a Venn diagram to plan a paragraph
Writing a comparison paragraph

Think and Discuss

1. What is the tallest building in your area? What is the oldest?
2. What do you think are the most amazing buildings in the world?
Why are they special?

▲ Workers crowd a building site at the Nagarjuna Sagar Dam in Andhra Pradesh State, India.

Exploring the Theme

Read the information and discuss the questions.

1. Why do humans build monuments and other large structures? List as many reasons as you can.

2. What are some examples of monuments? Why are they important?

3. Which of the monuments mentioned below have you heard of? Which would you most like to visit?

Building Big

Throughout history, humans have felt a need to build huge structures. Some large structures that have a special purpose are known as monuments.

There are many reasons for building monuments. Some are tombs for great people. For example, ancient Egyptians built pyramids to protect their kings after death. Centuries later, the ruler Shah Jahan built the Taj Mahal in India to remember his dead wife. Some monuments remind us of great leaders in the past, such as Mount Rushmore's giant carvings of American presidents. Other monuments have religious purposes, such as Göbekli Tepe, one of the oldest religious structures on Earth. The purpose of some monuments, such as the ancient stone circle of Stonehenge in England, is still a mystery.

UNESCO (the United Nations Educational, Scientific, and Cultural Organization) protects many of these important structures as World Heritage Sites.

Builders work on the giant faces of George Washington (left) and Thomas Jefferson (right), two of four former U.S. presidents carved on Mount Rushmore, South Dakota, USA. Construction on the monument began in 1927 and took 14 years to complete.

A | **Building Vocabulary.** Find the words in **blue** in the reading passage on pages 145–148. Read the words around them and try to guess their meanings. Then match the sentence parts below to make definitions.

1. _____ An **architect** is

2. _____ If you **commit** yourself **to** something,

3. _____ If you **illustrate** ideas,

4. _____ If you get **inspiration** from something,

5. _____ A **successor** is

6. _____ **Sculpture** is

7. _____ A **structure** is

8. _____ An artistic **style** is characteristic of

9. _____ A **symbol** is

10. _____ A **theme** is

a. a shape or design that represents an idea.

b. you explain or give examples of the ideas.

c. a kind of art that is produced by carving or shaping stone, wood, clay, or other materials.

d. it gives you new ideas.

e. an important idea or subject found throughout a piece of writing or a work of art.

f. something made of parts connected together in an ordered way.

g. a particular period or group of people.

h. a person who takes another person's role or job after he or she has left.

i. a person who plans and designs buildings.

j. you give your time and energy to it.

B | **Using Vocabulary.** Answer the questions. Share your ideas with a partner.

1. What is the **style** of the building you are in right now? Is it modern? Is it traditional?
2. What tasks or activities are you **committed to** right now?
3. From whom or what do you get **inspiration**? Explain your answer.

C | **Brainstorming.** If the style of a building is inspired by nature, what might it look like? List your ideas.

The ceiling is painted to look like the sky at night.

_____

_____

D | **Predicting.** Read the title and subheads of the reading passage on pages 145–148 and look at the pictures. Then work with a partner to find words in the passage that help you answer these questions.

1. What kind of person is the passage probably about? _____
2. What kind of building is the reading passage about? _____
3. What is special about the building? _____

_____

Word Partners

Use **style** with (*n.*) **leadership** style, **learning** style, style **of music**, **writing** style; (*adj.*) **distinctive** style, **particular** style, **personal** style.

Unfinished Masterpiece[1]

▲ Workers using ropes climb the tall columns inside Barcelona's La Sagrada Família.

track 2-07

A IT'S A STRUCTURE that isn't finished, yet two million people visit it every year. Antoní Gaudí began building his church, La Sagrada Família, in 1881. Work continues to this day.

B The architect Antoní Gaudí was born in 1852 near the town of Reus, in the Catalonian region of Spain. As a child, he was interested in the natural wonders of the Catalonian countryside. When he grew up, he went to Barcelona to study architecture. Gaudí designed many structures in Barcelona, but he was most committed to La Sagrada Família. In fact, by 1910, he stopped working on any other projects.

Inspired by Nature

C Early in his career, Gaudí experimented with many styles, but eventually developed his own ideas about architecture. The natural world was the main inspiration for Gaudí's designs. "Nothing is art if it does not come from nature," he believed. Gaudí understood that the natural world is full of curved[2] forms, not straight lines. With this idea in mind, he based his structures on a simple idea: If nature is the work of God, then the best way to honor God is to design buildings based on nature.

D The architect's love of nature combined with his religious beliefs guided the design of La Sagrada Família. Gaudí designed the inside of La Sagrada Família to feel like a forest. Inside the church, pillars[3] rise up like trees. The theme continues outside. The outside of the church is decorated with sculptures of native wildlife. For example, a turtle—a symbol of the sea—and a tortoise—a symbol of the land— are carved[4] into the base of two columns. Carvings of other animals, such as reptiles and birds, appear throughout the structure.

---

[1] A **masterpiece** is an extremely good work of art.
[2] If something is **curved**, it is not straight.
[3] **Pillars** are tall, round structures that support buildings.
[4] If something is **carved**, it is cut from wood or stone into a shape or pattern.

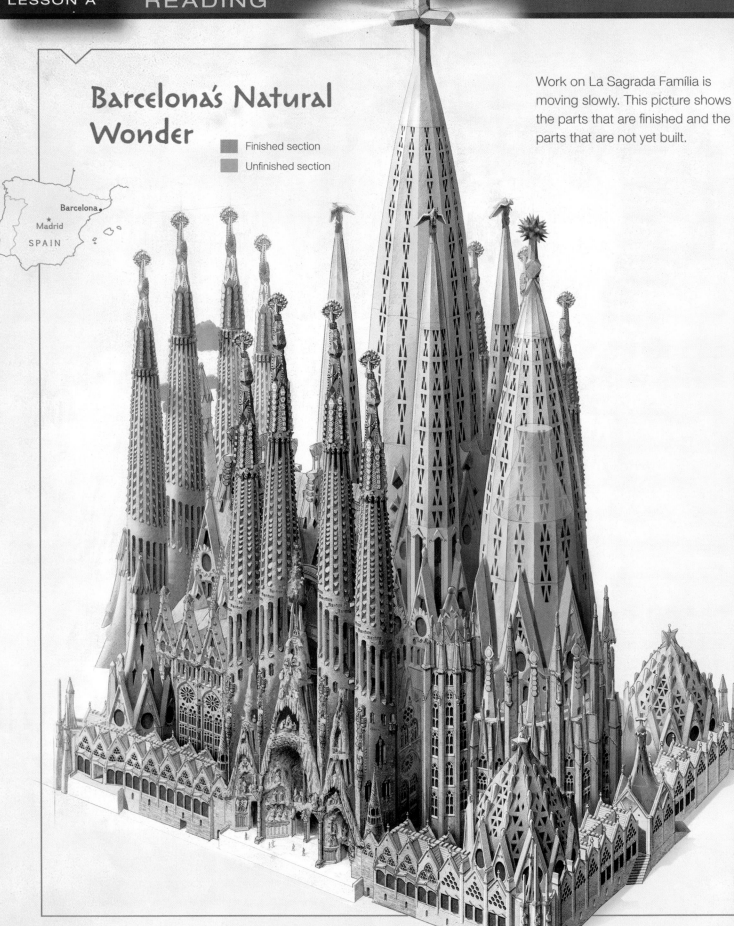

Barcelona's Natural Wonder

■ Finished section
■ Unfinished section

Barcelona •
★ Madrid
SPAIN

Work on La Sagrada Família is moving slowly. This picture shows the parts that are finished and the parts that are not yet built.

Forms in nature influenced Gaudí's architectural style. There are many examples of his nature-inspired designs throughout the church.

Natural Windows

Gaudí's windows are similar to shapes found in nature, such as in this algae, a tiny sea animal.

Pyrite crystal ▲

Tower Tops

Some of the decorations on La Sagrada Família are modeled on Gaudí's study of crystals, grains, and grasses.

Vine Lines

Gaudí often used vine shapes to decorate the walls of the church.

▼ Passion fruit vine

Spiral Stairways

The spiral is a common shape in nature. It exists in plants and animals. Gaudí used spirals in many parts of the church.

Garden snail ▼

Tree Structures

Gaudí made a "forest" inside the church by creating columns that look like trees. He even carved shapes that look like places where branches were removed.

An End in Sight

E   Gaudí died in 1926. Before his death, he made three-dimensional[5] models of his plans for the building, hoping that others could complete his masterpiece. Many of these models were lost during the Spanish Civil War,[6] but some survived. These models have helped Gaudí's successors. For example, Mark Burry, an architect from New Zealand, has worked on La Sagrada Família for 31 years. He uses computer technology and the surviving models to bring Gaudí's plans to life.

F   Gaudí's work illustrates a timeless truth. As the architectural historian Joan Bassegoda wrote: "The lesson of Gaudí is . . . to look at nature for inspiration . . . nature does not go out of fashion."[7] In fact, you might say Gaudí's architectural style was ahead of its time. The architect's nature-inspired designs can be seen as an early example of the modern science of biomimetics—a science that uses designs in nature to solve modern problems.

G   Work on La Sagrada Família is expected to be finished in 2026, 100 years after Gaudí's death. Gaudí was once asked why La Sagrada Família was taking so long to complete. "My client[8] is not in a hurry," he said.

▲ Antoní Gaudí (1852–1926)

1893

A Work in Progress

The first stage of building La Sagrada Família was completed in 1893. The church's main towers will be completed in 2020; six years later, all work will be complete.

2020

◄ **1933**

1978 ►

◄ **2010**

---

[5] A **three-dimensional** object can be measured in three directions: height, length, and depth.

[6] The **Spanish Civil War** was a revolt against the government of Spain (1936–1939).

[7] To **go out of fashion** means to become unpopular.

[8] A **client** is someone for whom a professional does some work.

A | **Understanding the Gist.** Look back at your answers for exercise **D** on page 144. Were your predictions correct?

B | **Identifying Main Ideas.** What are the main ideas of the following paragraphs? Use the questions to help you answer.

1. Paragraph C: What were Gaudí's ideas about architecture?

   _____

   _____

2. Paragraph D: How is La Sagrada Família an example of Gaudí's architectural style?

   _____

   _____

3. Paragraph E: How did Gaudí help his successors?

   _____

   _____

C | **Identifying Supporting Details.** Complete the chart with examples of how the design of La Sagrada Família is inspired by nature.

	Object in Church	Shape or Object in Nature
Inside	pillars	trees
Outside		

D | **Critical Thinking: Reflection.** Write answers to the questions.

1. What do you think about Gaudí's design for La Sagrada Família? Do you know any other buildings that have an unusual design?

2. Look again at the last line of the passage. What do you think Gaudí means?

3. According to Joan Bassegoda, "Nature does not go out of fashion." What are some things that were in style in the past and are still popular today? Why do you think they are still popular?

Strategy

When you scan, **look for paraphrases** of key words, as well as the key words themselves. For example, *began building* is a paraphrase for *started work on*.

Reading Skill: *Scanning for Specific Information*

Scanning helps you find details quickly. When you scan, you move your eyes quickly across and down a page and you only look for particular things. For example, to get information about times and dates, look for numbers, and to get information about people and places, look for capitalized words. Read the words around the numbers or capitalized words to understand the context.

For example, to answer the question "When did Gaudí start work on La Sagrada Família?", first scan the text to find a year. Then read the words near the year for information about "starting work."

Antoní Gaudí began building his church, La Sagrada Família, in 1881.

First, your eyes go to *1881*. Then your eyes go to *began building*. You have found the answer to the question—*in 1881*.

A | **Scanning for Details.** The passage below is about the mysterious statues in Rapa Nui (Easter Island) called *moai*. Scan the paragraph to find the answers to these questions. Underline the words in the paragraph that give you the answers.

1. How far is Rapa Nui from Chile? _____
2. When did people probably first come to Rapa Nui? _____
3. Where did the people of Rapa Nui come from? _____
4. How tall are the statues? How much do they weigh? _____

♪ The Moai of Rapa Nui

track 2-08

Rapa Nui (Easter Island) is an island in the Pacific Ocean located 2,300 miles (3,700 kilometers) west of Chile. It's home to the mysterious *moai* statues, enormous figures carved from stone. It's not clear when the island was first settled. Experts guess that a few brave sailors somehow sailed west to Rapa Nui from Polynesian islands around AD 800. Experts do know that the Rapa Nui culture was at its height between the 10th and 16th centuries. They think the Rapa Nui people carved and built the *moai* in this period. There are 900 *moai* statues across the island. They are about 13 feet (4 meters) tall and weigh as much as 14 tons. Most scholars think that the *moai* were created to honor ancestors, chiefs, or other important people.

B | **Scanning for Details.** Look back at the reading on pages 145–148. Scan the text to find answers to these questions. Write each answer and note the paragraph where you found the information.

1. When did Gaudí start working *only* on La Sagrada Família?

_____ Paragraph: _____

2. Who worked on La Sagrada Família in recent years?

_____ Paragraph: _____

3. When will La Sagrada Família be completed?

_____ Paragraph: _____

4. What happened to Gaudí's models during the Spanish Civil War?

_____ Paragraph: _____

THE PYRAMIDS OF GIZA

Before Viewing

▲ For thousands of years, the Pyramids of Giza were the tallest structures on Earth. Archaeologists have learned much about how and when they were built, but many mysteries still remain.

A | Brainstorming. What do you think was the purpose of the pyramids in ancient Egypt? Check your answer(s).

_____ places to live   _____ places to see art

_____ places for dead bodies   _____ places to honor Egyptian gods

_____ places for travelers to stay   _____ other: _____

B | Using a Dictionary. You will hear the words in **bold** in the video. Match each word with the correct definition. Use your dictionary to help you.

archaeologist   possessions   pharaoh   tombs   the afterlife

1. _____ a king in ancient Egypt
2. _____ the belief in some religions of the existence of life after death
3. _____ stone structures containing the bodies of dead people
4. _____ things that a person owns or has with them
5. _____ a person who studies societies and peoples of the past by examining the remains of their buildings and other objects

While Viewing

A | Watch the video about the Pyramids of Giza. As you watch, check and correct your answer(s) to exercise **A** above.

B | As you view the video, think about the answers to these questions.

1. For how long have the Pyramids of Giza existed?
2. What is the Pyramid of Khufu made of?
3. About how long did it take to build the Pyramid of Khufu?
4. What does the face of the Sphinx look like?

After Viewing

A | Discuss answers to questions 1–4 above with a partner.

B | Critical Thinking: Synthesizing. Compare the Pyramids of Giza with La Sagrada Família. Think about the following:

- how long it took / is taking to build the structures
- how old the structures are
- the design of the structures
- the purpose of the structures

A | **Building Vocabulary.** Read the sentences below. Look at the words around the words and phrases in **bold** to guess their meanings. Circle the best definition and write the part of speech for each word or phrase.

1. Experts discovered a **site** that is 4,000 years old. They think it is an ancient tomb.

    a. a newly-built city   b. a place with a particular purpose

    Part of speech: _____

2. The Pyramids of Giza **consist of** heavy blocks. Each block weighs about two and a half tons.

    a. are formed from   b. are inspired by

    Part of speech: _____

3. Experts think it took only about 20 years to **construct** the Great Pyramid of Khufu.

    a. discover   b. build

    Part of speech: _____

4. Experts continue to **debate** the purpose of some ancient monuments. There are many opinions because there is not yet enough evidence.

    a. discuss   b. agree on

    Part of speech: _____

5. When archaeologists **excavate** a site, they use special tools to find items buried underground.

    a. carefully remove earth from   b. take pictures of

    Part of speech: _____

6. Experts think the tall column may **represent** a person because it looks like a human being.

    a. be a problem for   b. be a symbol of

    Part of speech: _____

7. Some building projects **require** hundreds of people. Many people must work together to get the job done quickly.

    a. hurt   b. need

    Part of speech: _____

8. A wedding is a religious **ritual** for many people. The event often occurs in a holy place.

    a. ceremony   b. document

    Part of speech: _____

Word Link

trans = across: **trans**port, **trans**portation, **trans**fer, **trans**it, **trans**late. Note that *transport* can be both a noun and a verb, but the stress is different: (*n.*) **trans**port, (*v.*) trans**port**.

9. Ancient people went to the **temple** to honor their gods.

a. place for entertainment   b. place for religious activities

Part of speech: _____

10. How did ancient people **transport** heavy stones? At the time, they didn't even have wheels.

a. move   b. carve

Part of speech: _____

B | Using Vocabulary. Answer the questions in complete sentences. Then share your sentences with a partner.

1. Colors **represent** different things to different people. What does the color red represent to you?

_____

_____

2. What are some issues in the news today that people are **debating**?

_____

_____

3. What are some methods of **transporting** heavy objects over a long distance?

_____

_____

4. Have you ever tried to **construct** anything? What was it?

_____

_____

5. What is an important **site** in your area? What is its purpose?

_____

_____

C | Scanning/Previewing. On the next two pages, look at the pictures and scan for names of places. What is the reading passage mainly about?

The passage is about two _____.

One is in _____ and the other is in _____.

Amazing Structures

🎧 *track 2-09*

A PEOPLE HAVE CREATED monuments for various reasons, inspired by different sources. Two of the greatest architectural achievements are on opposite sides of the world, in Turkey and Mexico.

"In 10 or 15 years," predicts archaeologist Klaus Schmidt, "Göbekli Tepe will be more famous than Stonehenge."

Turkey

Göbekli Tepe

Where:
Southeastern Turkey

When built:
Approx. 11,590 B.C.

B **Göbekli Tepe** is one of the oldest man-made structures on Earth. It was already nearly 8,000 years old when both Stonehenge[1] and the pyramids of Egypt were built. The structure consists of dozens of stone pillars arranged in rings. The pillars are shaped like capital Ts, and many are covered with carvings of animals running and jumping. They are also very big—the tallest pillars are 18 feet (5.5 m) in height and weigh 16 tons (more than 14,500 kg). In fact, archaeologists think that Göbekli Tepe was probably the largest structure on Earth at the time.

How Was It Built?

C At the time that Göbekli Tepe was built, most humans lived in small nomadic[2] groups. These people survived by gathering plants and hunting animals. They had no writing system and did not use metal. Even wheels did not exist. Amazingly, the structure's builders were able to cut, shape, and transport 16-ton stones. Archaeologists found Stone Age[3] tools such as knives at the site. They think hundreds of workers carved and put the pillars in place.

Why Was It Built?

D Archaeologists are still excavating Göbekli Tepe and debating its meaning. Many think it is the world's oldest temple. Klaus Schmidt is the archaeologist who originally excavated the site. He thinks that people living nearby created Göbekli Tepe as a holy meeting place. To Schmidt, the T-shaped pillars represent human beings. The pillars face the center of the circle and perhaps represent a religious ritual.

Workers (top right) dragged stone pillars to the construction site. Builders carved the pillars and placed them in circles.

The Temple of Kukulkan,
Chichén Itzá

Chichén Itzá is an ancient city made of stepped pyramids, temples, and other stone structures. The largest building in Chichén Itzá is the Temple of Kukulkan, a pyramid with 365 steps. A kind of calendar, the temple shows the change of seasons. Twice a year on the spring and autumn equinoxes,[4] a shadow falls on the pyramid in the shape of a snake. As the sun sets, this shadowy snake goes down the steps to eventually join a carved snake head on the pyramid's side.

Chichén Itzá

Where:
Yucatán, Mexico

When built:
750–1200 A.D.

How Was It Built?

The Mayans constructed the pyramids with carved stone. To build a pyramid, Mayan workers created a base and added smaller and smaller levels as the structure rose. Building the pyramids required many workers. Some pyramids took hundreds of years to complete. As at Göbekli Tepe, builders worked without wheels or metal tools.

Why Was It Built?

Chichén Itzá was both an advanced city center and a religious site. Spanish records show that the Mayans made human sacrifices[5] to a rain god here. Archaeologists have found bones, jewelry, and other objects that people wore when they were sacrificed. Experts also know that the Mayans were knowledgeable astronomers.[6] They used the tops of the pyramids to view Venus and other planets.

[1] **Stonehenge** is a prehistoric monument in southern England, built around 2600 B.C.
[2] If a person or group is **nomadic**, they travel from place to place rather than living in one place all the time.
[3] The **Stone Age** was a very early period in human history when people used tools and weapons made of stone, not metal.
[4] An **equinox** is a time in the year when day and night are of equal length.
[5] A **sacrifice** is a religious ceremony in which people or animals are killed.
[6] An **astronomer** is a person who studies stars, planets, and other objects in space.

A | Understanding the Gist. Look back at your answers for exercise **C** on page 153. Were your ideas correct?

B | Scanning for Specific Information. Work with a partner. Scan the reading passage on pages 154–155 for information to complete the chart.

Name	When was it built?	How was it built?
Göbekli Tepe	11,590 B.C.	
Chichén Itzá		

C | Critical Thinking: Evaluating Arguments. According to the writer, what was the purpose of each structure? What evidence does the writer give? Scan the reading again and write your answers.

Göbekli Tepe

Purpose: _____

Evidence: _____

_____

Chichén Itzá

Purpose: _____

Evidence: _____

_____

Does the writer give enough supporting evidence? Share your ideas with a classmate.

D | Critical Thinking: Analyzing Similarities and Differences. In what ways are the structures you read about similar? In what ways are they different? Use your ideas from exercises **B** and **C**. Complete the Venn diagram.

CT Focus

To identify comparisons, you need to scan for and select relevant details from different parts of the text, for example, names of people and places, years, dimensions, and other specific details.

Göbekli Tepe   Chichén Itzá

used for rituals

E | Critical Thinking: Synthesizing. In a small group, compare one of the structures from the reading with either La Sagrada Família or the Pyramids of Giza.

GOAL: In this lesson, you are going to plan, write, revise, and edit a comparison paragraph on the following topic: **Compare two structures in terms of their age, size, purpose, and the length of time it took to build each one.**

A | Brainstorming. Look at the list of structures from this unit. Add one or more structures you know well. Brainstorm information about each one. Think about their age, size, purpose, construction, and any other characteristics. Then put a check next to the two structures you know the most about.

☐ La Sagrada Família _____

☐ Göbekli Tepe _____

☐ Chichén Itzá _____

☐ Other: _____

B | Journal Writing. Write in your journal about the two structures that you checked in exercise **A**. Write for three minutes.

C | Analyzing. Read the information in the box. Complete the sentences (1–3) using comparative adjectives.

Language for Writing: Using Comparative Adjectives

One way to make comparisons is to use the comparative forms of adjectives.

adjective + -er + than
more / less + adjective + than (with most adjectives that have two or more syllables)
Examples:
> Göbekli Tepe is **older than** Stonehenge.
> The design of La Sagrada Família is **more complex than** the design of St. Patrick's Cathedral.

Use (not) as + adjective + as to say things are (or are not) the same.
Example:
> The Empire State Building is **not as tall as** the Tokyo Sky Tree.

For further explanation and more examples of comparative adjectives, see page 217.

---

1. The Tokyo Sky Tree is 2,080 feet (634 meters) tall. The Canton Tower is 1,969 feet (600 meters) tall.

   The Tokyo Sky Tree is _____ the Canton Tower. (tall)

2. St. Paul's Cathedral has a traditional design. The design of St. Mary's Cathedral is partly traditional and partly modern.

   The design of St. Mary's Cathedral is _____ the design of St. Paul's Cathedral. (traditional)

3. The Great Wall of China is 5,500 miles (8,850 kilometers) long. Hadrian's Wall is 73 miles (120 kilometers) long.

   Hadrian's Wall is not _____ the Great Wall of China. (long)

D | Applying. Write five comparison sentences about places. Use your ideas from exercises **A** and **B** above.

Writing Skill: *Writing a Comparison Paragraph*

When you write a comparison paragraph, first choose a topic—that is, the items you wish to compare. Next, think of two or three points about the items that you want to discuss. Then think of one or two details to include about each point.

Transition words and phrases in your paragraph help the reader understand your ideas:
Similarities: *similarly, both, also, too*   **Differences:** *however, on the other hand, but*

> **Both** *Göbekli Tepe and Stonehenge are ancient monuments.* **However***, Göbekli Tepe is much older.*

> *The pyramids at Chichén Itzá showed the change in seasons.* **Similarly***, some experts think people used Stonehenge as a kind of calendar.*

E | **Critical Thinking: Analyzing.** Read the paragraph below comparing the two libraries. Use the notes on the right to help you complete the Venn diagram.

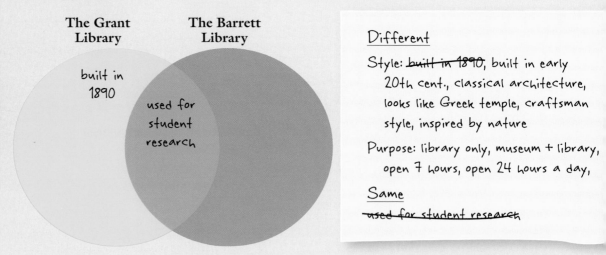

The Grant Library | The Barrett Library

built in 1890

used for student research

Different

Style: ~~built in 1890~~, built in early 20th cent., classical architecture, looks like Greek temple, craftsman style, inspired by nature

Purpose: library only, museum + library, open 7 hours, open 24 hours a day,

Same

~~used for student research~~

    The Grant Library and the Barrett Library are both important resources for BCU students, but there are some differences between the two structures. First, the buildings have very different styles. The Grant Library, built in 1890, is older than the Barrett Library. It was built in the classical style. For example, there are tall marble columns at the entrance, which make the library look like a Greek temple. The Barrett Library, on the other hand, has a newer design. It was built in the early 20th century in the craftsman style. It is made entirely of wood and blends in with the natural environment. The purposes of the two libraries are also different. Students can do research at both places, but the Barrett Library is also a museum, so it's open only seven hours a day. The Grant Library, however, is open 24 hours a day. So students can study there for a longer time. The two buildings have different styles and purposes, but both are excellent examples of the variety of architectural styles on the BCU campus.

F | **Critical Thinking: Analyzing.** Look again at the paragraph and answer the questions.

1. What are the two points about the buildings that the writer is comparing?
2. Find and underline two detail sentences for each of the points of comparison.
3. How many comparison words can you find? Circle them.

A | Planning. Follow the steps to plan your comparison paragraph.

Step 1 Label the two circles of the Venn diagram with the names of the two structures you are going to compare.

Step 2 Think of two or three points of comparison and write them below the Venn diagram.

Step 3 Write the similarities in the space where the two circles intersect (meet). Write the differences in the outer parts of the circles. Add details and examples. Don't write complete sentences.

Step 4 Write a topic sentence that tells the reader whether you are going to write about similarities, differences, or both.

_____   _____

Point 1: _____

_____

Point 2: _____

_____

Point 3: _____

_____

Topic sentence: _____

_____

B | Draft 1. Use your Venn diagram to write a first draft of your paragraph.

C | **Analyzing.** The paragraphs below compare the Golden Gate Bridge and the Brooklyn Bridge.

Which paragraph is the first draft? _____ Which paragraph is the revision? _____

a   The Golden Gate Bridge and the Brooklyn Bridge are both examples of amazing engineering. The two bridges have a similar design. They are both suspension bridges and both have tall towers. The Golden Gate Bridge is longer than the Brooklyn Bridge. The Golden Gate Bridge is 1.7 miles (2.7 kilometers) long. The Brooklyn Bridge is 1,595.5 feet (486.3 meters) long. It crosses the East River, connecting Manhattan with the borough of Brooklyn. It's the oldest suspension bridge in the United States and it became a National Historic Landmark in 1964. As for the Golden Gate Bridge, many people wonder where the name came from. The color of the bridge isn't in fact golden; instead, it's a brownish red color. The term "golden gate" actually refers to part of the Pacific Ocean that it crosses, the Golden Gate Strait.

▲ Golden Gate Bridge

> **Strategy**
>
> When you write a comparison paragraph, **use pronouns** (*it, they*, etc.) to avoid repeating the same nouns too often. Make sure it is clear to the reader what the pronoun is referring to.

b   The Golden Gate Bridge and the Brooklyn Bridge are both examples of amazing engineering. They have some features in common. First, they have a similar design. Both are steel suspension bridges—bridges with a deck that is hung from cables. Both have tall towers that hold the cables in place. However, there are some differences. At 1.7 miles (2.7 kilometers) long, the Golden Gate Bridge is longer than the Brooklyn Bridge, which is only 1,595.5 feet (486.3 meters) long. Also, the Golden Gate Bridge is more recent than the Brooklyn Bridge. The Golden Gate Bridge was completed in 1938. However, the Brooklyn Bridge was built in 1883 and is one of the oldest suspension bridges in the United States. The two bridges also have similar purposes. Both carry thousands of cars, pedestrians, and bicycles to and from busy areas of their city each day. The two bridges have some similarities, but are different in terms of age and size.

▲ Brooklyn Bridge

D | **Critical Thinking: Analyzing.** Work with a partner. Compare the paragraphs above by answering the following questions about each one.

	a		b	
1. Does the paragraph have one main idea?	Y	N	Y	N
2. Does the topic sentence introduce the main idea?	Y	N	Y	N
3. Are there at least two points of comparison?	Y	N	Y	N
4. Is there enough detail for the points of comparison?	Y	N	Y	N
5. Are there transition words to show similarities and differences?	Y	N	Y	N
6. Is there a concluding sentence?	Y	N	Y	N

E | **Revising.** Answer the questions above about your own paragraph.

F | Peer Evaluation. Exchange your first draft with a partner and follow these steps:

Step 1 Read your partner's paragraph and tell him or her one thing that you liked about it.

Step 2 List your partner's points of comparison.

Step 3 Complete the Venn diagram below showing the similarities and differences that your partner's paragraph describes.

Point 1: _____

Point 2: _____

Point 3: _____

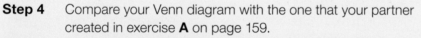

Step 4 Compare your Venn diagram with the one that your partner created in exercise **A** on page 159.

Step 5 The two Venn diagrams should be similar. If they aren't, discuss how they differ.

G | Draft 2. Write a second draft of your paragraph. Use what you learned from the peer evaluation activity, and your answers to exercise **E**. Make any other necessary changes.

▼ At almost 2,723 feet (830 meters), the Burj Khalifa became the world's tallest structure when it opened in 2010.

H | Editing Practice. Read the information in the box. Then find and correct one comparative adjective mistake in each of the sentences (1–5).

In sentences with comparative adjectives, remember to:

- use *more / less … than* with most adjectives that have two or more syllables.
- not use *more / less … than* with comparative adjectives ending in *-er*.
- not use *than* with *(not) as … as*.

---

1. The Chelsea Hotel is more smaller than Casa Mila.

2. La Sagrada Família is attractiver than St. Mary's Cathedral.

3. The construction of the Morrison Library was more expensiver than the construction of the Barrett Library.

4. The Tokyo Sky Tree is not as tall than the Burj Khalifa in Dubai.

5. The carvings on the columns in La Sagrada Família are not ancient as the columns of Göbekli Tepe.

I | **Editing Checklist.** Use the checklist to find errors in your second draft.

Editing Checklist	Yes	No
1. Are all the words spelled correctly?		
2. Is the first word of every sentence capitalized?		
3. Does every sentence end with the correct punctuation?		
4. Do your subjects and verbs agree?		
5. Did you use comparative adjectives correctly?		
6. Are other verb tenses correct?		

J | **Final Draft.** Now use your Editing Checklist to write a third draft of your paragraph. Make any other necessary changes.

UNIT QUIZ

p.142 1. Mount Rushmore is a famous _____ in South Dakota, USA.

p.144 2. A(n) _____ is an important idea or subject found throughout a work of art.

p.145 3. Antoní Gaudí's architectural style was inspired by _____.

p.150 4. Scanning helps you find _____ quickly.

p.151 5. The Pyramids of Giza were built as _____ for pharaohs.

p.154 6. Experts think that Göbekli Tepe was a **temple** / **tomb** / **city**.

p.157 7. Writers use adjectives like *older* and *larger* to make _____.

p.158 8. A Venn diagram helps you see **differences** / **similarities** / **both differences and similarities**.

Form and Function

ACADEMIC PATHWAYS

Lesson A: Distinguishing facts from theories
Lesson B: Synthesizing information from related texts
Lesson C: Paraphrasing and summarizing
Writing a summary

Think and Discuss

1. Why do some animals have fur, skin, or scales?

2. What human-made objects or machines were inspired by nature?

▲ An adult male kingfisher rises from a river in Labod, Hungary.

163

Exploring the Theme

Read the information below and discuss the questions.

1. What is an example of **(a)** a physical adaptation, and **(b)** a behavioral adaptation?
2. Do the animals below show physical or behavioral adaptation?
3. What are some other examples of adaptations in the natural world?

Adaptation

An adaptation is a change in an organism—a plant or an animal—that helps it survive in its environment. These changes are the result of mutation. Mutations are passed in an animal's genes from one generation to the next. As more organisms inherit (receive) the mutation, the change becomes a normal part of the species.

An adaptation can affect an organism physically. For example, some plants adapt to living in the desert by storing water in their stems. It can also affect behavior, such as migration. For example, gray whales give birth in warm water, but travel to cold water for food.

Sometimes an adaptation develops for one purpose, but is used for another. For example, feathers were probably adaptations for keeping warm, but were used later for flying.

The harmless **scarlet king snake** (right), adapted to look like the deadly coral snake (left). This adaptation helps keep it safe from predators.

Ruby-throated hummingbirds can eat both plants and animals. This allows them to get their food from many different sources.

▼ Young steppe eagle chicks share a nest at Cherniye Zemliye Reserve, Russia. The eagles' feathers—the result of many thousands of years of adaptation—will darken as the chicks grow older.

A | Building Vocabulary. Find words in **blue** in the reading passage on pages 167–168. Read the words around them and try to guess their meanings. Then write the correct word from the box to complete each sentence (1–10).

display	evidence	evolve	flexible	fossil
insulation	layer	primitive	speculate	theory

Word Partners

Use **theory** with:
(n.) **evidence for a** theory, **support for a** theory; (adj.) a **scientific** theory, a **convincing** theory; (v.) **develop a** theory, **propose a** theory, **put forward a** theory, **test a** theory.

1. If you _____ about something, you make a guess about its nature or about what might happen.

2. _____ is a material or substance used to keep something warm.

3. A(n) _____ is the remains of a prehistoric animal found inside a rock.

4. A(n) _____ is a formal idea that is intended to explain something and that can be tested.

5. A(n) _____ of material is a quantity of it that covers something, or is between two other things.

6. Something that is for _____ is designed to be seen.

7. _____ is anything that you see, experience, read, or are told that makes you believe something is true.

8. When things _____, they gradually change and develop into another form over time.

9. If something is _____, it moves into different positions easily without breaking.

10. If an animal is _____, it belongs to an early period in its development.

B | Using Vocabulary. Answer the questions. Share your ideas with a partner.

1. Describe something **flexible** in your classroom. What makes it flexible? (For example, what material does it consist of?)
2. What kinds of **evidence** do police look for to solve crimes?
3. Can you name a famous scientist who developed a **theory**? What kind of theory did he or she develop?

C | Brainstorming. Look at the pictures on page 167 and discuss this question with a partner: *Why are some birds' feathers so colorful?* Write down as many ideas as you can think of.

_____

_____

Strategy

A subhead (or section head) indicates the main theme of that section. Reading subheads can give you an overall idea of the theme of a passage and how it is organized, such as whether or not the information is divided into categories.

D | Predicting. Read the title and the subheads of the reading passage on pages 167–168. What is the reading passage mainly about?

a. three ways in which birds attract the opposite sex

b. three possible purposes of feathers

c. three methods birds use to fly

What are Feathers For?

A coat of feathers provides warmth ▲
to a resting greater flamingo.

track **2-10**

A

PALEONTOLOGISTS[1] THINK feathers have existed for millions of years. Fossils of a 125-million-year-old dinosaur called a theropod show that it had a thin layer of hair on its back—evidence of very primitive feathers. Discoveries such as this are helping scientists understand how and why feathers evolved.

Insulation

B

Some paleontologists speculate that feathers began as a kind of insulation to keep animals or their young warm. Paleontologists have found theropod fossils that have their front limbs[2] spread over nests. They think this shows that the dinosaurs were using feathers to keep their young warm. In addition, many young birds are covered in light, soft feathers, which keep the birds' bodies warm. Even when they become adult birds, they keep a layer of warm feathers closest to their bodies.

Attraction

C

Another theory is that feathers evolved for display—that is, to be seen. Feathers on birds show a huge range of colors and patterns. In many cases, the purpose of these beautiful feathers is to attract the opposite sex.

A red bird of paradise adult male uses its ▶
feather display to attract females.

[1] **Paleontologists** are scientists who study fossils.
[2] **Limbs** are arms or legs.

A gull takes flight. ▶

D   A peacock spreads his iridescent[3] tail to attract a peahen. Other birds use crests—feathers on their heads. A recent discovery supports the display idea: In 2009, scientists found very small sacs[4] inside theropod feathers, called melanosomes. Melanosomes give feathers their color. The theropod melanosomes look the same as those in the feathers of living birds.

Flight

E   We know that feathers help birds to fly. Here's how they work: A bird's feathers are not the same shape on each side. They are thin and hard on one side, and long and flexible on the other. To lift themselves into the air, birds turn their wings at an angle. This movement allows air to go above and below the wings. The difference in air pressure allows them to fly.

F   Paleontologists are now carefully studying the closest theropod relatives of birds. They are looking for clues to when feathers were first used for flight. A 150-million-year-old bird called *Anchiornis*, for example, had black-and-white arm feathers. These feathers were almost the same as bird feathers. However, unlike modern bird feathers, the feathers were the same shape on both sides. Because of this, *Anchiornis* probably wasn't able to fly.

G   Scientists also found a small, moveable bone in *Anchiornis* fossils. This bone allowed it to fold its arms to its sides. Modern birds use a similar bone to pull their wings toward their bodies as they fly upwards. Scientists speculate that feathered dinosaurs such as *Anchiornis* evolved flight by moving their feathered arms up and down as they ran, or by jumping from tree to tree.

H   Recent research therefore shows that feathers probably evolved because they offered several advantages. The evidence suggests that their special design and bright colors helped dinosaurs, and then birds, stay warm, attract mates, and finally fly high into the sky.

◀ Fossil evidence suggests that *Anchiornis* had black-and-white arm and leg feathers and a red crest.

[3] If something is **iridescent**, it has many bright colors that seem to be changing.
[4] A **sac** is a small part of an animal's body that is shaped like a little bag.

A | Understanding the Gist. Look back at your answer for exercise **D** on page 166. Was your prediction correct?

B | Identifying Main Ideas. According to the reading passage, what are three purposes of feathers? Write them in the first column in the chart below.

C | Identifying Supporting Details. Scan the reading for information to complete the chart.

1. How does the author support the ideas about the purposes of feathers? Find at least one modern-day example in the reading for each purpose. Write each one under "Examples."

2. What fossil evidence have scientists found relating to each purpose? Note the information under "Evidence."

Purpose	Examples	Evidence
1.	_____ have _____ that keep their bodies warm.	
2.		
3.	A bird's feathers are _____ on one side and _____ on the other—so they can lift themselves into the air.	Feathered dinosaurs such as Anchiornis had a _____ that allowed them to fold their arms to their sides. This may eventually have helped them use their feathers to fly.

D | Critical Thinking: Evaluating Evidence. Think about the scientific evidence in exercise **C** for each theory about feathers. Discuss the questions with a partner.

1. In your opinion, does the evidence help support the theories? Does it convince, or persuade, you? Why, or why not?

2. Do you think one theory is more convincing than the others?

CT Focus

When you evaluate evidence, consider whether it is *relevant* (does it relate to the main idea?), *logical* (does it make sense?), *sufficient* (does it give enough support for the idea?), *plausible* (is it believable and does it match what you already know?), and *reliable* (does the writer state where the evidence comes from?).

Reading Skill: *Identifying Theories*

Science writers use certain words and expressions to differentiate theories from facts. In science, a **fact** is an idea that has been proven to be true. A **theory** is an idea that is based on evidence and reasoning, but has not yet been proven. Scientists develop theories in order to explain why something happens, or happened in a particular way.

Science writers use verbs such as *think*, *speculate*, and *suggest* when they refer to theories.

Some paleontologists speculate that feathers started out as insulation.

Evidence suggests that their special design and bright colors helped both dinosaurs and birds stay warm.

Writers also use words such as *probably* and *perhaps* to indicate theories.

Because of this, Anchiornis probably wasn't able to fly.

A | **Analyzing.** Read the information about a fossil discovery in China. Underline the theories and circle the words that introduce them.

track 2-11

New Discovery Suggests Dinosaurs Were Early Gliders

Many scientists think that a group of dinosaurs closely related to today's birds took the first steps toward flight when their limbs evolved to flap.[1] They theorize that this arm flapping possibly led to flying as a result of running or jumping. But recently discovered fossils in China are showing a different picture.

Paleontologists discovered the fossils of a small, feathered dinosaur called *Microraptor gui* that lived between 120 and 110 million years ago. The Chinese team that studied the fossils doesn't think this animal ran or flapped well enough to take off from the ground. Instead, they think that this animal possibly flew by gliding[2] from tree to tree. They further speculate that the feathers formed a sort of parachute[3] that helped the animal stay in the air.

Not everyone agrees with this theory. Some researchers suggest that *M. gui*'s feathers weren't useful for flight at all. They think that the feathers possibly helped the animal to attract a mate, or perhaps to make the tiny dinosaur look bigger.

▲ Feathered dinosaurs such as *Microraptor gui* may have flown by gliding from tree to tree.

[1] If a bird or insect **flaps** its wings, the wings go up and down.
[2] When birds or airplanes **glide**, they float on air currents.
[3] A **parachute** is a device made of cloth that allows a person to jump safely from an airplane.

B | **Identifying Theories.** Look back at "What Are Feathers For?" Underline three theories and circle the words that introduce them.

The Draco lizard, or "Flying **Dragon**," can **escape** from predators by gliding from tree to tree.

Flying Reptiles

▲ A paradise tree snake prepares to **launch** itself from a **branch** in the Borneo jungle.

Before Viewing

A | Meaning from Context. Look at the photos and read the captions. Match each word or phrase in **bold** with a definition.

1. _____ a large lizard-like animal in stories and legends
2. _____ part of a tree that has leaves or fruit growing on it
3. _____ (to) send something into the air
4. _____ (to) succeed in getting away from something

B | Classifying. How would you describe the Draco lizard and the paradise tree snake? What characteristics do they share? Work with a partner to complete the diagram.

Draco Lizard   Tree Snake

While Viewing

A | Watch the video about flying reptiles. As you watch, add any new information you learn to the diagram.

B | As you view the video, think about the answers to these questions.

1. How far can the tree snake and the Draco lizard travel through the air?
2. What kind of shape does the snake use to take off? What shape does it use to turn in the air?
3. What does the narrator mean by ". . . but the snake doesn't seem put off by this display"?

After Viewing

A | Discuss answers to the questions 1–3 above with a partner.

B | Critical Thinking: Synthesizing. How are the reptiles in the video similar to, and different from, the feathered dinosaurs described on page 170?

A | Building Vocabulary. Read the sentences below. Use the context to help you identify the part of speech and meaning of each **bold** word or phrase. Write your answers. Check your answers in a dictionary.

1. Some animals see well at night because when it gets dark, their eyes **adjust**.

   Part of speech: _____

   Meaning: _____

2. Nature has given us ideas for products in many different areas of business and manufacturing. One example is the automobile **industry**.

   Part of speech: _____

   Meaning: _____

3. Many Chinese scientists are **involved** in archaeological digs in China. They are working with other scientists to study the connection between dinosaurs and birds.

   Part of speech: _____

   Meaning: _____

4. Airplane wings **mimic** birds' wings. They help a plane fly because they have a similar design.

   Part of speech: _____

   Meaning: _____

5. The scales on a shark's skin appear to be separate, but they actually **overlap** each other like birds' feathers.

   Part of speech: _____

   Meaning: _____

6. The first step in the **process** of biomimetics is to study the way an animal's body part works. The next step in the procedure is to think of a way humans can use it.

   Part of speech: _____

   Meaning: _____

7. Duck's feathers are oily. As a result, they **repel** water and keep the feathers dry.

   Part of speech: _____

   Meaning: _____

8. A toucan's beak, or bill, is very light because it is not **solid** inside. However, it is very strong.

   Part of speech: _____

   Meaning: _____

Word Partners

Use **involved** with: (*in* + *n.*) involved **in a process**, involved **in an accident**, involved **in politics**, involved **in a relationship**; (*adv.*) **actively** involved, **deeply** involved, **directly** involved, **emotionally** involved, **heavily** involved, **personally** involved.

9. The **surface** of a bird's beak is smooth, but underneath it is actually made of many small pieces of bone.

Part of speech: _____

Meaning: _____

10. The desert beetle's shell is **unique**. It's different from other beetle shells because it is specially designed to help it survive in a very dry environment.

Part of speech: _____

Meaning: _____

B | Using Vocabulary. Answer the questions in complete sentences. Then share your sentences with a partner.

1. Which objects in your room have rough **surfaces**? Which have very smooth surfaces?

_____

2. What are some objects that **repel** water?

_____

3. What **process** do you use to prepare for a test? Describe it.

_____

4. What is an example of something that you can **adjust** to easily?

_____

5. What are some characteristics that make humans a **unique** species?

_____

C | Previewing. Underline the key words in the subheads on pages 174–175. What animals are you going to read about?

_____

D | Applying. You read about biomimetics in Unit 8 (page 148). What connection might there be between biomimetics and the animals on pages 174–175? Note your ideas and discuss them with a partner.

_____

_____

Now predict what the reading passage on pages 174–175 is mainly about.

_____

_____

Design by Nature

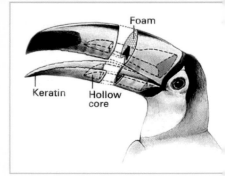

ALL LIVING organisms are uniquely adapted to the environment in which they live. Scientists study their designs to get ideas for products and technologies for humans. This process is called biomimetics. Here are three examples—in the air, on land, and in the water.

Toucan Bills and Car Safety

Toucan bills are so enormous that it's surprising the birds don't fall on their faces. One species of toucan, the toco toucan, has an orange-yellow bill six to nine inches (15–23 centimeters) long. It's about a third of the bird's entire length. Biologists aren't sure why toucans have such large, colorful bills. Charles Darwin[1] theorized that they attracted mates. Others suggest the bills are used for cutting open fruit, for fighting, or for warning predators to stay away.

One thing scientists are certain of is that the toucan's beak is well designed to be both strong and light. The surface is made of keratin, the same material in human fingernails and hair. But the outer layer isn't a solid structure. It's actually made of many layers of tiny overlapping pieces of keratin. The inside of the bill has a foam-like structure—a network of tiny holes held together by light, thin pieces of bone. This design makes the bill hard but very light.

Marc André Meyers is an engineering professor at the University of California, San Diego. He thinks the automotive and aviation industries can use the design of the toucan bill to make cars and planes safer. "Panels that mimic toucan bills may offer better protection to motorists involved in crashes," Meyers says.

---

[1] **Charles Darwin** was a 19th-century English naturalist who developed a theory of evolution by natural selection.

Beetle Shells and Collecting Water

▲ Stenocara beetle

E The Namib Desert in Angola, Africa, is one of the hottest places on Earth. A beetle called *Stenocara* survives there by using its shell to get drinking water from the air. Zoologist Andrew Parker of the University of Oxford has figured out how *Stenocara* collects water from desert air.

F The surface of *Stenocara*'s armor-like[2] shell is covered with bumps. The top of each bump is smooth and attracts water. The sides of each bump and the areas in between the bumps repel water. As the little drops of water join together and become larger and heavier, they roll down the bumps into the areas between them. A channel[3] connects these areas to a spot on the beetle's back that leads straight to its mouth.

G Parker thinks *Stenocara*'s bumpy armor can help humans survive better, too. He thinks the beetle's shell is a good model for designing inexpensive tent coverings. The shell might also be a model for roofs that can collect water for drinking and farming in dry parts of the world.

Shark Scales and Swimsuits

H Sharks are covered in scales made from the same material as teeth. These flexible scales protect the shark and help it swim quickly in water. A shark can move the scales as it swims. This movement helps reduce the water's drag.[4]

I Amy Lang, an aerospace engineer at the University of Alabama, studied the scales on the shortfin mako, a relative of the great white shark. Lang and her team discovered that the mako shark's scales differ in size and in flexibility in different parts of its body. For instance, the scales on the sides of the body are tapered— wide at one end and narrow at the other end. Because they are tapered, these scales move very easily. They can turn up or flatten to adjust to the flow of water around the shark and to reduce drag.

J Lang feels that shark scales can inspire designs for machines that experience drag, such as airplanes. Designers are also getting ideas from shark scales for coating ship bottoms and designing swimwear.

▲ Sharkskin scales inspired the design of the Speedo Fastskin swimsuit.

A close-up view of ▲ sharkskin shows tooth-like scales.

[2] If something is **armor-like**, it is similar to the metal clothing that soldiers wore in the past to protect themselves in battle.

[3] A **channel** is a long, narrow passage for water or other liquids to flow along.

[4] **Drag** is a force that opposes the motion of an object moving in water or air.

A | Understanding the Gist. Look back at your answer for exercise **D** on page 173. Were your predictions about the reading passage correct?

B | Identifying Main Ideas. Discuss your answers to these questions with a partner. Then complete the chart.

1. What parts of each animal does the reading passage describe?
2. What is the purpose (or possible purposes) of these parts for the animal?
3. What products or technologies for humans are they inspiring?

Animal Part	Purpose	Product or Technology
toucan _____bill_____		
beetle _____		
shark _____		bathing suits

C | Paraphrasing. Write a definition of *biomimetics* in your own words.

_____

_____

D | Critical Thinking: Applying. Which of the following are examples of biomimetics? Which are not? Discuss your answers with a partner.

1. using bird feathers in a jacket to stay warm in cold weather
2. inventing a material for making boats that has the same structure as a toucan bill
3. making a rain hat that mimics the structure of the *Stenocara* beetle's shell
4. attaching sharkskin to the bottom of a boat to make it go faster in the water

Strategy

When you look for theories, scan for words like *think*, *believe*, *suggest*, *feel*, and *theorize*, as well as qualifiers like *can*, *may*, and *might*.

E | Identifying Theories. Find and underline two theories in "Design by Nature."

F | Critical Thinking: Synthesizing. Look again at the first line of the reading: "All living organisms are uniquely adapted to the environment in which they live." Discuss this question in small groups: *How is each organism described in this unit uniquely adapted to its environment?*

GOAL: In this lesson, you are going to plan, write, revise, and edit a summary paragraph on the following topic: *Summarize a section of the reading passage on pages 174–175.*

A | **Brainstorming.** You are going to write a summary of a section of the reading passage on pages 174–175. Without looking back, try to remember the main ideas of each one. Note your ideas in the chart. Put a check next to the section that you remember the most about.

✓	Section	Main Ideas
	Toucan bills	
	Beetle shells	
	Shark scales	

B | **Journal Writing.** In your journal, write about what you remember from the section you checked in exercise **A**. Write for three minutes.

C | **Analyzing.** Read the information in the box. Use the best synonym to complete the sentences (1–3).

Language for Writing: Using Synonyms

When you write a summary of a passage, you should restate information as much as possible in your own words. One way to do this is to replace some of the original words or phrases with synonyms—words that have a similar meaning. This is also known as paraphrasing. For example, look at the two sentences below:

Original: *Some paleontologists speculate that feathers began as a kind of insulation to keep animals or their young warm.*
Paraphrase: *Some experts think that feathers started as a way to keep warm.*

paleontologists → *experts*   *speculate* → *think*
began → *started*   *insulation* → *a way to keep warm*

(Note: You don't change words that don't have synonyms: *feathers* → *feathers.*)

One way to find synonyms is to use a **thesaurus**, a type of dictionary that has synonyms and antonyms (words with opposite meaning). Not all synonyms are an exact match for a word, so it's important to understand the context in which you are using a word in order to choose the best synonym. For example, look at the following sentence:

The Stenocara *beetle collects drinking water from the atmosphere.*

Synonyms in a thesaurus for *atmosphere* might include: *air, sky, feeling,* and *mood*. Only *air* is correct in this context.

1. This design makes the bill <u>hard</u> but very light.
   a. difficult   b. firm

2. The bird's feathers are <u>stiff</u> on one side.
   a. inflexible   b. formal

3. The *Stenocara* beetle can survive in a very <u>dry</u> environment.
   a. uninteresting   b. arid

D | **Applying.** Use synonyms to rewrite five sentences from the reading section that you checked in exercise **A**.

Writing Skill: *Writing a Summary*

When you write a summary, you explain the key ideas of an original reading passage in your own words. A summary has the following characteristics:

- It's shorter than the original but has the same meaning.
- It includes all the key ideas, but fewer details.
- It does not contain new information; that is, information not in the original.

- It presents the key ideas in the same order as the original.
- It has a topic sentence that expresses the main idea of the original.
- It does not contain the summary writer's opinions.

To write a summary:
- First, read the original reading passage and highlight the key ideas as you read.
- Then, write the key ideas in your own words.

▲ A close-up view of a piece of Velcro shows its hook-and-loop design, inspired by a type of seedpod called a bur (below).

E | Identifying Key Ideas. Read the paragraph below about biomimetics. Then look at the key ideas from the paragraph. Match each one to one of the sentences in the summary.

Original

Scientists are studying the adaptations of living organisms in order to use their designs in products and technologies for humans. This process is called biomimetics. Velcro is one example of biomimetics. In 1948, a Swiss scientist, George de Mestral, removed a bur stuck to his dog's fur. De Mestral studied it under a microscope and noticed how well hooks on the bur stuck to things. He copied the design to make a two-piece fastening device. One piece has stiff hooks like the ones on the bur. The other piece has soft loops that allow the hooks to attach to it.

Key Ideas

☐ biomimetics: studying plants and animals to develop products and technologies for people

☐ George de Mestral observed how well a bur attached to dog's fur.

☐ an example of biomimetics: Velcro

☐ De Mestral mimicked the design of the bur and the fur to create a product.

Summary

a. Biomimetics involves studying the ways in which plants and animals adapt to their environments in order to develop useful products and technologies for people. b. An example of biomimetics is Velcro. c. A Swiss scientist, George de Mestral, observed how well a bur attached to his dog's fur. d. He created a two-part fastener by mimicking the loops on the bur and the softness of the dog's fur.

F | Identifying Synonyms. In the summary, underline synonyms for these words and phrases from the original paragraph.

a. organisms   b. humans   c. noticed   d. stuck   e. two-piece fastening device

A | Planning. Follow the steps to plan your summary.

Step 1 Choose a passage or section of a passage to summarize. Write the title in the chart below.

Step 2 Read the passage or section again that you are going to summarize. With a highlighter, mark the key ideas.

Step 3 Paraphrase the key ideas of the passage or section in the chart. Remember to keep the original ideas, but use your own words.

Step 4 Write a topic sentence that introduces the main idea of the original passage.

Summary

Title of original text: _____

Topic sentence: _____

_____

Key ideas: _____

_____

_____

_____

_____

_____

_____

B | Draft 1. Use your notes from exercise **A** to write a first draft.

C | **Analyzing.** The paragraphs below are summaries of the passage entitled "Adaptation" on page 164.

Which is the first draft? _____   Which is the revision? _____

ⓐ   An adaptation is a change in a plant or an animal that helps it survive in its environment. A change becomes a mutation when an organism inherits the change from its parent. Over time, a mutation can become a characteristic of the species. When this happens, it is an adaptation. There are two kinds of adaptation—physical and behavioral. A desert plant that can store its own water is an example of a physical adaptation, and whale migration is an example of behavioral migration. Occasionally an adaptation occurs for a particular reason, and then evolves to have a different function. Feathers are an example of this type of adaptation.

ⓑ   Adaptations are called mutations. As mutations are passed from one generation to the next, they become a typical part of a species. There are two kinds of adaptation—physical and behavioral. An example of a behavioral adaptation is when gray whales give birth in warm water, but travel to cold water for food. Canadian geese flying south during the winter is another example of behavioral adaptation. There's another strange kind of adaptation when something develops for one purpose but is used for another, like feathers.

D | **Critical Thinking: Analyzing.** Work with a partner. Compare the paragraphs above by answering the following questions about each one.

	ⓐ		ⓑ	
1. Is there a topic sentence that introduces the main idea of the original passage?	Y	N	Y	N
2. Does it include all the key ideas that were in the original?	Y	N	Y	N
3. Are the key ideas in the same order as the original?	Y	N	Y	N
4. Is there enough paraphrasing of the language of the original (i.e., use of synonyms)?	Y	N	Y	N
5. Are there any unnecessary details and opinions?	Y	N	Y	N
6. Does it contain information that is not in the original?	Y	N	Y	N

E | **Revising.** Answer the questions above about your own paragraph.

F | **Peer Evaluation.** Exchange your first draft with a partner and follow these steps:

Step 1   Read your partner's summary and say one thing that you liked about it.
Step 2   Look back at the original passage that your partner summarized and make a list of the key ideas in the original in the space below.

Summary

Title of original text _____

Topic sentence _____

Key ideas _____

_____

_____

_____

_____

_____

Step 3   Compare your list of key ideas with the list of key ideas that your partner made in exercise **A** on page 179.
Step 4   The two lists should be similar. If they aren't, discuss how they differ.

G | **Draft 2.** Write a second draft of your summary. Use what you learned from the peer evaluation activity, and your answers to exercise **E**. Make any other necessary changes.

H | **Editing Practice.** Read the information in the box. Circle the correct word in each of the sentences (1–5).

> In sentences using synonyms, remember to:
>
> • use a synonym that works in the same context as the original word.
> • choose a synonym that has the same part of speech as the original.

1. Feathers are one of nature's most **well-dressed / elegant** inventions.
2. The baby bird was covered in **light / easy**, soft feathers.
3. They think dinosaurs used feathers to keep their **young / new** warm.
4. They found theropods with their front limbs **broadcast / spread** over nests.
5. Drops of water roll down the bumps on the *Stenocara* beetle's **bomb / shell**.

WRITING TASK: Editing

I | Editing Checklist. Use the checklist to find errors in your second draft.

Editing Checklist	Yes	No
1. Are all the words spelled correctly?		
2. Is the first word of every sentence capitalized?		
3. Does every sentence end with the correct punctuation?		
4. Do your subjects and verbs agree?		
5. Did you use synonyms correctly?		
6. Are other verb tenses correct?		

J | Final Draft. Now use your Editing Checklist to write a third draft of your summary. Make any other necessary changes.

UNIT QUIZ

p.164 1. Adaptations can be physical or _____.

p.166 2. _____ is a material or substance that keeps something or someone warm.

p.170 3. The following statement is a **fact / theory**:
Scientists believe the dark spots on pepper moth wings are possibly an adaptation to air pollution.

p.170 4. Paleontologists found fossils in China that helped to explain how birds and _____ are related.

p.172 5. If you copy something, you _____ it.

p.174 6. The beak of the _____ is inspiring ways to make safer cars and planes.

p.177 7. *Start* and *begin* are _____ ; *start* and *end* are

_____.

p.178 8. When you write a summary, you **keep / change** the ideas of the original passage.

Mobile Revolution

ACADEMIC PATHWAYS

Lesson A: Taking notes on an expository text
Lesson B: Reading linked texts in a blog
Lesson C: Using a chart to plan a paragraph
Writing a problem-solution paragraph

Think and Discuss

1. Do you have a cell phone? What do you mainly use it for?

2. List the things you can do with a cell phone. Which is the most important? Why?

A Masai warrior uses a cell phone ▶ and an antenna to track radio-collared animals in Kenya (see page 191).

A. Look at the map and photos and discuss the questions.

   1. What do the colors of the map show about cell phone use worldwide?

   2. How many uses for the cell phone can you think of?

B. Look at the chart below and discuss the questions.

   1. How did cell phone subscriptions[1] change between 2000 and 2007? How did this compare with other technologies?

   2. What do you think the percentage of cell phone users is in your country? How is it changing? How about other technologies?

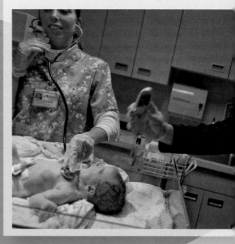

Parent in New Jersey, USA

Rise of the Cell Phone

Between 2000 and 2007, technology connected many more people than ever before. The number of people paying for a cell phone service more than quadrupled.[2] In the same period, the number of people with personal computers nearly doubled. The number of phone lines increased in that period, too. However, the growth of traditional phones was much slower than the rise of cell phones and personal computers.

PERCENTAGE OF WORLD'S HOUSEHOLDS WITH:

	Telephone lines	Cellular subscriptions	Personal computers	Internet subscriptions	Televisions
2007	19	51	15	7	89%
2000	16	12	8	2	79%

[1] A **subscription** is an amount you pay regularly to receive a service.

[2] If something **quadruples,** it becomes four times bigger.

Cattle rancher in Brazil

A Global Conversation

"Given a choice, people will demand the freedom to communicate wherever they are," said Martin Cooper on April 3, 2003. Thirty years earlier, Cooper, the inventor of the modern cell phone, made the first cellular phone call from a street in New York City. By 2010, there were over 4.6 billion cell phone users worldwide.

Financial dealer in Tokyo, Japan

Tourist in Kiel, Germany

Cell subscriptions per 100 people, 2007

- More than 100
- 80 – 100
- 60 – 79.9
- 40 – 59.9
- Less than 40
- No data available

Climbers at Nanga Parbat Base Camp, Pakistan

Businessmen in Doha, Qatar

Visitor to Pretoria Aquarium, South Africa

A | Building Vocabulary. Find the words in **blue** in the reading passage on pages 187–188. Read the words around them and try to guess their meanings. Then match the sentence parts below to make definitions.

1. _____ A **challenge** is

2. _____ If something is **current**,

3. _____ If a thing is **dependable**,

4. _____ **Health care** is

5. _____ If you **install** something,

6. _____ When you **monitor** something,

7. _____ If something is a **reality**,

8. _____ If something is **rural**,

9. _____ If you do something **thoroughly**,

10. _____ When you **update** something,

a. the various services for the prevention or treatment of illnesses and injuries.

b. it is true or actually exists.

c. you can be sure it will do what you need it to do.

d. you check its progress.

e. it is happening at the present time.

f. it is in the countryside and not in the city.

g. you connect or set up something, such as a computer program, so it is ready to use.

h. you do it carefully and in a detailed way.

i. a new and difficult thing that requires great effort and determination.

j. you add new information to it.

B | Using Vocabulary. Answer the questions. Share your ideas with a partner.

1. What are the main **challenges** that students in your country face when they study English?

2. What services in your community are **dependable** (e.g., electricity, Internet connections)?

3. What idea or dream do you want to make a **reality**?

C | Brainstorming. Scan the reading passage on pages 187–188 and list the country and region names that you find. Then discuss this question in small groups: *What are some possible communication problems that people have in these countries, especially if they live in rural areas?*

_____

_____

D | Predicting. Read the title and the subheads of the reading passage, and look at the photos and captions. What is the reading passage mainly about?

I think the reading passage is about a(n) _____ who _____

_____

that _____.

Word Partners

Use **challenge** with (*adj.*) **biggest** challenge, **new** challenge; (*v.*) **accept** a challenge, **face** a challenge, **present** a challenge.

Changing the World with a Cell Phone

track 2-13

A   **KEN BANKS** does not run health care programs in Africa. He also does not provide information to farmers in El Salvador. However, his computer software[1] is helping people do those things—and more.

Simple Solutions for Big Problems

B   Banks was working in South Africa in 2003 and 2004. He saw that there were many organizations in Africa that were trying to help people. They were doing good work, but it was difficult for them to communicate over great distances. They didn't have much money, and many didn't have Internet access. But they did have cell phones.

C   Banks had an idea. He created some computer software called FrontlineSMS. "I wrote the software in five weeks at a kitchen table," Banks says. The software allows users to send information from computers without using the Internet. It can work with any kind of computer. Users install the software on a computer. Then they connect a cell phone to the computer. To send information, users select the people they want to send it to and hit "send." The cell phone sends the information as a text message from the computer.

---

[1] **Software** is a computer program.

Solving Problems around the World

D FrontlineSMS software is free. It can work with an inexpensive laptop. It works with old cell phones, too. In fact, it can work almost anywhere in the world, even in places where electricity is not very dependable. Today, people are using FrontlineSMS to send important information in more than 50 nations.

E For example, Nigerians used it to monitor their 2007 election². Voters sent 10,000 texts to describe what was happening when they went to vote. In Malawi, a rural health care program uses FrontlineSMS to contact patients. As a result, workers no longer have to visit patients' homes to update medical records. The program saves thousands of hours of doctor time and thousands of dollars in fuel costs. In other parts of the world, such as Indonesia, Cambodia, Niger, and El Salvador, farmers now receive the most current prices for their crops³ by cell phone. As a result, the farmers can earn more money.

Making Ideas Reality

F FrontlineSMS is an example of taking an idea and turning it into a successful reality. So, what should you do if you have an idea for making the world a better place? Banks advises first researching your idea thoroughly. Try to find out if your idea offers something that people really need. The best way to do this kind of research is to go into the community and talk to people. Then take advantage of social media tools such as blogs, he advises. They allow you to get your message out and connect with people who have similar ideas.

▲ "FrontlineSMS gives [people] tools to create their own projects and make a difference."
- Innovator Ken Banks

G Technology is not a solution by itself, but it's a useful tool for solving many of the world's great challenges. Using today's technology, Banks says, makes it faster and easier than ever to make the world a better place.

² An **election** is a process in which people vote to choose a person or a group of people to hold an official position.
³ **Crops** are plants that are grown in large quantities to be harvested.

A | **Understanding the Gist.** Look back at your answer for exercise **D** on page 186. Was your prediction correct?

B | **Identifying Main Ideas.** Write answers to the questions. Use your own words.

1. How did Ken Banks get his idea for FrontlineSMS?

    _____

2. Why is FrontlineSMS a good solution for certain countries?

    _____

3. How has FrontlineSMS helped people in the following countries?

    Nigeria: _____

    Malawi: _____

    El Salvador: _____

4. According to Banks, what is the first thing you should do if you have an idea for making the world a better place? How can technology help?

    _____

    _____

C | **Identifying Sequence.** How does FrontlineSMS work? Number the steps from 1 to 5 to show the correct sequence.

_____ Users hit "send."

_____ The cell phone sends information as a text message from the computer.

_____ Then they connect a cell phone to the computer.

_____ Users select the people they want to send information to.

_____ Users install the FrontlineSMS software on a computer.

D | **Critical Thinking: Relating.** Think of situations in your past where you needed to get important information to a large group people. How did you do it? What kind of technology did you use? Was it successful? Share your ideas with a partner.

E | **Synthesizing.** With a partner, discuss your answers to the following questions: *What are some other examples you have read about of using technology to solve a problem? Which of these solutions use social media?* (For some examples, look back at Units 2 and 3 of this book.)

F | **Personalizing.** Think of a simple way to make your community a better place. Does your idea require technology? Describe your idea.

> **CT Focus**
>
> **Relating information to personal experience** means comparing situations that you read about to experiences in your own life. Ask yourself questions: *What would I do in that situation? Have I experienced something like that? How might this idea apply to my own life?*

Reading Skill: *Taking Notes*

Taking notes on a reading passage has two main benefits. First, it helps you to understand the information better. It also helps you to collect important information for writing assignments and for tests.

One note taking method is to identify the main idea and the supporting details of each paragraph, or section, as you read.

It is often helpful to use some kind of graphic organizer when you take notes. Use graphic organizers that best match the type of passage you are reading. Many reading passages are a mixture of text types, so you may want to use more than one graphic organizer:

T-chart: problem-solution, cause-effect, pros and cons (see page 67)

mind map (also *concept map* or *word web*): description, classification (see page 11)

Venn diagram: comparison (see page 156)

traditional outline: any type (see page 97)

time line or **flow chart:** process or events over time (see page 137)

simple chart or **grid:** any type (see below)

See page 210 for more suggestions on note taking.

A | **Taking Notes.** Complete the following chart with notes on "Changing the World With a Cell Phone."

Strategy

When you take notes, remember to **only note the key points**. Don't write complete sentences. Try to use your own words as much as possible.

Pararaph	Main Idea	Supporting Details
B	how Banks got the idea for FrontlineSMS	- lived in S. Africa in 2003-04 - trouble communicating w/out electricity, Internet, etc., but did have cell phones
C		
D		
E		
F		

B | **Applying.** Use the notes you took in exercise **A** to write a summary of "Changing the World— With a Cell Phone." See page 178 for tips on writing a summary.

Cell Phone Trackers

Nomadic Masai people in Kenya often share the same **territory** with African lions. This can be a problem when lions kill and eat the nomads' **livestock**. A potential solution is to put **radio collars** on the lions. The technology can help animals and humans to live peacefully in the same area.

Before Viewing

A | **Meaning from Context.** Look at the photo and read the caption. Match each word or phrase in **bold** with a definition.

1. _____ (*adj.*) traveling from place to place, with no settled home
2. _____ (*n.*) objects worn around the neck that can send electronic signals
3. _____ (*n.*) land that is controlled by someone or a group of people
4. _____ (*n.*) animals such as cows and sheep that are kept on a farm

B | **Brainstorming.** How might radio collars help to stop lions from killing and eating livestock? List your ideas.

_____

_____

While Viewing

A | Watch the video about lion tracking in Kenya. As you watch, check and correct your answers to exercise **B** above.

B | As you view the video, think about the answers to these questions.

1. What is the job of the "lion guardians"?
2. Who else receives money as part of the program?
3. Has the program been a success so far? What evidence is there?
4. What other technology is Antony Kasanga using to help solve the problem?

After Viewing

A | Discuss answers to questions 1–4 above with a partner.

B | **Critical Thinking: Synthesizing.** Do you think FrontlineSMS could help the Masai? Explain your answer.

A | Building Vocabulary. Read the sentences below. Look at the words around the **blue** words and phrases to guess their meanings. Circle the best definition and write the part of speech (noun, verb, or adjective).

1. Cell phone software that **analyzes** blood can help doctors take care of patients in rural areas.

   a. gives information about   b. removes

   Part of speech: _____

2. New **applications** of cell phone technology provide ways to improve the lives of people in rural areas.

   a. uses   b. documents

   Part of speech: _____

3. Cell phones **empower** women in poor countries because they can use them to start businesses.

   a. give information about something   b. provide a way to achieve something

   Part of speech: _____

4. Cell phones can **enrich** people's lives when they use them for education.

   a. make better   b. give money for

   Part of speech: _____

5. It is difficult to **imagine** a world without technology. In fact, many people have no idea what life was like before many technological innovations existed.

   a. use your mind to picture something   b. use writing to describe something

   Part of speech: _____

6. People who do not live near big cities sometimes feel **isolated** from the rest of the world.

   a. far away from   b. close to

   Part of speech: _____

7. Learning by cell phone is **practical** for people who do not have a lot of time or money.

   a. common   b. effective

   Part of speech: _____

8. You can improve the **prosperity** of people in poor countries by giving them ways to make money.

   a. a condition of doing well financially   b. a condition of good health

   Part of speech: _____

9. People in **remote** villages sometimes don't know what is happening in the world because they are so far from big cities.

   a. small   b. far away

   Part of speech:_____

10. Cell phone innovations can **transform** people's lives. For example, they can make it easier for sick people to get medical advice.

    a. change   b. harm

    Part of speech: _____

B | Using Vocabulary. Answer the questions in complete sentences. Then share your sentences with a partner.

1. What do you **imagine** your town or city will look like 50 years from now?

_____

_____

Word Partners

Use **imagine** with (v.) **can / can't** imagine something, **try to** imagine; (adj.) **difficult / easy / hard** to imagine; **possible / impossible** to imagine.

2. What is a **practical** way to learn a second language?

_____

_____

3. What is one way to **enrich** your life?

_____

_____

4. If you feel **isolated** from other people, what can you do to improve your situation?

_____

_____

5. Have you ever been to a **remote** area? What was it like?

_____

_____

C | Predicting. Read the subheads and first paragraph of the reading passage on pages 194–195. What do you think the reading passage is mainly about?

a. innovative cell phone companies

b. innovative new types of cell phones

c. innovative ways to use cell phones

track **2-14**

Updated January 15, 2012

Cell Phone Innovators

A People around the world are using cell phones in exciting and innovative ways. Here are some examples of how people are using cell phones to enrich and empower their own lives and the lives of others.

Mobile Learning

B Bangladeshis are learning English on cell phones through a program called BBC Janala. The program is based on a TV drama series and game show. Students access the audio lessons from their cell phones. BBC Janala teaches English to adults who do not have the time or the money to attend classes. Over four million people have used the cell phone program.

C The lessons are practical and focus on everyday situations. The characters are ordinary people. The lessons are just three minutes long and cost less than the price of a cup of tea. Students can access the cell phone lessons on any type of phone and at any time of the day or night. In addition to listening to the program, students can take quizzes and even record their own stories. There are weekly quizzes in the newspaper, so students have many opportunities to practice their English.

Mobile Microscopes

D Aydogan Ozcan is solving global health problems with a cell phone. Ozcan's UCLA research team developed a way to use cell phones to help diagnose[1] medical conditions. The phones work in the most remote and poorest parts of the world.

◄ A sample of blood is placed over the cell phone's camera **1**. Light shines from a black tube **2** through the sample and onto the camera's imaging processor.

[1] To **diagnose** is to identify a problem or an illness.

Ozcan wanted to make a diagnostic tool that was inexpensive and easy to use, so he found a way to use a cell phone as a microscope. A local technician uses the phone to take a picture of a small amount of a patient's blood. Then the technician uses the Internet to send the picture from the phone to a computer installed in a hospital. The computer uses software that Ozcan created to analyze the picture of the blood. Since the computer does the analysis, and not the local technician, there are fewer mistakes.

The future of medicine, Ozcan believes, depends not only on new technologies, but also on innovative applications of existing technologies. He predicts, "That's what will transform global health care in powerful, practical ways we've never before imagined."

▲ Aydogan Ozcan

Mobile Miners

Choco is a gold-mining region that extends from Panama through Colombia and into Ecuador. Because of dense[2] jungles and poor infrastructure,[3] these people are isolated from the rest of the world. Many people in the region earn their living by mining[4] for gold. They use ancient methods that do not harm the environment. They shake wet sand in pans and pick out tiny pieces of the valuable metal by hand. In the past, the problem was getting the gold out of the region and selling it in other parts of the world.

▲ Panning, a traditional mining method, involves picking out pieces of gold by hand.

A new text messaging project helps Choco miners sell their gold. Each day, the technology helps them keep track of the current price for gold in the world's gold markets. Now miners in these remote regions are connected to their most important buyer, the London gold market. The text messaging project is improving the economic and social prosperity of the people in the region by combining traditional mining methods with current technology.

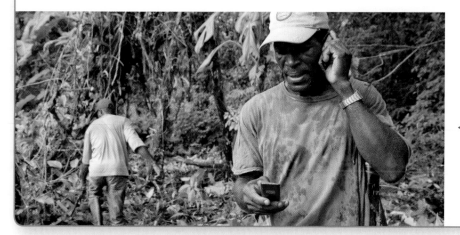

◀ By receiving text messages, Choco miners can keep in touch with the daily price for gold on global markets.

[2] If a place is **dense**, it contains a lot of things in a small area.
[3] **Infrastructure** refers to basic facilities such as transportation, communications, and buildings.
[4] **Mining** is the activity of getting useful minerals, such as gold, from the ground.

A | Understanding the Gist. Look back at your answer for exercise **C** on page 193. Was your prediction correct?

B | Critical Thinking: Analyzing. What problem does each cell-phone innovation in the reading passage on pages 194–195 solve? Complete the T-chart.

Problem	Solution
1. _____	learning English by cell phone
2. _____	using a _____ to diagnose health problems
3. working a long way from _____ _____	_____

C | Taking Notes. Use the chart to take notes on the key ideas from the reading.

Situation	Solution	Supporting Information
Mobile Learning	people in Bangladesh use cell phones to learn English	−lessons based on TV shows −practical and inexpensive
Mobile Microscopes		
Mobile Miners		

D | Applying. Use your notes in exercise **C** to write a summary of one of the situations in "Cell Phone Innovators."

E | Critical Thinking: Synthesizing. Discuss these questions in small groups: *Which cell phone innovation from this unit is the most useful or important? Why?*

GOAL: In this lesson, you are going to plan, write, revise, and edit a problem-solution paragraph on the following topic: *Think of a current problem (large or small) and propose a way that technology can help solve it.*

A | **Brainstorming.** Work with a partner. Use the T-chart to make a list of problems that you are interested in. Then think of possible solutions for each one using technology. Use ideas from the units in this book and/or your own ideas.

Problems	Solutions

B | **Journal Writing.** Write in your journal about one of the problems in exercise **A**. Write for three minutes.

C | **Analyzing.** Read the information in the box. Use the verbs in parentheses and the cues to complete the sentences (1–4).

Language for Writing: Using Modals to Discuss Abilities and Possibilities

Some modals express abilities and possibilities. These modals are useful for describing solutions.

Can shows present ability: *FrontlineSMS* **can** *work with any kind of computer.*

Will, could, may, and *might* show future possibility. The modal you choose depends on your degree of certainty. *Will* is most certain, *could* is less certain, and *may* and *might* are the least certain.

Radio collars **will** *solve the problem.* (I'm certain of this.)
Radio collars **could** *solve the problem.* (I'm less certain.)
Radio collars **might** *solve the problem.* (I'm the least certain.)

Note: Remember to use the base form of the verb after a modal.

For further explanation and more examples of modals, see page 218.

1. This solution _____ (save) people a lot of money. (future possibility; less certain)

2. Technicians _____ (make) fewer mistakes with Ozcan's cell-phone microscope. (future possibility; least certain)

3. FrontlineSMS _____ (help) farmers get better prices for their crops. (present ability)

4. BBC Janala _____ (help) students who do not have the time or the money to attend classes. (future possibility; most certain)

D | **Applying.** Use modals to write five sentences about your ideas in exercises **A** and **B** above.

Writing Skill: *Writing a Problem-Solution Paragraph*

In a problem-solution paragraph, you first describe the problem and then suggest the solution. When you describe the problem, give details and examples so the reader fully understands it. When you present the solution, provide a clear explanation of how it could, will, or might work. Try to give about the same amount of discussion to both the problem and the solution.

> The topic sentence states the problem and proposes the solution:
> *There is a problem of X in [place], but Y is a possible solution / can provide a solution (to this).*
> *X is a problem in [place], but a possible solution is [verb]-ing / to [verb] . . .*
> *Y is a possible way to solve the problem of X in [place].*
> *One way of solving / to solve the problem of X in [place] is [verb]-ing / to [verb] . . .*

Example:
> *Lions are a problem in Kenya, but a new cell-phone technology can provide a solution to this problem.*

The concluding sentence restates the problem and solution:
> *Therefore, FrontlineSMS is one way for farmers to solve the problem of lions killing livestock in Kenya.*

Strategy

Remember to use **transition words and phrases** when you describe a solution that involves a sequence of steps. See pages 128 and 136 for examples.

E | Identifying Problems and Solutions. Read the problem-solution paragraph. Find and label the following parts of the paragraph.

a. the solution
b. the problem
c. the conclusion
d. the topic sentence
e. a detail that describes the problem
f. another detail that describes the problem
g. sentences that explain how the solution works

Bad roads are a problem in my community, but cell phones can help solve this. Kingville is a remote village. It rains a lot there, and the rain often destroys the roads that go to the nearest big city. Some people in the village have cell phones and computers, but electricity is not dependable and people are not connected to the Internet. Therefore, people often do not know when the roads are gone. Missing roads are a serious problem because it makes it difficult to get out of the area in an emergency. The situation is especially dangerous when someone has to get to the hospital in the city. Cell phones using FrontlineSMS technology can be a solution to this problem. Here is how it could work: Citizens who live near the bad roads volunteer to be "road guards." They install FrontlineSMS on a computer and connect a cell phone to it. Then they can create a list of contacts. When it rains, road guards type a message about the road conditions on a computer and send the message. After that, the people on the contact list receive the information as a text message. At this point, they have time to plan another way into or out of the village. Although bad roads are a problem in my community, cell phones can provide a solution that not only saves time, but saves lives, too.

F | Critical Thinking: Analyzing. Answer this question about the paragraph in exercise **E**:
Is there an equal amount of discussion of both the problem and the solution?

A | Planning. Follow the steps to plan your problem-solution paragraph.

Step 1 Choose a problem and solution from your brainstorming notes on page 197.
Step 2 Write the problem and the solution in the chart below.
Step 3 Add details, examples, and/or reasons that explain the problem. Don't write complete sentences.
Step 4 Add information that shows how the solution works. Don't write complete sentences.
Step 5 Write a topic sentence that tells the reader about both the problem and the solution.

Topic sentence: _____

_____

Problem: _____

_____

Details, examples, or reasons:

_____

_____

_____

_____

_____

Solution: _____

_____

How the solution works:

_____

_____

_____

_____

_____

B | Draft 1. Use your chart to write a first draft of your paragraph.

C | Analyzing. The paragraphs below are about a problem at a community college.

Which is the first draft? _____   Which is the revision? _____

Strategy

One way to provide support for your solution is to describe **an alternative** and say why it isn't as good as your solution. See pages 115–116 for more information.

a   There is a serious problem with overcrowded classes at Bay City Community College, but Internet technology provides an easy, inexpensive solution. There are too many students who want to take English classes at Bay City Community College. As a result, classes are over-crowded and many students cannot get into the classes that they want to take. Although some people argue we should add more classes, that's not the answer, as the college can't afford to hire more teachers. Therefore, the best solution is to use existing classroom technology and webcast the classes to students who cannot get into the class. Webcasting is inexpensive because the school already has the equipment. English students who watch the webcast instead of coming to class do not have all the benefits of being in class, but they could pay a lower fee. Therefore, more students will be able to take English, and the college will get more money. It is clear that webcasting is an easy and inexpensive solution to the problem of overcrowding at Bay City Community College.

b   There is a serious problem with overcrowded classes at Bay City Community College. There are too many students who want to take English classes at Bay City Community College. Classes are overcrowded, and it's impossible to understand the teacher. In addition, there aren't enough classes, so many students have to wait several semesters before they can get into the English classes. Students need to take these classes before they can sign up for other programs at the college, so their education is delayed. In addition, because of the overcrowding problem, many students drop out or have to take English at other schools. The main cause of the problem is the budget crisis. There isn't enough money to hire more teachers or add more classes. In fact, most classes at Bay City Community College are overcrowded. For example, the computer science classes are very crowded. One solution is to provide more online classes.

D | Critical Thinking: Analyzing. Work with a partner. Compare the paragraphs above by answering the following questions about each one.

	a		b	
1. Does the paragraph have one main idea?	Y	N	Y	N
2. Does the topic sentence introduce both the problem and the solution?	Y	N	Y	N
3. Are there details, examples, and reasons to explain the problem?	Y	N	Y	N
4. Is there a clear explanation of how the solution works?	Y	N	Y	N
5. Is there an equal amount of discussion of both the problem and the solution?	Y	N	Y	N
6. Is there a concluding sentence?	Y	N	Y	N

E | Revising. Answer the questions above about your own paragraph.

F | Peer Evaluation. Exchange your first draft with a partner and follow these steps:

Step 1   Read your partner's paragraph and tell him or her one thing that you liked about it.
Step 2   Complete the T-chart to show the problem and the solution that your partner's paragraph describes.

Problem:	Solution:
Details, examples, or reasons:	How the solution works:

Step 3   Compare your chart with the chart that your partner did in exercise **A** on page 199.
Step 4   The two charts should be similar. If they aren't, discuss how the information is different.

G | Draft 2. Write a second draft of your paragraph. Use what you learned from the peer evaluation activity, and your answers to exercise **E**. Make any other necessary changes.

H | Editing Practice. Read the information in the box. Then find and correct one mistake in using modals in each of the sentences (1–5).

> In sentences with modals for possibility or ability, remember to:
> • use the base form of the verb after a modal
> • use the most appropriate modal for the degree of certainty (e.g., use *will* and *can* for a higher degree of certainty, *could*, *might*, and *may* if you are less certain).

1. With FrontlineSMS, you can to send a message to many people at one time.
2. Cell phone technology will makes it easy for people to talk on the phone wherever they are.
3. Online classes could to save the school a lot of money.
4. New technology may improving the lives of people who live in remote regions.
5. I am certain that cell phone-based learning might help students in other developing countries.

I | **Editing Checklist.** Use the checklist to find errors in your second draft.

Editing Checklist	Yes	No
1. Are all the words spelled correctly?		
2. Is the first word of every sentence capitalized?		
3. Does every sentence end with the correct punctuation?		
4. Do your subjects and verbs agree?		
5. Did you use modals correctly?		
6. Are verb tenses correct?		

J | **Final Draft.** Now use your Editing Checklist to write a third draft of your paragraph. Make any other necessary changes.

UNIT QUIZ

p.184 ▷ 1. Between 2000 and 2007, the percentage of households with
_____ doubled.

p.186 ▷ 2. If something is a(n) _____, it actually exists or is true.

p.188 ▷ 3. Cell phone technology is helping farmers in El Salvador get the most
_____ for their crops.

p.188 ▷ 4. People in Nigeria are using cell phones to _____ elections.

p.190 ▷ 5. Taking notes helps you to get information for writing assignments and
to _____.

p.192 ▷ 6. When you _____ someone's life, you change it for the better.

p.194 ▷ 7. Aydogan Ozcan invented a cell phone that works as a(n) _____.

p.197 ▷ 8. *Will* and *might* are _____ that are used to show
_____.

Longevity Leaders

Narrator: The elderly are found across all countries and cultures. And their numbers are increasing as people live longer.

There are over seven billion people in the world today. And this number could reach nine billion by the year 2050. There will be more elderly in the world than ever before.

We will see aging populations all over the world in the 21st century.

Andrew: In places like the United States, Europe, even China, we see populations that are getting much older much faster.

Narrator: But how old is old?

In the natural world, there are animals that live for centuries. Some researchers believe that some whales can live for 200 years or more. Giant tortoises are known to live for 150 years or more. Elephants are known to live for up to 70 years.

Humans live longer than most animals. They can live to a maximum of about 120 years. Of course most humans don't live that long. But there are places in the world where people live longer—and healthier—lives.

This is Sardinia, an island off the coast of Italy. It has a very high number of centenarians. These are people who live to see their 100th birthday. One example is Antonio Bruno, who was still healthy and happy at 103 years old.

National Geographic magazine writer Dan Buettner visited some of the world's longest-living communities to discover the secrets of longevity. He went to Okinawa, where people live longer and healthier lives than anywhere else in the world.

Dan: They live about 22 percent longer than Americans. They have about four times as many 100-year-olds than we do.

Narrator: Buettner found that centenarians' lifestyles were similar, even if their cultures were different.

They tend to stay active and eat locally grown food. They have hobbies, like this Okinawan woman who works in her garden every day. Most centenarians also have access to good medical care . . . and they have the support of their friends and family.

These centenarians seem to be very healthy . . . but how much longer will such healthy lifestyles last? Younger people are eating more processed foods, and may be less active than their parents and grandparents. With increasing globalization, these traditional lifestyles are fast disappearing.

People today are turning to medical science to help live longer lives. Some scientists have started to treat aging as a disease instead of a natural part of human life.

For now though, there are few centenarians, like this 102-year-old, in the world. However, if we follow their example—eat healthy, stay active, and keep our families close—then we may see more centenarians in our future. And our future may be very long indeed.

Solar Cooking

Narrator: It's a cold day in Borrego Springs, California, but Eleanor Shimeall is cooking outside. But she's not using electricity, gas, or any of the fuels we normally use in the kitchen.

Eleanor: I'm gonna check on this chicken and rice and see whether it's cooking. Ah, it's doing a good job.

Narrator: Instead, Eleanor is using the sun to make her meal. She has done this almost every day for the last 23 years. With sunshine, solar stoves can be used to cook everything from meat and fish, to bread and vegetables. This method is becoming popular with people who care about the environment.

Solar stoves can help save energy at home, and save lives in the developing world.

Dr. Metcalf: With sunshine, you have an alternative to fire. And that's important for two and a half billion people to learn about because they're running out of traditional fuels.

Narrator: Dr. Bob Metcalf is one of the people who started Solar Cookers International, a small group in Sacramento, California. SCI has taught people about solar cooking for the last 15 years, especially in the poor areas of Africa where people cannot afford a normal stove. They hope this innovation will also benefit women.

Dr. Metcalf: They have to walk about two to three miles or so to collect wood. And then they have to tend the fire, and the smoke from that fire—it burns their eyes and chokes their lungs.

Narrator: According to the World Health Organization, this pollution leads to the deaths of two million women and children each year.

With help from other groups, SCI has already trained more than 22,000 families to cook with the sun.

Woman #1: Oh, this is good. It's very good. The consistency is good, the texture is fine—no problem.

Woman #2: We're all amazed that a cardboard box can cook.

Narrator: People get their own solar stove to take home after each training. The stove costs about five dollars, lasts almost two years, and works just like the more expensive models.

Dr. Metcalf: Shiny things direct the sunshine onto a dark pot that then absorbs the sunshine, and changes that light energy into heat energy. And heat energy doesn't get out of the clear plastic bag, it doesn't get out of the window.

Narrator: There are also indications that solar cooking can help purify water.

About 6,000 people die every day from drinking dirty water. A solar cooker can heat water to a temperature that makes it safe to drink, and so preventing many deaths in developing countries.

From Nepal to Nicaragua, there are similar solar projects happening across the world. Some are even using much larger equipment, like this huge pizza cooker in Cuba.

But SCI hopes more communities will eventually use solar stoves. These efficient cookers have the power to help two and a half billion people. And maybe such creative yet simple solutions could lead to more devices powered by the sun.

Woman: OK, solar cooker!

Lamu: Tradition and Modernity

UNIT 3

Narrator: Lamu in Kenya, Africa, is a unique place. Stepping onto this island is like stepping back in time. Evidence of the past remains . . . along with old ways of doing things.

Lamu is the oldest town in Kenya, and the place where Swahili culture was born. On its old and very narrow streets, one of the most popular ways to get around is by donkey.

In 2001, Lamu town was placed on the United Nations list of World Heritage Sites. Many of the buildings are hundreds of years old. The most obvious influence is Arabic, but Lamu and its people absorb whatever cultures they come in contact with.

Badawy: Karibou, welcome.

Narrator: Sheik Ahmad Badawy's family has lived here for a few hundred years.

Badawy: Lamu is the cradle of Swahili civilization. This is where everybody depends on learning about the Swahili culture.

Narrator: It's a culture built on trade. Lamu was a busy economic center from as far back as the 14th century. Ships from China, India, Arabia, and Portugal sailed in and out, trading wood, spices, and many other goods. These traders all left a bit of themselves behind.

Badawy: That's how the culture is developed. Culture is dynamic. You blend in and when you blend in, it still retains the features of the Swahili people.

Narrator: These old interactions can be seen in faces on the street. But trading has decreased greatly in modern times, and the economy of Lamu has not grown. Community worker Amina Soud sees potential in the island's people.

Amina: We are trying to reach the people with the things they are used to, they are accustomed to. So when you go with it, they will just listen as it is and in the process, they will get the message that we want them to get.

Narrator: The message is that Lamu doesn't want to stay in the past. The hope—that people here will participate in the world beyond their island. Sheik Badawy, who owns an Internet café, wants this, too.

Badawy: You don't make money out of that . . . not really make money. But you connect and bring about what we call the tools that are needed to be with the world.

Narrator: But the relationship between modern and traditional is uneasy. Can Lamu change without losing its culture?

Badawy: Would you like to see it changed?

I don't think so. It's noise-free. So that the only noise you can get is from the microphone of the mosque, which is something sweet, I think.

Narrator: As Lamu looks to the future, its people also want to retain a strong connection with their past.

Amina: It is every day. I am telling you it is part of our life, it is our identity.

Saving Bluefin Tuna

UNIT 4

Narrator: Japanese scientist Shukei Masuma is on a mission. He is trying to save the bluefin tuna from becoming extinct. Their numbers have declined significantly over the last decade, largely due to overfishing.

Masuma's solution? To breed them in captivity. He feeds the tuna himself. Here, he visits the huge pools where adults are separated from the young. Says Masuma: "I'm realizing more and more how difficult it is to uncover knowledge about the bluefin. At this point, I'm relying on all my strength and energy."

When evening comes, he waits at the edge of the pool. He hopes to see the beginning of bluefin life. Once the big fish have laid their eggs, Masuma slowly puts the eggs into special tanks. From this stage on, he will take care of them. His goal is to keep them alive until they are old enough to be returned to the sea. He hopes his tuna will grow large enough to breed in the wild.

It's a difficult job. Many hatchlings, or baby fish, do not survive. But after years of hard work, Masuma has found a stable temperature and the right food for his hatchlings. Now he is able to breed them in large numbers. He shows ocean scientist Sylvia Earle how life begins for these giant fish

Sylvia: Already you see the eyes. Is that what these are—the eyes beginning to form?

Masuma: Eyes, they have formed . . . and heart is beating, of course.

Sylvia: Masuma, you were the first to actually pull off this great miracle.

Masuma: Thank you very much.

Narrator: Someday, Masuma will send these hatchlings back into the ocean. There, they will hopefully have a positive effect on the population. But first they have to avoid getting caught.

Scientists estimate that the bluefin tuna population in the Atlantic Ocean is now only one-fifth of its population in the 1970s. And their numbers have dramatically decreased in the Mediterranean Sea and the Pacific Ocean.

The future for the species does not look good. Unless we greatly reduce the number of fish we catch each year, these giants of the sea will eventually die out.

Memory School

UNIT 5

Narrator: London's taxi drivers are the Olympic athletes of memory. Drivers navigate the streets of London using a complex mental map with thousands of landmarks and other locations. These taxi drivers have helped researchers at University of London study how memory works.

Each new cab driver must pass a very difficult exam called "the knowledge," which takes about two years to prepare for. It's a good opportunity for scientists to study how the brain is able to adapt when it has to retain large amounts of information.

Passenger: Thanks, mate. Can you take me to Albert Hall?

Barry: When somebody gets in your cab, they'll say, "Take me to so-and-so." It's got to be like that . . . you've got to know instantly where you're going, which way to be pointing. So there's a lot of retention, you've got to retain a lot of what you've learned as well.

Narrator: Scientists suspected that a part of the brain called the hippocampus might be the key to the taxi drivers' success.

Teacher: Matt, now run me to the nearest police station.

Student: Leave by Waterloo Bridge, forward Lancaster Place . . .

Narrator: Drivers-in-training at the Knowledge Point School use this part of the brain a lot in classes.

Teacher: Dave, give me the name of a restaurant on Portland Road with a lady's name.

Student: Chutney Mary's.

Teacher: Hereford Road—where would you give me?

Student: Veronica's.

Narrator: After class, students take their knowledge to the streets. Visual processing takes up more space in the brain than all the other senses combined. So direct experience is a very important part of training.

James: You start off learning all the roads. Then you have to learn all the places on every road. With all the routes that you have to do for the knowledge, you couldn't possibly do it on a map. You have to get out on your bike, in the rain, the cold, the snow. You learn it bit by bit.

Narrator: But how does the brain retain and order all that information? All this internal effort has an external effect—a physical change in the brain itself.

From their study, scientists concluded that taxi drivers have a larger hippocampus than the average person. In fact, the biggest differences were seen in taxi drivers who had been working a long time.

Andy: It's almost like you've somehow, somewhere up in your brain, you've created enough space to sort of slip this map in, a little bit of software.

Narrator: This study suggests that the adult brain can physically change depending on what a person needs. Doctors hope this information can be used to help restore the minds of stroke victims, Alzheimer's patients, and those suffering other forms of brain damage.

UNIT 6

The Frog Licker

Narrator: Off the southeastern coast of Africa lies the island of Madagascar.

Madagascar is known for its wide-eyed lemurs, but it also has one of the world's most colorful amphibians—the Mantella poison frog.

Poison frogs aren't born poisonous. Instead, they are proof of the old saying: "You are what you eat." Their toxins are actually a side effect of their diet, which is made up of ants, millipedes, and mites. But which insects, specifically? And will the loss of these insects endanger the frogs?

Meet scientist Valerie C. Clark. Valerie encounters *Mantella betsileo*, a very widespread species of poison frog. This one appears to be carrying eggs.

Valerie: How do I know? Because it's just very, very fat, and this is the season for love.

Narrator: Clark and her colleagues use GPS data to record the frog's location, and other useful information.

Valerie: We're right at sea level.

Narrator: They also need to collect as many insects as possible to try to track down exactly what these frogs are eating.

First, Valerie's team chops up the leaves, then puts them into mesh bags—ones that have lots of little holes. They hang the bags up inside another bag, with a little plastic bag filled with alcohol attached to the bottom. As the soil dries out inside the mesh bag, the insects escape to find water and fall out. These become their samples.

How do you test the toxins in a frog's skin? There are a couple of methods. One way is to wipe their backs with tissue soaked in alcohol. But another way is what Clark calls the "quick lick" taste test.

Valerie: Well, let's see. Oh, it's definitely bitter.

Narrator: Bitterness equals toxic.

It seems like a risky thing to do, but Mantella are only mildly toxic to humans. They are brightly colored to warn predators to stay away.

These toxins in the frogs' skin may be harmful to other animals, but may be very valuable to humans. They could be an important contribution to medical science, providing pain relief and cures for diseases.

Valerie: By sampling frogs for their toxic chemicals, we're effectively taking a shortcut to the many, many chemicals that exist in countless insects in the rainforest.

Narrator: Back in the village, the results look promising.

Valerie: Oh! Here we go!

I'm very excited about these samples. This is certainly making up the great portion of the Mantella diet and has great potential to end up being some of the sources of their chemicals.

Narrator: The frogs need to eat many types of insects for their toxins to work. The bigger the forest, the more insects to choose from. If we start cutting down rainforest and affecting the ecosystem, it reduces our chances of finding new drug cures.

Valerie: So the more primary forest that we have, the better chance we have of finding new drug leads.

Narrator: Near the end of her journey, Clark has collected 500 tubes of insects. These could lead her to some sources of the frogs' toxins.

The message is clear. In order to save the poison frogs of Madagascar, people will have to save the rainforest with its amazing diversity of insects.

UNIT 7
Lightning

Narrator: A lightning storm. It's an incredible natural event—one that scientists are still learning about.

On hot summer days, it's common to see flashes of lightning in the sky. It's estimated that lightning occurs 50 to 100 times a second around the world. Regions with the most lightning strikes include Central Africa, the Himalayas, and South America.

Lightning is often seen flashing between storm clouds and the earth. These flashes of light are pure electricity. Scientists aren't exactly sure how lightning escapes from the cloud. They think it occurs because of movement of air within rain clouds.

Lighter particles moving toward the top of clouds become positively charged, while heavier particles heading toward the bottom become negatively charged. In conditions where positive and negative charges grow big enough, lightning occurs between these regions.

Most lightning occurs within the cloud, but some strike the earth in bright flashes. In these cases, the lightning escapes the cloud and extends toward the ground in a branching pattern, like a tree.

Just one lightning strike contains hundreds of millions of volts, and lasts less than a second.

Lightning seems to take the form of a single flash, but it's actually several flashes reaching up into the clouds. Lightning reaches temperatures of more than 28,000 degrees Celsius. This heat causes air around the lightning to expand, which creates the sound of thunder.

In the U.S., lightning occurs most frequently in Florida. Its hot, wet climate is particularly suited for creating thunder clouds.

Lightning kills a significant number of people each year—nearly 100 people on average in the U.S., more than hurricanes or tornadoes.

During thunderstorms, reduce your risk of getting struck by finding shelter inside a building or in vehicles. If caught outside, avoid high ground and isolated trees.

Lighting is a natural and common event, but one that can be deadly.

UNIT 8
The Pyramids of Giza

Narrator: The Pyramids of Giza are lasting symbols of ancient Egypt.

It is hard to believe that, even after 4,000 years, we still don't know everything about the pyramids. Experts are hard at work trying to learn more about these amazing structures. Archaeologists believe the pyramids served as tombs for the pharaohs, or kings, of Egypt. Each pyramid was constructed to guard the pharaoh's body and possessions, and to transport him into the afterlife.

The largest and oldest pyramid stands almost 140 meters tall. Thousands of workers built the pyramid for the pharaoh Khufu, who ruled about 4,500 years ago. The pyramid consists of over two million stone blocks, each weighing almost 2,300 kilograms. Yet it took only 20 years to complete.

The middle pyramid is the tomb of the Pharaoh Khafre, Khufu's son and successor. It is guarded by the Great Sphinx, located nearby. Over 70 meters long, the Sphinx is a sculpture combining the body of a lion and the head of a man. Experts think it represents Pharaoh Khafre himself.

The last and smallest of the three great pyramids is the tomb of the pharaoh Menkaure, Khafre's son. There is still a lot of excavation to be done around the area. Many of the surrounding tombs and temples have yet to be studied fully.

Here, scientists continue to make new discoveries that will help us understand more about the ancient Egyptians' lives and rituals.

In ancient times, the pyramids were thought to be one of the seven wonders of the world. Thousands of years later, they continue to inspire us.

Flying Reptiles

Narrator: The paradise tree snake is a special kind of snake. Not because it can climb trees. Many snakes are able to use their rough, overlapping scales to push against tree bark and move upwards.

No. What makes this species so unique is its ability . . . to fly!

These are flying snakes. They fly from tree to tree. In the dense forests of Indonesia, it's the quickest and most efficient way to get from here to there.

First, the snake hangs off the end of the branch in a "J" shape. Then it launches itself, "flying" through the air and down to the ground or another tree. The snake can flatten itself to about twice its normal width. This makes it more of a glider than a flyer.

By twisting its flexible body into an "S" shape, the snake can even make turns. This helps the snake cross distances of up to 100 meters.

Other animals have evolved in similar ways. This is the Draco lizard, or "flying dragon."

It is prey for the paradise tree snake and other predators of the jungle.

The lizard puffs itself up as a warning, but the snake doesn't seem put off by this display.

So the lizard spreads its wings and takes off.

These wings are actually thin folds of skin that extend from its body. The Draco uses them to glide from tree to tree, up to 10 meters apart.

Like the snake, this ability to "fly" helps it move around the forest quickly and easily.

As for the tree snake, looks like it'll have to find another prey—one that won't escape so easily.

Cell Phone Trackers

Narrator: Lions are beautiful, deadly, and kings of the African grassland. But nowadays, African lions must share their territory with an even more powerful animal—humans.

This is Kenya's Mbirikani Ranch—almost 5,000 square miles (8,000 square kilometers) of rural grassland. It is collectively owned by about 10,000 Masai.

These nomadic people live on the land, along with their livestock. Their cattle make a tasty—and easy—meal for hungry lions. In this remote area, Masai have to protect their livestock. Over the years, they've killed about 150 lions.

Antony Kasanga's challenge is to help his fellow Masai, as well as the lions. He finds evidence of lions nearby, and then finds a carcass—the body of a dead lion.

Antony (translated): This lion was killed two days ago. And it was speared in the morning, and it ran away with wounds. And they found the carcass later in the evening.

Narrator: Fortunately, these sad deaths are becoming increasingly rare at Mbirikani. This is because a new program pays the Masai to protect the lions, rather than kill them.

Antony and his colleagues are called "lion guardians." They keep these predators away from Masai cattle. The key is knowing where the lions are.

Seamus Maclennan is a biologist working with the lion guardian program. Many of the lions have radio collars, so he can analyze their movements.

Seamus: We're on the southern boundary of the ranch. This is the Mbirikani group ranch where the lion guardians work. I'm hoping to find one of our collared lions, or maybe two of them, down in this area here.

Narrator: Using a receiver to pick up signals from a radio collar, he's able to locate some lions.

Seamus: The male that we have just seen going behind those bushes there, he passes through from time to time. He has a collar. What I'm going to do now is just record his GPS location and a few details about what we saw today.

Narrator: Using the same radio technology, Masai guards in the program can monitor lion activity.

Using cell phones, the guardians can inform other Masai when the lions are around, so the Masai can move their livestock away from the lions. This technology also helps guardians monitor the number of lions in the area, and whether any hunters try to kill them.

As part of the lion-guardian program, money is given to people whose livestock have been killed or injured by lions. In order to receive the money, the Masai have to watch their livestock during the day and keep them behind special fences at night.

The program has been a success so far. There are now fewer lion killings on the Mbirikani Ranch than in other areas.

It's also empowered guards like Antony and transformed their relationship with the lions. He's started a blog about his experiences with lions and is helping to raise money for the project through online donations.

Both lions and humans call this grassland home. With the new technology, they can now live peacefully side by side . . . and perhaps even benefit from each other.

Contents

Tips for Reading and Note Taking

Tips for Writing and Research

Tips for Reading and Note Taking

Reading fluently

Why develop your reading speed?

Reading slowly, one word at a time, makes it difficult to get an overall sense of the meaning of a text. As a result, reading becomes more challenging and less interesting than if you read at a faster pace. In general, it is a good idea to first skim a text for the gist, and then read it again more closely so that you can focus on the most relevant details.

Strategies for improving reading speed:

- Try to read groups of words rather than individual words.
- Keep your eyes moving forward. Read through to the end of each sentence or paragraph instead of going back to reread words or phrases within the sentence or paragraph.
- Read selectively. Skip functional words (articles, prepositions, etc.) and focus on words and phrases carrying meaning—the content words. See page 48 for an example.
- Use clues in the text—such as highlighted text (**bold** words, words in *italics*, etc.)—to help you know which parts might be important and worth focusing on.
- Use section headings, as well as the first and last lines of paragraphs, to help you understand how the text is organized.
- Use context and other clues such as affixes and part of speech to guess the meaning of unfamiliar words and phrases. Try to avoid using a dictionary if you are reading quickly for overall meaning.

Thinking critically

As you read, ask yourself questions about what the writer is saying, and how and why the writer is presenting the information at hand.

Important critical thinking skills for academic reading and writing:

- Analyzing: Examining a text in close detail in order to identify key points, similarities, and differences.
- Evaluating: Using evidence to decide how relevant, important, or useful something is. This often involves looking at reasons for and against something.
- Inferring: "Reading between the lines;" in other words, identifying what a writer is saying indirectly, or *implicitly*, rather than directly, or *explicitly*.
- Synthesizing: Gathering appropriate information and ideas from more than one source and making a judgment, summary, or conclusion based on the evidence.
- Reflecting: Relating ideas and information in a text to your own personal experience and preconceptions (i.e., the opinions or beliefs you had before reading the text).

Note taking

Taking notes of key points and the connections between them will help you better understand the overall meaning and organization of a text. Note taking also enables you to record the most important ideas and information for future use such as when you are preparing for an exam or completing a writing assignment.

Techniques for effective note taking:

- As you read, underline or highlight important information such as dates, names, places, and other facts.
- Take notes in the margin—as you read, note the main idea and supporting details next to each paragraph. Also note your own ideas or questions about the paragraph.
- On paper or on a computer, paraphrase the key points of the text in your own words.
- Keep your notes brief—include short headings to organize the information, key words and phrases (not full sentences), and abbreviations and symbols. (See next page for examples.)
- Note sources of information precisely. Be sure to include page numbers, names of relevant people and places, and quotations.
- Make connections between key points with techniques such as using arrows and colors to connect ideas and drawing circles or squares around related information.
- Use a graphic organizer to summarize a text, particularly if it follows a pattern such as cause—effect, comparison—contrast, or chronological sequence. See page 190 for more information.
- Use your notes to write a summary of the passage in order to remember what you learned.

Useful abbreviations

approx.	approximately		incl.	including	
ca.	about, around (date / year)		info	information	
cd	could		p. (pp.)	page (pages)	
Ch.	Chapter		para.	paragraph	
devt	development		re:	regarding, concerning	
e.g./ex.	example		wd	would	
etc.	and others / and the rest		yr(s)	years(s)	
excl.	excluding		C20	20th century	
govt	government				
i.e.	that is; in other words				
impt	important				

Useful symbols

→	leads to / causes
↑	increases / increased
↓	decreases / decreased
& or +	and
∴	therefore
b/c	because
w/	with
=	is the same as
>	is more than
<	is less than
~	is approximately / about

Learning vocabulary

More than likely, you will not remember a new word or phrase after reading or hearing it once. You need to use the word several times before it enters your long-term memory.

Strategies for learning vocabulary:

- Use flash cards. Write the words you want to learn on one side of an index card. Write the definition and/or an example sentence that uses the word on the other side. Use your flash cards to test your knowledge of new vocabulary.
- Keep a vocabulary journal. When you come across a new word or phrase, write a short definition of the word (in English, if possible) and the sentence or situation where you found it (its context). Write another sentence of your own that uses the word. Include any common collocations. (See the Word Partners boxes in this book for examples of collocations.)
- Make word webs (or "word maps").
- Use memory aids. It may be easier to remember a word or phrase if you use a memory aid, or *mnemonic*. For example, if you want to learn the idiom *keep an eye on someone*, which means to "watch someone carefully," you might picture yourself putting your eyeball on someone's shoulder so that you can watch the person carefully. The stranger the picture is, the more you will remember it! See page 88 for more on mnemonics.

Common affixes

Some words contain an affix at the start of the word (*prefix*) and/or at the end (*suffix*). These affixes can be useful for guessing the meaning of unfamiliar words and for expanding your vocabulary. In general, a prefix affects the meaning of a word, whereas a suffix affects its part of speech. See the Word Link boxes in this book for specific examples.

Prefix	Meaning	Example
commun-	sharing	communicate
con-	together, with	construct
em- / en-	making, putting	empower, endanger
ex-	away, from, out	external
in-	not	independent
inter-	between	interactive
minim-	smallest	minimal
pre-	before	prevent
re-	back, again	restore
sur	above	surface
trans-	across	transfer
un-	not	uninvolved

Suffix	Part of Speech	Example
-able	adjective	dependable
-al	adjective	traditional
-ate	verb	differentiate
-ed	adjective	involved
-eer	noun	volunteer
-ent / -ant	adjective	confident, significant
-er	noun	researcher
-ful	adjective	grateful
-ical	adjective	practical
-ity	noun	reality
-ive	adjective	positive
-ize	verb	socialize
-ly	adverb	definitely
-ment	noun	achievement
-tion	noun	prevention

Tips for Writing and Research

Features of academic writing

There are many types of academic writing (descriptive, argumentative/persuasive, narrative, etc.), but most types share similar characteristics.

Generally, in academic writing you should:

- write in full sentences.
- use formal English. (Avoid slang or conversational expressions such as *kind of*.)
- be clear and coherent—keep to your main point; avoid technical words that the reader may not know.
- use signal words and phrases to connect your ideas. (See examples on page 214.)
- have a clear point (main idea) for each paragraph.
- be objective—most academic writing uses a neutral, impersonal point of view, so avoid overuse of personal pronouns (*I, we, you*) and subjective language such as *nice* or *terrible*.
- use facts, examples, and expert opinions to support your argument.
- show where the evidence or opinions come from. (*According to the 2009 World Database Survey,. . . .*)
- show that you have considered other viewpoints. (See examples of making concessions on page 115.)

Generally, in academic writing you should <u>not</u>:

- use abbreviations or language used in texting. (Use *that is* rather than *i.e.*, and *in my opinion*, not *IMO*.)
- use contractions. (Use *is not* rather than *isn't*.)
- be vague. (*A man made the first cell-phone call a few decades ago. -> An inventor named Martin Cooper made the first cell-phone call in 1973.*)
- include several pronoun references in a single sentence. (*He thinks it's a better idea than the other one, but I agree with her.*)
- start sentences with *or*, *and*, or *but*.
- apologize to the reader. (*I'm sorry I don't know much about this, but . . .*) In academic writing, it is important to sound confident about what you are saying!

Proofreading tips

Capitalization

Remember to capitalize:

- the first letter of the word at the beginning of every sentence.
- proper names such as names of people, geographical names, company names, and names of organizations.
- days, months, and holidays.
- the word *I*.
- the first letter of a title such as the title of a movie or a book.
- the words in titles that have meaning (content words). Don't capitalize *a*, *an*, *the*, *and*, or prepositions such *as to*, *for*, *of*, *from*, *at*, *in*, and *on*, unless they are the first word of a title (e.g., *The King and I*).

Punctuation

Keep the following rules in mind:

- Use a question mark (?) at the end of every question. Use a period (.) at the end of any sentence that is not a question.
- Exclamation marks (!), which indicate strong feelings such as surprise or joy, are generally not used in academic writing.
- Use commas (,) to separate a list of three or more things (*She speaks German, English, and Spanish.*).
- Use a comma after an introductory word or phrase. (*Although painful to humans, it is not deadly. / However, some species have fewer than 20 legs.*)
- Use a comma before a combining word (coordinating conjunction)—*and*, *but*, *so*, *yet*, *or*, and *nor*—that joins two sentences (*Black widow bites are not usually deadly for adults, but they can be deadly for children.*).
- Use an apostrophe (') for showing possession (*James's idea came from social networking sites.*).

- Use quotation marks (" ") to indicate the exact words used by someone else. (*In fact, Wesch says, "the Web is us."*)
- Use quotation marks to show when a word or phrase is being used in a special way, such as a definition. (*The name centipede means "100 legs."*)

Other Proofreading Tips:

- Print out your draft instead of reading it on your computer screen.
- Read your draft out loud. Use your finger or a pen to point to each word as you read it.
- Don't be afraid to mark up your draft. Use a colored pen to make corrections so you can see them easily when you write your next draft.
- Read your draft backwards—starting with the last word—to check your spelling. That way, you won't be distracted by the meaning.
- Have someone else read your draft and give you comments or ask you questions.
- Don't depend on a computer's spell-check. When the spell-check suggests a correction, make sure you agree with it before you accept the change.
- Remember to pay attention to the following items:
  - Short words such as *is*, *and*, *but*, *or*, *it*, *to*, *for*, *from*, and *so*.
  - Spelling of proper nouns.
  - Numbers and dates.
- Keep a list of spelling and grammar mistakes that you commonly make so that you can be aware of them as you edit your draft.

Watch out for frequently confused words:

- *there, their,* and *they're*
- *its* and *it's*
- *by, buy,* and *bye*
- *your* and *you're*

- *to, too,* and *two*
- *whose* and *who's*
- *where, wear, we're,* and *were*
- *then* and *than*

- *quit, quiet,* and *quite*
- *write* and *right*
- *affect* and *effect*
- *through* and *threw*

- *week* and *weak*

Research and referencing

Using facts and expert quotes from journals and online sources will help to support your arguments in a written assignment. When you research information, you need to look for the most relevant and reliable sources. You will also need to provide appropriate citations for these sources; that is, you need to indicate that the words are not your own but rather come from someone else.

In academic writing, it is necessary for a writer to cite sources of all information that is not original. Using a source without citing it is known as **plagiarism**.

There are several ways to cite sources. Check with your teacher on the method or methods required at your institution.

Research Checklist

- [ ] Are my sources relevant to the assignment?
- [ ] Are my sources reliable? Think about the author and publisher. Ask yourself, "What is the author's point of view? Can I trust this information?" (See also CT Focus on page 128.)
- [ ] Have I noted all sources properly, including page numbers?
- [ ] When I am not citing a source directly, am I using my own words? In other words, am I using appropriate paraphrasing, which includes the use of synonyms, different word forms, and/or different grammatical structure? (See page 177 for more on paraphrasing.)
- [ ] Are my sources up-to-date? Do they use the most recent data available? Having current sources is especially important for fields that change rapidly, such as technology and business.
- [ ] If I am using a direct quote, am I using the exact words that the person said or wrote?
- [ ] Am I using varied expressions for introducing citations, such as *According to X, As X says, X says / states / points out / explains . . .?* (See also CT Focus on page 127.)

Common signal phrases

Making an overview statement

It is generally agreed that . . .
It is clear (from the chart/table) that . . .
Generally, we can see that . . .

Giving supporting details and examples

One/An example (of this) is. . .
For example,. . . / For instance, . . .
Specifically, . . . / More specifically, . . .
From my experience, . . .

Giving reasons

This is due to . . .
This is because (of) . . .
One reason (for this) is . . .

Describing cause and effect

Consequently, . . . / Therefore, . . .
As a result, . . . /
As a consequence, . . .

This means that . . .
Because of this, . . .

Giving definitions

. . . which means . . .
In other words,. . .
That is . . .

Linking arguments and reasons

Furthermore, . . . / Moreover, . . .
In addition, . . . / Additionally, . . .
For one thing, . . . / For another example, . . .
Not only . . . but also . . .

Describing a process

First (of all), . . .
Then / Next / After that, . . .
As soon as . . . / When . . .
Finally, . . .

Outlining contrasting views

On the other hand, . . . / However, . . .
Although some people believe (that) . . .
it can also be argued that . . .
While it may be true that . . .,
nevertheless, . . .
Despite this, . . . / Despite
(the fact that) . . . Even though . . .

Softening a statement

It seems/appears that . . .
The evidence suggests/indicates that . . .

Giving a personal opinion

In my opinion, . . .
I (generally) agree that . . .
I think/feel that . . .
Personally, I believe (that) . . .

Restating/concluding

In conclusion, . . . / In summary, . . .
To conclude, . . . / To summarize, . . .

Grammar Reference

Unit 1

Language for Writing: Review of the Simple Present

Affirmative and Negative Statements

Affirmative Statements		Negative Statements		
Subject	Verb	Subject	*Do/Does Not*	Verb (Base Form)
I You We They	**live** in Singapore.	I You We They	**do not don't**	**live** in Mexico.
He She It	**lives** in Singapore.	He She It	**does not doesn't**	

Affirmative and Negative Statements with *Be*

Affirmative Statements			Negative Statements		
Subject	*Am/Are/Is*		Subject	*Am/Are/Is*	
I	**am**		I	**am not**	
You We They	**are**	happy. here. at work.	You We They	**are not aren't**	happy. here. at work.
He She It	**is**		He She It	**is not isn't**	

Unit 2

Language for Writing: Review of the Simple Past

Affirmative and Negative Statements

Affirmative Statements		Negative Statements		
Subject	**Verb (Past Form)**	**Subject**	*Did Not*	**Verb (Base Form)**
I You We They He She It	**started** a project. **walked** home. **studied**. **went** to school.	I You We They He She It	**did not** **didn't**	**start** a project. **walk** home. **study**. **go** to school.

Spelling Rules for Regular Verbs

1. Add -*ed* to most verbs. 2. If a one-syllable verb ends in *e*, add -*d*. 3. If a one-syllable verb ends in a consonant + vowel + consonant (not *w*, *x*, or *y*), double the consonant and add -*ed*. 4. If a two-syllable word ends in consonant + vowel + consonant, double the last consonant only if the stress is on the last syllable. 5. If a verb ends in consonant + -*y*, drop the -*y* and add -*ied*	talk—talked like—liked stop—stopped prefer—preferred edit—edited study—studied

Past Forms of Commonly Used Irregular Verbs

become—became begin—began build—built break—broke bring—brought buy—bought choose—chose come—came do—did draw—drew eat—ate	fall—fell find—found forget—forgot get—got give—gave go—went have—had hear—heard know—knew lose—lost make—made	read—read say—said see—saw speak—spoke spend—spent take—took teach—taught tell—told think—thought understand—understood write—wrote

Affirmative and Negative Statements with *Be*

Affirmative Statements			Negative Statements		
Subject	*Was/Were*		**Subject**	*Was/Were Not*	
I He She It	**was**	happy. sad. a doctor. a student. here. at work.	I He She It	**was not** **wasn't**	happy. sad. a doctor. a student. here. at work.
You We They	**were**		You We They	**were not** **weren't**	

Unit 3

The Present Perfect

Subject	*Have/Have Not*	Verb (Past Participle)	Time Marker (optional)
I You We They	**have** **have not / haven't**	**been** here **seen** her **called** him	since last year. for three months. recently.
He She It	**has** **has not / hasn't**		

Time Markers

Use *since* + a point in time, *for* + a length of time, *in the* + time period to describe something that began in the past and continues to the present.

I've lived in Denmark **since** 2010.
He hasn't been here **for** three years.
We've met a lot of people **in the past month**.

Use *already* in affirmative statements to emphasize that something happened at an unspecified time in the past. Use *yet* in negative statements to talk about something that has not happened before now.

I've seen that movie **already**.　　　　I haven't seen that movie **yet**.
She's **already** eaten.　　　　　　　　She hasn't eaten **yet**.

Use words such as *a few times*, *twice*, or a number to describe something that happened more than once in the past.

We've been to Mexico a **few times**.
Mark has called **twice**.
They've sent us **five** emails.

Use *recently* or *lately* to emphasize that something happened or didn't happen at an unspecified time in the recent past.

Sarah has called several times **recently**.
I haven't seen James **lately**.

Past Participle Forms of Commonly Used Irregular Verbs

be—been	find—found	say—said
become—become	forget—forgotten	see—seen
begin—begun	get—gotten	show—shown
build—built	give—given	sing—sung
break—broken	go—gone	sleep—slept
bring—brought	have—had	speak—spoken
buy—bought	hear—heard	spend—spent
choose—chosen	know—known	take—taken
come—come	lose—lost	teach—taught
do—done	make—made	tell—told
draw—drawn	meet—met	think—thought
eat—eaten	put—put	understand—understood
fall—fallen	read—read	write—written

Unit 5

Spelling Rules for Forming Gerunds

When forming gerunds, follow these rules for adding -ing to verbs:

1. Most verbs: add -ing:
   sleep → sleeping   think → thinking   remember → remembering

2. Verbs that end with a consonant followed by -e: drop the -e and add -ing:
   memorize → memorizing   store → storing   use → using

3. One-syllable verbs ending with a consonant + vowel + consonant: double the final consonant and add -ing:
   get → getting   stop → stopping   put → putting
   (Exceptions: Verbs that end in -w, -x, or -y; for example, say → saying)

4. Two-syllable verbs ending with a consonant + vowel + consonant, where the second syllable is stressed: double the final consonant and add -ing:
   admit → admitting   begin → beginning   prefer → preferring

Unit 8

Comparative Adjectives

1. With one-syllable adjectives, add -er:

Adjective	Comparative Form	Example
tall	taller	The Burj Khalifa is taller than the Empire State Building.
hard	harder	Granite is harder than wood.
large	larger	The columns in the outside are larger than the columns on the inside.

2. With two-syllable adjectives ending in -y, change the -y to -i and add -er:

Adjective	Comparative Form	Example
easy	easier	Is art easier than mathematics?
busy	busier	The Morrison Library is busier than the Barrett Library.

3. With most adjectives of two or more syllables, not ending in -y, use more:

Adjective	Comparative Form	Example
attractive	more attractive	The Morrison Library is more attractive than the Barrett Library.
famous	more famous	La Sagrada Familia is more famous than Park Guell.

4. Some adjectives have irregular comparative forms:

bad → worse   good → better
Mark's handwriting is worse than Mary's handwriting.   The new design is better than the old design.

5. You can also make comparisons with as . . . as to describe things that are equal, or not as . . . as to describe things that are not equal:

The Golden Gate Bridge is as beautiful as the Brooklyn Bridge.
However, the Golden Gate Bridge is not as old as the Brooklyn Bridge.

Unit 10

Modals		
Use modals with the base form of a verb.		
Affirmative and Negative Statements		
Subject	**Modal (*not*)**	**Verb**
I You We They He She It	can / can't could / couldn't may / may not might / might not	**save** hundreds of lives. **make** learning English easier and more affordable.

Vocabulary Index

*These words are on the Academic Word List (AWL). The AWL is a list of the 570 most frequent word families in academic texts. The list does not include words that are among the most frequent 2,000 words of English. For more information on the AWL, see http://www.victoria.ac.nz/lals/resources/academicwordlist/.

Academic Literacy Skills Index

Critical Thinking

Analyzing 7, 18, 28, 38, 56, 58, 67, 74, 75, 76, 78, 88, 95, 96, 98, 115, 116, 118, 127, 128, 135, 138, 157, 158, 160, 170, 177, 180, 196, 197, 198, 200

Applying a Method 87

Brainstorming 4, 9, 11, 15, 24, 29, 44, 49, 55, 64, 69, 71, 75, 89, 95, 104, 115, 124, 135, 144, 151, 157, 166, 177, 186, 197

Evaluating 67, 108, 127, 128, 134, 156, 169, 171

Guessing meaning from context 7, 9, 49, 67, 89, 109, 171, 191

Making connections/comparisons 2, 42, 27, 102, 134, 156, 164

Making inferences 47, 54, 87, 127

Peer-Evaluating 97, 139

Personalizing/Reflecting 1, 21, 22, 41, 61, 81, 101, 121, 141, 142, 149, 163, 183, 189

Predicting 4, 24, 31, 44, 51, 64, 71, 84, 91, 104, 109, 111, 124, 131, 144, 166, 186, 193

Ranking and justifying 22, 34

Synthesizing 9, 14, 29, 34, 49, 68, 69, 74, 89, 94, 109, 114, 129, 134, 151, 156, 171, 176, 189, 191, 196

Grammar

By + gerund 95, 99

Comparative adjectives 157, 161

Imperative and simple present verb forms 139

Modals 197, 201

Present perfect tense 55, 59

Simple past tense 35, 39

Simple present tense 15, 19

Synonyms 181

Verb forms for describing process 135

Reading Skills/Strategies

Identifying:

cause and effect 88, 94

figurative language 107

key details 7, 14, 27, 34, 47, 54, 74, 87, 94, 107, 114, 123, 127, 134, 178

main idea 8, 54, 67, 94, 149, 169, 176, 189

pros and cons 108

purpose 74

sequence 128, 134, 189

supporting ideas/details 28, 34, 36, 134, 149, 169

synonyms 178

theories 170, 176

Scanning for specific information 150, 153, 156

Understanding the gist 7, 14, 27, 34, 47, 48, 54, 67, 74, 87, 94, 107, 114, 127, 134, 149, 156, 169, 176, 189, 196

Understanding references 114

Visual Literacy

Interpreting graphic information

- graphs/charts 68, 75, 76, 78, 83, 93

- infographics 42, 73, 146-7, 148, 174, 184

- maps 42, 62, 68, 123, 185

Using graphic organizers

- Venn diagrams 156, 158, 159, 161, 171

- T-charts 84, 87, 196, 197

- time lines/flowcharts 137

- mind maps 11

Acknowledgments

The authors and publisher would like to thank the following reviewers for their help during the development of this series:

UNITED STATES AND CANADA

Gokhan Alkanat, Auburn University at Montgomery, AL; Nikki Ashcraft, Shenandoah University, VA; Karin Avila-John, University of Dayton, OH; John Baker, Oakland Community College, MI; Shirley Baker, Alliant International University, CA; Michelle Bell, University of South Florida, FL; Nancy Boyer, Golden West College, CA; Kathy Brenner, BU/CELOP, Mattapan, MA; Janna Brink, Mt. San Antonio College, Chino Hills, CA; Carol Brutza, Gateway Community College, CT; Sarah Camp, University of Kentucky, Center for ESL, KY; Maria Caratini, Eastfield College, TX; Ana Maria Cepero, Miami Dade College, Miami, FL; Daniel Chaboya, Tulsa Community College, OK; Patricia Chukwueke, English Language Institute – UCSD Extension, CA; Julia A. Correia, Henderson State University, CT; Suzanne Crisci, Bunker Hill Community College, MA; Lina Crocker, University of Kentucky, Lexington, KY; Katie Crowder, University of North Texas, TX; Joe Cunningham, Park University, Kansas City, MO; Lynda Dalgish, Concordia College, NY; Jeffrey Diluglio, Center for English Language and Orientation Programs: Boston University, MA; Scott Dirks, Kaplan International Center at Harvard Square, MA; Kathleen Dixon, SUNY Stony Brook - Intensive English Center, Stony Brook, NY; Margo Downey, Boston University, Boston, MA; John Drezek, Richland College, TX; Qian Du, Ohio State University, Columbus, OH; Leslie Kosel Eckstein, Hillsborough Community College, FL; Anwar El-Issa, Antelope Valley College, CA; Beth Kozbial Ernst, University of Wisconsin-Eau Claire, WI; Anrisa Fannin, The International Education Center at Diablo Valley College, CA; Jennie Farnell, Greenwich Japanese School, Greenwich, CT; Rosa Vasquez Fernandez, John F. Kennedy, Institute Of Languages, Inc., Boston, MA; Mark Fisher, Lone Star College, TX; Celeste Flowers, University of Central Arkansas, AR; John Fox, English Language Institute, GA; Pradel R. Frank, Miami Dade College, FL; Sherri Fujita, Hawaii Community College, Hilo, HI; Sally Gearheart, Santa Rosa Jr. College, CA; Elizabeth Gillstrom, The University of Pennsylvania, Philadelphia, PA; Sheila Goldstein, Rockland Community College, Brentwood, NY; Karen Grubbs, ELS Language Centers, FL; Sudeepa Gulati, long beach city college, Torrance, CA; Joni Hagigeorges, Salem State University, MA; Marcia Peoples Halio, English Language Institute, University of Delaware, DE; Kara Hanson, Oregon State University, Corvallis, OR; Suha Hattab, Triton College, Chicago, IL; Marla Heath, Sacred Heart Univiversity and Norwalk Community College, Stamford, CT; Valerie Heming, University of Central Missouri, MO; Mary Hill, North Shore Community College, MA; Harry Holden, North Lake College, Dallas, TX; Ingrid Holm, University of Massachusetts Amherst, MA; Katie Hurter, Lone Star College – North Harris, TX; Barbara Inerfeld, Program in American Language Studies (PALS) Rutgers University/New Brunswick, Piscataway, NJ; Justin Jernigan, Georgia Gwinnett College, GA; Barbara Jonckheere, ALI/CSULB, Long Beach, CA; Susan Jordan, Fisher College, MA; Maria Kasparova, Bergen Community College, NJ; Maureen Kelbert, Vancouver Community College, Surrey, BC, Canada; Gail Kellersberger, University of Houston-Downtown, TX; David Kent, Troy University, Goshen, AL; Daryl Kinney, Los Angeles City College, CA; Jennifer Lacroix, Center for English Language and Orientation Programs: Boston University, MA; Stuart Landers, Misouri State University, Springfield, MO; Mary Jo Fletcher LaRocco, Ph.D., Salve Regina University, Newport, RI; Bea Lawn, Gavilan College, Gilroy, CA; Margaret V. Layton, University of Nevada, Reno Intensive English Language Center, NV; Alice Lee, Richland College, Mesquite, TX; Heidi Lieb, Bergen Community College, NJ; Kerry Linder, Language Studies International New York, NY; Jenifer Lucas-Uygun, Passaic County Community College, Paterson, NJ; Alison MacAdams, Approach International Student Center, MA; Julia MacDonald, Brock University, Saint Catharines, ON, Canada; Craig Machado, Norwalk Community College, CT; Andrew J. MacNeill, Southwestern College, CA; Melanie A. Majeski, Naugatuck Valley Community College, CT; Wendy Maloney, College of DuPage, Aurora, IL; Chris Mares, University of Maine – Intensive English Institute, Maine; Josefina Mark, Union County College, NJ; Connie Mathews, Nashville State Community College, TN; Bette Matthews, Mid-Pacific Institute, HI; Richard McDorman, inlingua Language Centers (Miami, FL) and Pennsylvania State University, Pompano Beach, FL; Sara McKinnon, College of Marin, CA; Christine Mekkaoui, Pittsburg State University, KS; Holly A. Milkowart, Johnson County Community College, KS; Donna Moore, Hawaii Community College, Hilo, HI; Ruth W. Moore, International English Center, University of Colorado at Boulder, CO; Kimberly McGrath Moreira, University of Miami, FL; Warren Mosher, University of Miami, FL; Sarah Moyer, California State University Long Beach, CA; Lukas Murphy, Westchester Community College, NY; Elena Nehrebecki, Hudson Community College, NJ; Bjarne Nielsen, Central Piedmont Community College, North Carolina; David Nippoldt, Reedley College, CA; Nancy Nystrom, University Of Texas At San Antonio, Austin, TX; Jane O'Connor, Emory College, Atlanta, GA; Daniel E. Opacki, SIT Graduate Institute, Brattleboro, VT; Lucia Parsley, Virginia Commonwealth University, VA; Wendy Patriquin, Parkland College, IL; Nancy Pendleton, Cape Cod Community College, Attleboro, MA; Marion Piccolomini, Communicate With Ease, LTD, PA; Barbara Pijan, Portland State University, Portland, OR; Marjorie Pitts, Ohio Northern University, Ada, OH; Carolyn Prager, Spanish-American Institute, NY; Eileen Prince, Prince Language Associates Incorporated, MA; Sema Pulak, Texas A & M University, TX; Mary Kay Purcell, University of Evansville, Evansville, IN; Christina Quartararo, St. John's University, Jamaica, NY; James T. Raby, Clark University, MA; Anouchka Rachelson, Miami-Dade College, FL; Sherry Rasmussen, DePaul University, IL; Amy Renehan, University of Washington, WA; Daniel Rivas, Irvine Valley College, Irvine, CA; Esther Robbins, Prince George's Community College, PA; Bruce Rogers, Spring International Language Center at Arapahoe College, Littleton, CO; Helen Roland, Miami Dade College, FL; Linda Roth, Vanderbilt University English Language Center, TN; Janine Rudnick, El Paso Community College, TX; Paula Sanchez, Miami Dade College – Kendall Campus, FL; Deborah Sandstrom, Tutorium in Intensive English at University of Illinois at Chicago, Elmhurst, IL; Marianne Hsu Santelli, Middlesex County College, NJ; Elena Sapp, INTO Oregon State University, Corvallis, OR; Alice Savage, Lone Star College System: North Harris, TX; Jitana Schaefer, Pensacola State College, Pensacola, FL; Lynn Ramage Schaefer, University of Central Arkansas, AR; Ann Schroth, Johnson & Wales University, Dayville, CT;

Margaret Shippey, Miami Dade College, FL; Lisa Sieg, Murray State University, KY; Samanthia Slaight, North Lake College, Richardson, TX; Ann Snider, UNK University of NE Kearney, Kearney, NE; Alison Stamps, ESL Center at Mississippi State University, Mississippi; Peggy Street, ELS Language Centers, Miami, FL; Lydia Streiter, York College Adult Learning Center, NY; Steve Strizver, Miami Beach, FL; Nicholas Taggart, Arkansas State University, AR; Marcia Takacs, Coastline Community College, CA; Tamara Teffeteller, University of California Los Angeles, American Language Center, CA; Adrianne Aiko Thompson, Miami Dade College, Miami, FL; Rebecca Toner, English Language Programs, University of Pennsylvania, PA; Evina Baquiran Torres, Zoni Language Centers, NY; William G. Trudeau, Missouri Southern State University, MO; Troy Tucker, Edison State College, FL; Maria Vargas-O'Neel, Miami Dade College, FL; Amerca Vazquez, Miami Dade College, FL; Alison Vinande, Modesto Junior College, CA; Christie Ward, IELP, Central CT State University, Hartford, CT; Colin Ward, Lone Star College - North Harris, Houston, TX; Denise Warner, Lansing Community College, Lansing, MI; Rita Rutkowski Weber, University of Wisconsin – Milwaukee, WI; James Wilson, Cosumnes River College, Sacramento, CA; Dolores "Lorrie" Winter, California State University Fullerton, Buena Park, CA; Wendy Wish-Bogue, Valencia Community College, FL; Cissy Wong, Sacramento City College, CA; Sarah Worthington, Tucson, Arizona; Kimberly Yoder, Kent State University, ESL Center, OH.

ASIA

Nor Azni Abdullah, Universiti Teknologi Mara; Morgan Bapst, Seoul National University of Science and Technology; Herman Bartelen, Kanda Institute of Foreign Languages, Sano; Maiko Berger, Ritsumeikan Asia Pacific University; Thomas E. Bieri, Nagoya College; Paul Bournhonesque, Seoul National University of Technology; Joyce Cheah Kim Sim, Taylor's University, Selangor Darul Ehsan; Michael C. Cheng, National Chengchi University; Fu-Dong Chiou, National Taiwan University; Derek Currie, Korea University, Sejong Institute of Foreign Language Studies; Wendy Gough, St. Mary College/Nunoike Gaigo Senmon Gakko, Ichinomiya; Christoph A. Hafner, City University of Hong Kong; Monica Hamciuc, Ritsumeikan Asia-Pacific University, Kagoshima; Rob Higgens, Ritsumeikan University; Wenhua Hsu, I-Shou University; Helen Huntley, Hanoi University; Debra Jones, Tokyo Woman's Christian University, Tokyo; Shih Fan Kao, JinWen University of Science and Technology; Ikuko Kashiwabara, Osaka Electro-Communication University; Alyssa Kim, Hankuk University of Foreign Studies; Richard S. Lavin, Prefecturla University of Kumamoto; Mike Lay, American Institute Cambodia; Byoung-Kyo Lee, Yonsei University; Lin Li, Capital Normal University, Beijing; Bien Thi Thanh Mai, The International University – Vietnam National University, Ho Chi Minh City; Hudson Murrell, Baiko Gakuin University; Keiichi Narita, Niigata University; Orapin Nasawang, Udon Thani Rajabhat University; Huynh Thi Ai Nguyen, Vietnam USA Society; James Pham, IDP Phnom Penh; John Racine, Dokkyo University; Duncan Rose, British Council Singapore; Greg Rouault, Konan University, Hirao School of Management, Osaka; Simone Samuels, The Indonesia Australia Language Foundation, Jakarta; Yuko Shimizu, Ritsumeikan University; Wang Songmei, Beijing Institute of Education Faculty; Richmond Stroupe, Soka University; Peechaya Suriyawong, Udon Thani Rajabhat University; Teoh Swee Ai, Universiti Teknologi Mara; Chien-Wen Jenny Tseng, National Sun Yat-Sen University; Hajime Uematsu, Hirosaki University; Sy Vanna, Newton Thilay School, Phnom Penh; Matthew Watterson, Hongik University; Anthony Zak, English Language Center, Shantou University.

LATIN AMERICA AND THE CARIBBEAN

Ramon Aguilar, Universidad Tecnológica de Hermosillo, México; Lívia de Araújo Donnini Rodrigues, University of São Paolo, Brazil; Cecilia Avila, Universidad de Xapala, México; Beth Bartlett, Centro Cultural Colombo Americano, Cali, Colombia; Raúl Billini, Colegio Loyola, Dominican Republic; Nohora Edith Bryan, Universidad de La Sabana, Colombia; Raquel Hernández Cantú, Instituto Tecnológico de Monterrey, Mexico; Millie Commander, Inter American University of Puerto Rico, Puerto Rico; José Alonso Gaxiola Soto, CEI Universidad Autonoma de Sinaloa, Mazatlán, Mexico; Raquel Hernandez, Tecnologico de Monterrey, Mexico; Edwin Marín-Arroyo, Instituto Tecnológico de Costa Rica; Rosario Mena, Instituto Cultural Dominico-Americano, Dominican Republic; Elizabeth Ortiz Lozada, COPEI-COPOL English Institute, Ecuador; Gilberto Rios Zamora, Sinaloa State Language Center, Mexico; Patricia Veciños, El Instituto Cultural Argentino Norteamericano, Argentina; Isabela Villas Boas, Casa Thomas Jefferson, Brasília, Brazil; Roxana Viñes, Language Two School of English, Argentina.

EUROPE, MIDDLE EAST, AND NORTH AFRICA

Tom Farkas, American University of Cairo, Egypt; Ghada Hozayen, Arab Academy for Science, Technology and Maritime Transport, Egypt; Tamara Jones, ESL Instructor, SHAPE Language Center, Belgium; Jodi Lefort, Sultan Qaboos University, Muscat, Oman; Neil McBeath, Sultan Qaboos University, Oman; Barbara R. Reimer, CERTESL, UAE University, UAE; Nashwa Nashaat Sobhy, The American University in Cairo, Egypt; Virginia Van Hest-Bastaki, Kuwait University, Kuwait.

AUSTRALIA

Susan Austin, University of South Australia, Joanne Cummins, Swinburne College; Pamela Humphreys, Griffith University.

Special thanks to Dan Buettner, Jane Chen, Barton Seaver, and James Vlahos for their kind assistance during this book's development.

This series is dedicated to Kristin L. Johannsen, whose love for the world's cultures and concern for the world's environment were an inspiration to family, friends, students, and colleagues.

61: David Doubilet/National Geographic, **62:** Hannele Lahti/National Geographic, **62-63:** Jason Edwards/National Geographic **63:** George Steinmetz/National Geographic, **63:** Paul Chesley/National Geographic, **63:** David Doubilet/National Geographic, **65:** Brian J. Skerry/National Geographic, **65:** Brian J. Skerry/National Geographic, **65:** Brian J. Skerry/National Geographic, **69:** Anderson, John (California)/National Geographic, **69:** David Doubilet/National Geographic, **70:** David Doubilet/National Geographic, **70-71:** Jason Edwards/National Geographic, **72:** Katie Stoops, **81:** Rebecca Hale/National Geographic, **82-83:** Maggie Steber/National Geographic, **83:** Anne Keiser/National Geographic, **85:** Gerd Ludwig/National Geographic Stock, **85:** The Granger Collection, NYC, **86:** Getty Images, **86:** David Alan Harvey/National Geographic, **88:** Steve and Donna O'Meara/National Geographic, **89:** Annie Griffiths/National Geographic, **92:** Justin Guariglia/National Geographic, **92:** PinonRoad/iStockphoto, **92:** Lisovskaya Natalia/Shutterstock, **93:** Courtesy of Dr. Arthur W. Toga, Laboratory of Neuro Imaging at UCLA, **100:** Syakobchuk Vasyl,2009/ Used under license from Shutterstock.com, **101:** Cary Wolinsky/National Geographic, **102:** Brooke Whatnall/National Geographic, **102:** Joel Sartore/National Geographic, **103:** David Doubilet/National Geographic, **103:** Amy White & Al Petteway/National Geographic, **103:** Joel Sartore/National Geographic, **105:** Takacs, Zoltan/National Geographic, **106:** Bruce Dale/National Geographic Image Collection, **106:** Mattias Klum/National Geographic, **109:** Rebecca Hale/National Geographic, **109:** Joel Sartore/National Geographic, **112:** Cary Wolinsky/National Geographic, **112:** Sarah Leen/National Geographic, **113:** AP Photo, **113:** Cary Wolinsky/ National Geographic, **121:** Smith, Fred K./National Geographic, **122-123:** Jim Richardson/National Geographic, **123:** Campo, Colorado/National Geographic, **123:** Mark Thiessen/National Geographic, **125:** Mike Theiss/National Geographic, **128:** Campo, Colorado/National Geographic, **129:** Ricardo Mohr/National Geographic Image Collection, **132:** Mark Thiessen/National Geographic, **141:** John Scofield/National Geographic, **142-143:** National Geographic, **145:** Stephen Chao/National Geographic, **146-147:** Fernando G. Baptista/National Geographic Magazine, **148:** Apic/Getty Images, **148:** Chris Hill/National Geographic, **149:** Fernando G. Baptista/National Geographic Magazine, **150:** Stephen Alvarez/National Geographic, **151:** Kenneth Garrett/ National Geographic, **154:** ©2011/Vincent J. Musi/National Geographic Image Collection, **155:** Simon Norfolk/National Geographic, **160:** Raymond Gehman/National Geographic, **160:** Richard Nowitz/National Geographic, **161:** Victor Hideo Kobayashi/National Geographic, **163:** Joe Petersburger/National Geographic, **164:** Robert Sisson/National Geographic, **164:** IM Brandenburg/ Minden Pictures/National Geographic, **164-165:** Wild Wonders of Europe LTD/National Geographic, **167:** Tim Laman/National Geographic, **167:** Tim Laman/National Geographic, **168:** Abigail Eden Shaffer/National Geographic, **168:** Xing Lida/National Geographic, **170:** John Sibbick/National Geographic, **171:** National Geographic, **171:** National Geographic, **172:** Norbert Wu/Minden Pictures/ National Geographic, **174:** Norbert Wu/Minden Pictures/National Geographic, **174:** Shawn Gould/National Geographic, **175:** Martin Harvey/Corbis, **175:** Robert Clark/National Geographic, **175:** Photo Researchers/National Geographic, **175:** Brian J. Skerry/National Geographic, **178:** Robert Clark/National Geographic, **178:** Robert Clark/National Geographic, **179:** Martin Harvey/ Corbis, **183:** Seamus MacLennan/National Geographic, **184:** Lynn Johnson/National Geographic, **184:** Steve Winter/National Geographic, **185:** Jim Richardson/National Geographic, **185:** Justin Guariglia/National Geographic, **185:** Tommy Heinrich/National Geographic, **185:** Robb Kendrick/National Geographic, **185:** Elizabeth Stevens/National Geographic, **187:** Justin Guariglia/National Geographic, **187:** Josh Nesbit, Medic Mobile, **188:** TechChange, **188:** Bedford, James/National Geographic Stock, **191:** Amy Howard/National Geographic, **192:** Seamus MacLennan/National Geographic, **194:** Ken Banks, kiwanja.net, **194:** Ozcan Research Group at UCLA, **195:** Ozcan Research Lab at UCLA, **195:** Frans Lanting/National Geographic, **195:** Guillaume Collanges, **209:** David Doubilet/National Geographic

Map and Illustration Images

2: National Geographic Maps; **5:** National Geographic Maps; **6:** National Geographic Maps; **12-13:** Illustrations Blue Zones LLC; **21:** Ken Eward/National Geographic Stock; **22-23:** Mr. Griff Wason/National Geographic Image Collection; **25:** Workshop Loves You; **25:** National Geographic Maps; **27:** Workshop Loves You; **42-43:** National Geographic Maps; **43:** Oliver Uberti/National Geographic Image Collection; **49:** National Geographic Maps; **52:** National Geographic Maps; **62-63:** Benjamin Halpern and others, National Center for Ecological Analysis and Synthesis, University of California, Santa Barbara; **66:** Martin Gamache/National Geographic Image Collection; **72-73:** Mariel Furlong/Alejandro Tumas/National Geographic Image Collection; **75:** Page2, LLC; **76:** Page2, LLC; **78:** Page2, LLC; **83:** Anne Keiser/National Geographic; **83:** Page2, LLC; **93:** National Geographic Maps; **100:** Syakobchuk Vasyl, 2009/ Used under license from Shutterstock.com, **109:** National Geographic Maps; **123:** National Geographic Maps/National Geographic Image Collection; **126:** Gary Hincks/ Photo Researchers, Inc.; **130:** Bruce Morser/National Geographic Image Collection; **132-33:** Bruce Morser/National Geographic Image Collection; **146-147:** Fernando G. Baptista/National Geographic Magazine; **148:** Fernando G. Baptista/National Geographic Magazine; **149:** Fernando G. Baptista/National Geographic Magazine; **154:** National Geographic Maps; **154:** Fernando G. Baptista/National Geographic Magazine; **155:** National Geographic Maps; **168:** Xing Lida/ National Geographic; **170:** John Sibbick/National Geographic; **174:** Shawn Gould/National Geographic; **178:** Robert Clark/National Geographic; **184-185:** National Geographic Maps